John Bird Finch, Charles Arnold McCully

The People versus the Liquor Traffic

Speeches of John B. Finch, Delivered in the Prohibition Campaigns of the United States and

Canada

John Bird Finch, Charles Arnold McCully

The People versus the Liquor Traffic
Speeches of John B. Finch, Delivered in the Prohibition Campaigns of the United States and Canada

ISBN/EAN: 9783743417496

Manufactured in Europe, USA, Canada, Australia, Japa

Cover: Foto ©Suzi / pixelio.de

Manufactured and distributed by brebook publishing software (www.brebook.com)

John Bird Finch, Charles Arnold McCully

The People versus the Liquor Traffic

VERSUS

THE LIQUOR TRAFFIC.

SPEECHES OF

JOHN B. FINCH,

DELIVERED IN THE

PROHIBITION CAMPAIGNS OF THE UNITED STATES AND CANADA.

TWENTY-FOURTH (REVISED) EDITION.

WITH AN INTRODUCTION BY J. N. STEARNS.

EDITED BY CHARLES ARNOLD McCULLY.

"Once to every man and nation comes the moment to decide,
In the strife of Truth with Falsehood, for the good or evil side;
Some great cause, God's new Messiah, offering each the bloom or blight,
Parts the goats upon the left hand, and the sheep upon the right,
And the choice goes by forever 'twixt that darkness and that light."

NEW YORK:
PUBLISHED BY THE R. W. G. LODGE,
B. F. PARKER, R. W. G. SECRETARY.
1887.

INTRODUCTION.

CONSTITUTIONAL PROHIBITION is fast becoming the watchword of the hour. The people of the nation are becoming more and more restive under the increasing burden of the liquor traffic, and are determined to take the question into their own hands. This is a government of the people, for the people, and by the people. The license system has been tried for more than two hundred years, and under its fostering care the evils of intemperance have grown to colossal proportions. High-licensed whiskey destroys manhood and debases womanhood, and beggars children just as quickly and as fast as the lowest of the low-priced licenses. The evil is in the drink. The traffic is on trial for its life. The people, in their sovereign capacity at the ballot-box, are the highest tribunal and the fountain of all power. This is the next great question before the American people to be settled at the ballot-box. The conflict between the saloon and the home will continue with increasing force and power until it is settled, and settled right. When settled by the voice of the people in their sovereign capacity, it should go into the bed-rock of the Constitution. Already the States of Kansas, Maine, Iowa, and Rhode Island have, by overwhelming majorities, given prohibition place in the fundamental laws of the State. Iowa was cheated out of a constitutional amendment by a technicality, but the agitation has given her an iron-clad prohibitory law which has been of untold benefit to the State. A majority of **votes were undoubtedly cast** for the amendment in

Michigan, but the people of that State, too, have by fraud been deprived of the fruits of their victory.

The Legislatures of Texas, Tennessee, West Virginia, Oregon, and Pennsylvania have voted to submit a prohibitory amendment to a direct vote of the people, and in a dozen more States constitutional prohibition is the leading question before the people. Hence it is all-important that the people should be thoroughly informed and enlightened upon every phase of this most important subject. Of all the men who have been before the American public to discuss this question, Mr. John B. Finch stands foremost for clear perception, sound logic, apt illustration, and convincing argument. The lectures which are gathered in this volume, though delivered in different parts of the country to meet special emergencies, will be found to contain argument and statistics of very great value in the Constitutional Amendment campaigns now being carried on in different parts of the country. Mr. Finch has dedicated his great talents and wide-spread influence to the cause of Prohibition. He has made it his life study, and this volume goes forth as his free-will offering for the cause, to which he has dedicated himself.

The prohibition of the traffic in intoxicating beverages, is the only proper solution and righteous settlement of this whole question. Wherever honestly tried it has proved the greatest of blessings. In Maine, Kansas, and Iowa, the volume of liquor sold and drank has been reduced tenfold. Blessings follow in its train. Prosperity comes in when liquor goes out. Prohibition by Constitutional Amendment, vitalized by Prohibitory Statutes stringently enforced, will usher in an era of peace, prosperity and happiness never before known or realized in the civilized world.   J. N. STEARNS.

NEW YORK, *May* 1, 1887.

CONTENTS.

	PAGE
INTRODUCTION,	iii
I. WHY CONSTITUTIONAL PROHIBITION,	1
II. A STATEMENT OF THE CASE,	13
III. WHY THE INDICTMENT IS PRESSED,	35
IV. AN EXAMINATION OF THE ISSUES,	65
V. EXAMINATION OF THE ISSUES AND DEFENCE,	83
VI. THE DEFENCE REVIEWED,	109
VII. THE QUESTIONS ASKED BY THE JURY ANSWERED,	133
VIII. THE DEFENCE ANSWERED,	155
IX. WHAT, WHY, AND HOW,	194
X. COMPENSATION,	218
XI. THE PRACTICABILITY OF THE MOVEMENT PROVED BY ITS SUCCESS,	238

THE PEOPLE

VERSUS

THE LIQUOR TRAFFIC.

I.

WHY CONSTITUTIONAL PROHIBITION.

An Address delivered at the banquet of the Boston Social Temperance Union, in Tremont Temple, December, 1883.

LADIES AND GENTLEMEN: A joint committee of the different temperance organizations and churches undertook, last winter, to secure the submission to the electors of an amendment to your State Constitution, prohibiting the manufacture and sale of alcoholic beverages. This winter the campaign is to be renewed, and your Secretary, Mr. Jewell, has asked me, as one living in that section of our country where the movement for constitutional prohibition originated, to give you the reason which induced Western workers to adopt that plan of work. I do this with pleasure, because practical trial and experience have convinced me of its practicability and desirability. You, Eastern workers, fully conversant with your people and social customs, can judge for yourselves whether the reasons which led us to adopt the plan are good reasons for its adoption here.

It seemed to us that any plan of work to produce permanent results must accomplish three things: 1. Unite all enemies of the liquor traffic. 2. Thoroughly educate and prepare the people for correct legislation; 3. Guarantee a thorough trial of the law before its change or repeal. The purpose of the work is the prevention of the evil results of the alcoholic liquor traffic by the destruction of the traffic. The traffic being a social institution, is entitled to protection the same as other social institutions so long as its results are a blessing to society. The demand for its destruction is based, not on the fact that it is called the liquor traffic, but because it has proved itself an enemy of the purposes for which society exists. The traffic was allowed to develop by society to bless man, and has always debauched and degraded him. It is aggressive in its viciousness, and the people are forced to adopt measures to defend themselves. No sane man will undertake to defend the record, or to justify the effects of the traffic. All persons admit the desirability, but some question the practicability of its destruction. Its destruction can only come after the people are fully convinced of the truth of the charges against it, because its destruction means a social revolution which can only be accomplished by the affirmative act of the people. The constitutional is the American method of revolution. "Government is aboriginal with man," wrote a great statesman; which was simply saying that a man was a social animal, that society was necessary for his development, and that the conflicting interests of the members of society make necessary an institution of justice called the State. As man develops socially, intellectually, morally, the government must develop to meet and settle the new social problems which man's changing conditions constantly bring to the front. The lower orders of government have never made provision for this development, and the people in them have developed like lower orders of life, which, when the covering, or skin, prevents further growth, throw it off, and take a new one. The pathway of advancement in such governments has been a pathway of assassination, of tumult, of revolution. The men who settled Massachusetts were loyal to the British form of government, and only became disloyal when common dangers, common suffering, and common interests had destroyed stratified society, and developed a brotherhood. A government good enough for a society composed of nobles, gentlemen, and peasants was not adapted to the new social conditions developed by the peculiar social life of the colonies, and the people became restless, riotous, and when the king refused their prayers for new forms, rebellious. Seven years of suffering, agony, and bloodshed threw off the old form of government, and soon delegates met to determine the conditions of the new. They were broad, liberal men. They did not think that all political wisdom would die with them, but, on the contrary, said, "This people will develop, new social problems will constantly arise, and the government we are forming must be so arranged as to meet and settle them, or the people will reject it as worthless, and form one that will assist to advance, not impede mankind." They realized they could only prevent revolution by providing for peaceable evolution. In the constitutions framed and adopted, Bancroft says: "To perfect the system, and forever prevent revolution, power is reserved to the people, by amendments of their constitution, to remove every imperfection which time may lay bare, and to adapt it for unforeseen contingencies." American constitutions provide that when any great question affecting the social happiness or prosperity of the people is to be determined, the legislature shall, by constitutional amendment, submit it to the people, for them to examine and determine; that they shall have ample time to discuss, examine, and form correct opinions, and then, on a day set apart, shall go to the ballot-box and deposit their written opinions, and a majority of those opinions shall decide the action of the government. The provision makes American progress an evolution by ballots, instead of a revolution by bullets.

The alcoholic liquor traffic is an old institution, and the charges urged against it are that its whole results debauch and degrade society. The Prohibitionists say that it is a school of crime, vice, and immorality; and that a republican form of government, based on intelligence and morality, must destroy the traffic to preserve its own existence. These charges are grave ones, and if sustained no excuse can be offered for allowing the traffic to continue. The question is one of fact. Is the traffic guilty? Do Prohibitionists tell the truth? The jury to determine the matter must be the people, because in free America all political power is inherent in the people. The existence of the business must be sanctioned by law, or prohibited by law, and the people are the only law-makers. Bancroft says: "As the sea is made up of drops, American society is composed of separate, free, and constantly moving atoms, ever in reciprocal action—advancing, receding, crossing, struggling against each other, and with each other, so that the institutions and laws of the country rise out of the masses of individual thought, which, like the waters of the ocean, are rolling on evermore." Laws are of two kinds—organic, which are adopted by the people by direct vote; and functional, which the people adopt by delegated vote; and the question for Prohibitionists to determine is, whether it is better to have the people act directly or by delegation in settling the existence or non-existence of the liquor traffic. Its destruction means a great social change, and I do not believe it wise or best to attempt it by statutory law. Statutory law is passed by representatives of the people, using the people's power. The representatives are few in number, subject to influence of popular passion and excitement, to say nothing of other means of influence which it is charged are used. The legislators as a class are partisans, who unite party success with all questions of public policy; and the laws they pass are subject to modification or repeal at any time by themselves or succeeding legislatures. On the contrary, constitutional law can only be adopted by the whole people, after calm and mature deliberation, the provisions for amendment preventing unwise and hasty action. The law once adopted it is guaranteed a fair trial, because its repeal is just as difficult as its adoption. The constitution belongs to the whole people. It does not speak of Republicans, Democrats, or Prohibitionists. An amendment is submitted, not to Prohibitionists as Prohibitionists, not to Democrats as Democrats, not to Republicans as Republicans, but to electors as electors. The issue raised by the amendment asked by the committee, would be, Shall the constitution be amended? The electors would ask, "Why amend the constitution?" To which the Prohibitionists would reply, "To destroy the alcoholic liquor traffic." "Ought the traffic to be destroyed?" the elector would ask. "Yes," would answer the Prohibitionists. "No," would answer the drunkard-maker; and the issue would be joined before the jury, which must finally settle the question. Each elector will be called on to express his opinion, and wishing to do so intelligently, will investigate the whole matter. The drunkard-makers have always said, "Temperance men are fanatics and fools," and the campaign will give them opportunity to go before the people and disprove, if they can, the charges against their business, and convict the temperance men as slanderers and maligners. The people will read, examine, think; and whatever is their decision, public opinion will occupy that plane. A statute law expresses only the will of the legislature, and is always open to the attack, "The people are not educated up to that point"; but an amendment adopted is the will of the people, because it is adopted by the people. A statute law being easily changed or repealed, those opposed to it are encouraged to defy it, hoping thereby to bring it into contempt and secure its repeal, which they are enabled to do by the fact that moral people, having won a victory over the viler elements of society on a special line, have so much other work to do that their attention is called from the field, thereby giving the outlaws, who have no other interest, the opportunity to assassinate the law, and again fasten on society.

One of the strongest arguments in favor of written constitutions is, that they, to a very great extent, guard against this danger. Lieber says: "Constitutions form in times of political apathy, if not too great a passage, a bridge to pass over to better times. When civic consciousness is too weak, and patriotism too low to repel encroachments by their own action, they are still sometimes sufficient to do so with the aid of a well-settled and clearly pronounced constitution. It gives a strong feeling of right and a powerful impulse of action to have the written law clearly on one's side; and though power, if it comes to the last, will disregard the written law as well as the customary, yet it must come to the last before it dares pass the Rubicon, and to declare revolution." Prohibition by statute was adopted in Massachusetts, and the drunkard-makers determined to bring it into contempt. Year by year the law was drawn tighter, and its violation made more difficult. The outlaws were desperate, and in an hour when it was least expected, by fraud, trickery, and political combinations they sent to the State House the notorious P. L. L. Legislature, and the law was destroyed; not because it was a failure, but because it was a success, and was effectually destroying the business of the men who elected the Legislature. No person familiar with the history of the reform in this State, believes that the law would have been repealed if it had been necessary to refer it to the people, and to give them time to examine the facts. The law was the victim of political conspiracies and combinations.

In Kansas the prohibitory principle was placed in the constitution. The drunkard-makers, adopting the tactics of their Eastern allies, refused to obey the law in many places, and organized secretly to overthrow it. The decent people, having outlawed the business, thought the question settled, and took up other issues. The outlaws, having but one object, traded, conspired, and combined with every other class or clique that would combine with them; and covering their real purpose with the cry of anti-monopoly, anti-third term and other issues in regard to which Prohibitionists are not agreed, they defeated St. John, and, as they thought, prohibition. Their triumph was short-lived; for they found that though Prohibitionists were divided as regarded other issues, they were a unit in their hatred of the liquor traffic, and the principle being in the constitution, to repeal it would again strip the question of all side issues, and draw the line with the defenders of the home on one side, and the defenders of the grog-shop on the other. They had captured the earthworks of statutory law, but the principle they wished to destroy was in the citadel of the constitution, defended by the lovers of home, country, and civilization, and no political compromise or bargain could destroy it. The constitution could only be amended by the people, and this would force the traffic to meet its record of crime, vice, and rebellion. The liquor men having everything to gain, and nothing to lose, would force the issue, but politicians did not dare, and the State was and is safe. In the treatment of chronic sores by cauterizing or cutting, the pain of the operation, and the inflammation caused, may lead the patient to resist the operation; yet these new conditions, which make the sore for a time appear worse than before treatment, are necessary to generate healthy action. So the resistance and excitement following the outlawry of the saloon may for a time make things seem worse than before, but these symptoms indicate healthy action in the place of listless carelessness, and all that is necessary to make the work permanent, is to hold on until the public mind has time to settle, and the generation come up who know not the grog-shop. Joseph Cook once said, in substance: "A swamp may, after it has been drained, be more offensive for a time than before; but that is no reason for again turning on the water. The thing to do is to keep it drained until sunlight and pure air have cleansed and purified it" The liquor traffic is an ulcer on the body politic; no change in its treatment should be made without mature deliberation; and when the change is made, it should be made in such shape as to insure a full and fair trial of the new treatment. The change proposed is to change the power vested in the legislature from full power to be used as the legislature pleases, to limited power to be used as the people direct. The Legislature of Massachusetts now has plenary power to deal with the liquor traffic. This power they have had since the adoption of the constitution, and in the light of history I stand here to say the experience of all these years proves that the legislature is no place to deposit discretionary power in dealing with the alcoholic liquor traffic. The power exercised by the legislature is the people's power delegated by the people to the legislature; and the people have the right to recover any right or power which they have delegated whenever they think they can better their condition by so doing. The change will be that the people will say what the public policy shall be, and direct the Legislature to make the principle in the organic law operative by functional law. If the principle does not prove practical, the people can at any time change it, but it can never be changed until the people will it.

So long as discretionary power is vested in the legislature, the drunkard-makers will annually use thousands of dollars if necessary to prevent right action; and when discretionary power is taken from them, one of the worst sources of legislative corruption will be dried up, because the legislature can act in but one way, and it will be useless to try to bribe them. With prohibition a settled principle in the constitution, every legislator who swears to support the constitution must vote in favor of a prohibitory law, making the principle operative, or be a perjurer and a rebel.

I am aware that some will object that the constitution is no place to define what shall and what shall not be crimes. The eminent constitutional authority last quoted says: "Constitutions are the assemblage of those publicly acknowledged principles which are deemed fundamental to the government of a people. They refer either to the relation in which the citizen stands to the State at large, and consequently to the government, or to the proper delineation of the spheres of authority." The constitution lays down principles of government, and to attack or violate those principles is a crime against the constitution and the government. The defining and adopting the principles, makes its violation a crime against the government. To adopt a constitutional amendment prohibiting the liquor traffic, is to make the principle of prohibition fundamental, and to change the spheres of authority to conform to the newly adopted principle. This was done in regard to African slavery. The people adopted the principle that no slavery should exist in the States, and left to Congress and the Legislatures of the States the power to enact functional laws to carry out the will of the people. The principle of monogamy is deemed fundamental by many of our States, and will soon undoubtedly be placed in the Constitution of the United States. That life and property should be protected is one of the fundamental principles of all constitutions, and the legislatures are left to pass functional laws to make the principle operative. A gentleman recently asked me, "Would you prohibit murder in the constitution?" In reply I asked, "Suppose your legislature should pass a law licensing murder, would it be constitutional?" Of course he said "No"; and thereby answered himself that it was prohibited by the constitution. The people of Iowa, finding lotteries dangerous to their best interests, declared it a fundamental principle of their government that lotteries should not exist; and the State has not been cursed with them since the principle was adopted by the people. When the people become convinced that a principle is right, the place for it is in the constitution. That there are objections to changes in constitutions I am aware; but they are not as strongly urged as were the objections to written constitutions supplanting the unwritten ones. The constitution that cannot develop is a fraud, and a good basis for a despotism. To the objection that the amendment specifies a single institution, the answer is, that this institution is a special evil which is threatening the life of the government by debauching and degrading the units of the government. The question of its overthrow is the question of the existence or non-existence of republican institutions; and that the prohibition of the existence of such an institution is fundamental to the existence of the government it jeopardizes, is self-evident.

The verdict, for or against the traffic, will be made by the voters. They, desiring to act intelligently, will investigate the whole matter. Books, documents, and papers will be read, and accusers and defenders of the traffic will discuss the matter in every town and city of the State. The time necessary for its adoption prevents rash or injudicious action, and when the verdict is made, it will be an intelligent verdict, and will be enforced, because it will be the verdict of the people; and woe to the politicians or party who disregard the VOX POPULI.

The plan commends itself, because:

1. The method is in accordance with the provisions made by the Constitution for social and political development.

2. It provides for the trial and arraignment of the

liquor traffic for its crimes before the people, and gives ample time for examination and investigation of the whole matter before action is taken.

3. It makes a simple issue: the crimes of the traffic against society—and summons all voters to decide on the merits of the case.

4. The trial will thoroughly educate the people, so they will be ready to defend and uphold their own action.

5. The amendment adopted ensures a fair trial of the principle, and guards against its assassination in hours of political apathy.

6. The placing of the principle in the Constitution is in accordance with the theory of American constitutions.

The best form of an amendment undoubtedly is:

SEC. 1. The manufacture and sale of alcoholic liquors as a beverage are prohibited.

SEC. 2. The Legislature (the General Court in Massachusetts) shall pass laws necessary to enforce this prohibition.

The use of the word "intoxicating" is not best, as it leaves the Courts or the Legislature to define the word and render prohibition a farce, as in your State, where the Courts hold that liquors containing less than three per cent. of alcohol are not intoxicating, thereby permitting the sale of lager-beer and other lesser alcoholics. The word "alcoholic" makes the chemist's test of the liquors the only thing necessary to condemn them. The question frequently asked: "What will be done about liquors to be manufactured and sold for other purposes?" is best answered by an examination of the power granted the Legislature by the Constitution as it now is, and as it will be with the amendment a part of the Constitution. The Legislature is created by the Constitution, and given general power to legislate, subject to three limitations, viz.: The Constitution of the United States; Laws passed in accordance with the Constitution of the United States; Limitations in the State Constitution. In the celebrated license cases which were taken, if my memory is right, from Massachusetts to the Supreme Court of the United States, that court held: "There is nothing in the Constitution of the United States to prevent it (the State) from regulating or restraining the traffic, or prohibiting it altogether if it thinks proper." The power to deal with the traffic is thus wholly a State power, and the State having delegated the power to the Legislature, it has and will exercise that power until the people define and limit the power by constitutional amendment. When the amendment is a part of the Constitution, the Legislature will return all power not taken away by the amendment; and as that only prohibits the manufacture and sale of alcoholic liquors as a beverage, the power to regulate, restrain, or prohibit the manufacture and sale for other purposes will remain in the Legislature, and that body may say under what restrictions the manufacture and sale for such purposes shall be carried on.

Petitioning for the submission of an amendment, simply asks the Legislature to submit the whole matter to the people. One issue alone is raised: "Shall people govern themselves?" The legislator is not asked to vote for or against prohibition, simply to say whether his constituents shall decide for themselves; and any legislator who refuses to submit the question, not only insults every voter in his district, but is a traitor to the principles of Republican Government, and should be defeated by the votes of honest men if he ever again seeks office.

Thus I have briefly stated the reason why Western workers insist on the adoption of the principle by the people before the passage of statutory law.

You are the ones who are to say what you will do with the matter, and I can only urge upon you the necessity of doing something. The duty of the hour is action, and the leaders should be in the front of the fight. Inaction and idleness produce the same results as treason to the principle. The liquor interests are active and aggressive, and the defenders of the home should be equally so. I have no faith in, or sympathy for leaders who say: "We are discouraged, and fear we can accomplish nothing." Suppose your wife is on a sick-bed, and you call a doctor, who on coming and examining her would say to her, "There is very little chance for you to live; I am discouraged"; would you not kick him out of doors? What you would expect him to say, and what he would say if he had good sense, would be, "While there is life there is hope; keep up good courage and you will pull through." This Government is terribly sick, and the political leader who will go upon the public platform and injure public vitality by discouraging the units of society, is an unsafe leader, and should have sense enough to resign, or, failing to do so, should be requested to take a back seat. What we want is men and women who, for the love of home and country, will enter the struggle to win; and after carefully studying the plan of action, draw the sword and throw away the scabbard, determined only to cease the struggle when victory comes to bless our homes and country.

II.

A STATEMENT OF THE CASE.

An Address delivered before the Northwestern Convocation of Temperance Workers at Lake Bluff, Illinois, August 27, 1881.

LADIES AND GENTLEMEN: Some months since I received a letter from our mutual friend, Dr. Jutkins, in which he requested me to deliver an address at this Convocation. I replied that I should attend the Convocation, but preferred to remain silent, as a learner at the feet of older men. Another letter gave me to understand that no excuse would be accepted, therefore an address was prepared for this occasion; but, since coming upon the grounds, I have heard much which leads me to think it better to leave the manuscript, and talk to you as one worker to other workers, on the present aspects of the reform.

I shall talk to you plainly, positively; and if I bore you, charge it to Dr. Jutkins, for he alone is responsible for my appearing before you.

In discussing the question of temperance, one fact more than all others I would impress on your minds at the commencement; that is, that the question of the existence of the drink traffic and drink habit must be settled in this country. It cannot be laughed down, sneered down, jeered down, or blackguarded down, and there is not money enough in the blood-stained coffers of the liquor power of this nation to buy enough votes to long prevent the entire defeat of the liquor oligarchy at the hands of this people.

This statement may be considered over-sanguine, and yet, ladies and gentlemen, it seems to me that the man or woman who insists that this great movement is caused by mere temporary excitement, must be a careless student of social problems. From the day the temperance movement started in this country it has never gone backwards.

A few months since, curiosity prompted me to write to State officers in different States whose Legislatures were in session last winter, asking them for the record of legislative sessions ten years ago, and also the record of the sessions held during the last winter, and I found this to be true—that, of the Legislatures of ten years ago, there was not one which discussed the question of the prohibition of the liquor traffic, while the Legislatures of the past winter, without a single exception, devoted a large part of their time to the discussion of this question.

The St. Louis *Globe Democrat* (and, by the way, the *Globe Democrat* is not noted as a very strong temperance paper, the history of both its former and present managers proving that they sympathize largely with the whiskey and beer traffic) in the month of April last, contained an editorial nearly a column in length, in which it was asserted that the temperance question was THE religio-politico question of this age, and the editor went on to say that the man who thought this movement was an agitation by a few idle visionaries or old women, was dreaming on the crater of a social volcano. Then, after explaining and giving fully his reasons for such conclusions, the editor said that the Legislature of the State of Missouri would no more dare, at its next session, to refuse to submit the question of the prohibition of the manufacture and sale of alcoholic liquors to the voters of that State, than it would dare commit any other kind of political suicide.*

In my State, the frontier State of Nebraska, ten years ago, a member of the Legislature who did not drink liquor was an exception; to-day a member who does is an exception. To-day a man could not be elected in Nebraska, on any party ticket, if it was known he was a tippler.

---

* The amendment to the State Constitution passed the Assembly of Missouri, but was defeated in the Senate, at the session of the Legislature mentioned in this speech. The liquor-dealers went to party politicians, and told them that if they allowed the amendment to pass, the liquor interest would defeat their parties. This was one cause of the formation of the Prohibition party in the States.

The Legislature met last winter, and during the entire session I saw no member under the influence of liquor. I understood there was a member drunk, but his friends said he was suffering with brain fever, and kept him out of sight until he became sober.

Ten years ago, those who called on the ladies in Omaha, who kept open house on New-Year's, found wine on nearly every table; for the past three years (and I have means of knowing the truth of what I affirm) not a family in Omaha, nor in the city of Lincoln, has placed wine before its guests on that day. Even our German friends have, to a great extent, banished it from their homes in obedience to the demands of better educated public opinion.

As I look over the rapid advance that has been, and is being made in this country, I have no doubt that the temperance question will come up in every spring election, every Town election, every City election, every County election, every State election, and every National election until it is settled; each year it will come with louder knocks, and each year with more urgent demands. Politicians and party leaders will be taught that they cannot trifle with this question, that home interests and moral principles are dearer to honest men than party fealty or party success. This truth leads to another one, viz.:

"A question is never settled until it is settled right."

Put the two together: it must be settled, it must be settled right, and we can proceed to an intelligent discussion of the issues.

My friends, whether you believe in the use of alcoholic liquor or not, the issues in this case must be investigated, and you must make up your minds to meet them and settle them like thinking men and women. Compromise, upon a question of principle, is always a victory for the devil. If you know you are right; if your conscience, your reason tells you so, and then for the sake of temporary peace, you make concessions to the side that you know to be wrong, you will find sooner or later that you have involved yourself in greater trouble, and probably in a worse fight, one that will not be settled until you retrace the wrong steps which you have taken. Tell one lie and you will find it necessary to tell others to prevent detection of the first. The history of the world is simply recorded demonstrations of these truths.

After the American Colonies were settled, the Parliament of Great Britain insisted that the right was vested in the King, by and with the consent of Parliament, to levy taxes upon the people of the Colonies: the Colonists at once demurred, and insisted that if Parliament, or the King, by and with consent of Parliament, had the right to levy taxes, then the Colonies must be represented in the Parliament which gave the consent. The Parliament of Great Britain levied heavy taxes on the Colonies. The result was inevitable. Parliament was seeking to establish what the majority of the Colonies believed to be a false principle of government. To resist such tyrannical action, Clubs of Liberty were organized throughout the Colonies. The English Premier saw the storm his action had raised, and wished, if possible, to allay it; the result was the repeal of all the heavy taxes and the concession that the taxes levied should only be upon commerce, and should be applied to the use of the Colony where they were levied. By this act, Parliament conceded everything but the principle—a small tax levied by Parliament to be applied to the use of the Colony where the tax was laid. But the agitation did not cease.

A leading American was asked in Boston, "Would you plunge the Colonies in war for a few pence on a pound of tea?" The answer was, "It is not the amount of the tax, but the accursed principle upon which Parliament bases the claim of right to levy ANY tax, that we are fighting." It was fought out on that line, and King George lost one of the brightest jewels in his crown.

This principle has also been demonstrated at a much later date. The representatives of the United States, assembled for the first time as a Congress of an independent nation, declared: "We hold these truths to be self-evident: that all men are created equal; that they are endowed by their Creator with certain inalienable rights; that among these are life, liberty, and the pursuit of happiness." Jefferson, in his original draft of the Declaration of Independence, emphasized the words "All men," by this charge: "He (the King) has waged cruel war against human nature itself, violating its most sacred rights of life and liberty, in the persons of a distant people who never offended him, captivating and carrying them into slavery in another hemisphere, or to incur miserable death in their transportation hither. This piratical warfare, the opprobrium of infidel powers, is the warfare of the Christian king of Great Britain. Determined to open a market where men should be bought and sold, he has prostituted his negative, for suppressing every legislative attempt to prohibit or restrain this execrable commerce. And that this assemblage of horrors might want no fact of distinguished dye, he is now exciting those very people to rise in arms among us, and to purchase that liberty of which he has deprived them, by murdering the people upon whom he also obtruded them, thus paying off former crimes committed against the liberties of one people with the crimes which he urges them to commit against the lives of another."

Slavery existed in the Colonies. The representatives, fearing the people, would not ratify the Declaration, the clause which Jefferson had written was stricken out, and the general term, "All men," was left undefined and unemphasized. The long years of mental and physical struggle for freedom during the Revolutionary War extended the mental horizon of American statesmen, and they began to perceive that "All men" might possibly include Africans, and thus the question which statesmen thought they had settled by the compromise made at the time of adopting the Declaration, forced itself into the convention which met to amend the defective Articles of Confederation. There the wrong of slavery was not denied, but the feelings of the delegates were expressed by one who said: "We have a wolf by the ears, and we dare not hold on or let go!" To do right seemed to endanger a national form of government, and another compromise followed. The word slavery was so obnoxious to men emerging from a long and bloody war for their own liberties that they would not allow it to appear in the Constitution of the United States. They allowed it to exist in the States as a thing to be passed by rather than noticed, and, although slavery has gone from the land it has never been necessary to change a word in the original Constitution. "Regulate and restrain" was the policy adopted.

Madison, speaking of this compromise half apologetically, said: "It were doubtless to be wished that the power of prohibiting the importation of slaves had not been postponed until the year 1808, or rather, that it had been suffered to have immediate operation, but it is not difficult to account, either for this restriction on the general Government, or for the manner in which the whole clause is expressed. It ought to be considered a great point gained in favor of humanity that a period of twenty years may terminate forever within these States a traffic which has so long and so loudly upbraided the barbarism of modern policy; that within that period it will receive a considerable discouragement from the general Government, and may be totally abolished by the concurrence of the few States which continue the unnatural traffic."

The delegates labored under the delusion that their action had placed the question where it would settle itself; but soon prostituted principle woke from the slumber of exhaustion to hear the ringing words of John Randolph, like a fire-bell in the night:

"I know there are gentlemen, not only from the Northern but from the Southern States, who think this unhappy question — for such it is — of Negro slavery, which the Constitution has vainly tried to blink by not using the term, should never be brought to public notice, more especially that of Congress, and most especially here. Sir, with every due respect to the gentlemen who think so, I differ from them *toto cælo*. Sir, it is a thing which cannot be hid; it is not a dry-rot which you can cover with a carpet until the house tumbles about your ears; you might as well try to hide a volcano in full operation; it cannot be hid; it is a cancer in your face, and must be treated *secundum artem;* it must not be tampered with by quacks who never saw the disease or the patient."

Brave, prophetic words. The volcano of an awakening public conscience could not, indeed, be suppressed. Compromise followed compromise, the old ulcer on the body politic grew deeper, the moral pulse of the nation grew feebler, but God was not asleep; the cry of the bondman had reached His ear, the stench of human blood had offended His nostril. To-day, along the mountains, plains, and valleys of the sunny Southland, the cold sod is heavy over the forms of the grandest, bravest men of the nation, men who wore the blue, men who wore the gray, whose blood was poured out as a libation upon the nation's altar to atone for an accursed compromise, which might, at one time, have been stricken out with a pen. In the reddest of American blood it is written: "A QUESTION IS NEVER SETTLED UNTIL IT IS SETTLED RIGHT."

With this truth, taught by experience, as a starting-point we are ready to continue the investigation. This is not a personal matter between the drunkard-maker and the temperance advocate. Whether the drunkard-maker is a scoundrel or a gentleman weighs not an atom in settling the merits of the case. For the purposes of this investigation, it matters not whether he is a devil or an angel of light. If he is an angel he cannot make a devilish principle a good one; if he is a devil he cannot make a God-given principle a bad one.

The question to be considered is, the cause of, and remedy for, the evils of intemperance. If the whole brood of drunkard-makers could be drowned in Lake Michigan to-morrow, another brood would spring up in three months, equally as bad as the one destroyed, unless we could destroy the accursed *system* that produced them; sear the neck of the license hydra, with public opinion in the hands of prohibition Iolaus.

Some cry, "Attack the liquor-seller!" When asked why, they answer, "He is a mean man." What if he is? The meaner and viler the drunkard-maker, the better he represents his mean, vile business; and I prefer a man should be a good representative of his trade. The American people must enter upon the investigation of this question, determined to examine fully all of its phases, to weigh carefully the arguments advanced by both sides, investigate the alleged facts produced by advocates who represent the home and the grog-shop, and then, on the weight of evidence presented, base their verdict. Anything less would not be reasonable, anything else would not be honest. In trying such issues, blackguardism, sneers, and reckless statements are out of place. I have been often impressed, when listening to those who represent the drunkard-makers, that a blackguard is as much out of place in the field of honest, manly discussion as a monkey would be in the tabernacle of the Lord. A man engaged in either intellectual or physical combat should never throw mud when he has rocks at hand, and when individuals stoop to use the mud of epithets in a discussion of this kind, it is *prima facie* evidence that they have nothing else to use. The copious use of epithets like " Fanatic," " Zealot," " Fool," and " Visionary," is not argument, but rather an indication of a cerebral vacuum in the head of the talker. When you see a man standing on the street corner, sticking his thumb in his vest-pocket and calling temperance people vile names, just remember it does not require a high order of brains to abuse people. A parrot can blackguard. " If you have no case, abuse the opposing attorney," is the motto of pettifoggers the world over.

Temperance advocates have no use for the style of argument used by the drunkard-makers and their apologists. Temperance men believe they are advocating correct principles, and that the facts and arguments upon which they base their claims are so nearly self-evident, that a presentation in a fair, candid way will convince thinking, intelligent people that prohibition is the only remedy for the drink curse. They believe the people are intelligent, and fully capable of passing judgment upon any question of governmental policy; that the people are the court of last resort, and that all questions must be determined by them. In accordance with this idea they go to the people as to a jury, presenting an indictment against the drink traffic, and ask that the traffic be tried, and a verdict rendered in accordance with the evidence. The object and purpose of the work they have never concealed. From the day the temperance reform started in this country, the prohibitionists have declared from platform and pulpit their purpose, and that purpose is to bury the liquor traffic in the way the old Welsh woman said she would bury the devil: "With face down, so that should he ever come to life, the more he digs the deeper he will get."

·Ladies and gentlemen, such is the purpose of the temperance men of this country—a calm, deliberate, dispassionate purpose—formed after a full investigation of all the facts in the case. You say at once, "This involves social changes, legal changes, changes in the very structure of this government." I answer, "Yes." You ask, "On what charges do you base the demands for this change?" Let me write the answer; dip my finger in the blood of some man killed by beer or whiskey, and write it on this wall:

1st. From the day the liquor traffic was allowed to come into this country from the despotisms of Europe, it has existed as a bitter, blighting, damning curse on everything decent, virtuous, and pure. Its history proves it the enemy of law, order, morality, Christianity, and civilization.

2d. The American dram-shop is the cause of more than six-sevenths of the pauperism and four-fifths of the crime in the nation. It is the hot-bed where outlaws germinate; the cradle where vice is rocked.

3d. Liquor-drinking makes the slums of great cities, and is responsible for the horrible condition of mankind in the slums.

The temperance leaders stand before the people of the world, present the indictment, and say to the liquor interest: "Come into the court of the people and plead." It does not matter whether the temperance advocate is a scoundrel or a gentleman, Mr. Beerseller. The only question the liquor interest of this country must meet is the question raised by this indictment. If the charges are false, the temperance men are liars, slanderers, maligners, and the people should put them on a rail, ride them out of the towns, and dump them into the lake. If the charges are true, no man can justify the license of a damnable traffic guilty of such social crime. It is simply a question of fact. Do the temperance men lie, or do they tell the truth? They have always proclaimed and pressed the charges. They have stood upon the public platforms and said to the keepers of the dram-shops: "Dare you come before the people and deny these charges?" How do the liquor-dealers meet the charges?

Supposing a young man living in Lake Bluff should steal a horse, and start to go to Wisconsin. He is arrested this side of the Wisconsin line, brought back and put in the county jail. The grand jury meet and find an indictment charging him with felony. The young man is brought into court to make his plea. The people prefer he should be acquitted. I believe it is a fact that the American people always sympathize with the criminal; in other words, they prefer that the man should be innocent, rather than that he should be guilty. You see a man led into a court-room, charged with the crime of murder, and the people hope that the charge is not true. The boy is brought in, the clerk reads the indictment, and asks the simple question: "Are you guilty or not guilty?" It is a question of fact between him and the people; he is expected to do one of two things, either plead guilty and accept the punishment of outraged law, or not guilty, thereby challenging the allegations of the people, and forcing their attorney to produce the proof.

The indictment is read, he is asked for his plea, "Guilty or not guilty?" but instead of making it he draws back, begins to whimper, and says: "If I had not stolen the horse some other man would!"

The court would say: "That has nothing to do with the question; it is a question involving your character, reputation, and liberty, a simple question of fact; are you guilty or not guilty?"

The prisoner continues to whimper, and says: "People have always stolen horses, and they will always steal horses, and it is not fair to pitch into me."

No court would accept such a plea. I can imagine the indignation of the court when for the third time he is asked: "Are you guilty or not guilty?"

The prisoner, drawing back among a crowd of roughs,

answers, "And if I am guilty, what are you going to do about it? All prohibitory laws for the suppression of stealing have failed. Persons steal in every section of this land. You cannot stop it. Prohibition is a failure. Let me tell you what I will do. If you will let me go and continue stealing, I will give you half the money I received for the horse."

If the judge, in face of such a threat, should accept the bribe and release the prisoner, how quickly the people would move to impeach such a judge and depose him for corrupt practices.

The temperance leaders draw the indictment on which the liquor business is brought into the court of the people. They insist and demand that the traffic shall plead; not sneak into its dens of infamy, not crouch with the bludgeon in the hands of drunken assassins, not bulldoze and intimidate law-abiding citizens; but, like any other criminal, come and plead to the indictment before the people. Bring the traffic, in the person of its representatives, into court. Read the indictment. Mr. Liquor-dealer, what is your plea?

The liquor-dealer commences to whimper, and says:
"These temperance people are all hypocrites."

"Come, now, brace up and be a man: true or false?"

He says, "If I don't sell, some other fellows will."

"What has the question of another individual's guilt to do with the question of the guilt of the whole traffic? The question is simply, Is your business guilty? That is all. If it is not guilty, the business will go on all the stronger; if it is guilty, it must die. Guilty or not guilty?"

"The people have always drank; they always will drink, and it is not fair to pitch into me."

"Guilty or not guilty, Mr. Liquor-seller? That is all."

He draws back, and says:

"Well, if I am, what are you going to do about it? If you say I shall not sell, I will sell in defiance of law. You never have stopped the sale, and never can stop it. When you say I shall not do it, I will hoist the flag of rebellion on the head of a beer-keg, and defy you to stop me. Let me tell you what I will do: If you will permit me to sell, despite the social results of my traffic, I will give you $500 out of the money I get out of the business."

And the people of Chicago and the people of this country reach out their hands and say:

"Pass over a part of the crime-tainted proceeds; divide the blood-money with us, and we will license you and swear you are respectable."

See again how the liquor-dealers meet the charges. They dare not meet them like honest men.

In Kansas I had the pleasure of visiting the State to help in the struggle for prohibition. I went down into the Democratic part of the State. Strange as it may seem to some of you, my political opinions lead me to support that party. I did not stand on a platform during the campaign that I did not ask the liquor men to come to the platform and discuss the question. I said: "If temperance men are wrong, get your ablest men and bring them here upon the platform, prove us in the wrong, and you have beaten us." Did they come? Never.

I was one day returning to my home in Lincoln, from Atchison, Kansas, when a gentleman from Chicago, by the name of Hass, came and sat down beside me. After shaking hands, he said:

"Vell, Finch, vat are you down here for?"

I said I had been doing a little work.

"Vat kind of vork?"

"Persuading the people to pass the prohibition amendment."

"You dink you bass him?"

"No; I do not think so."

"Vat you mean?"

"I know it will be passed."

He looked at me, and said: "Vell, Finch, you vas a pretty smart fellow about some dings, but you vas a dam vool about dot."

After he had finished laughing at his own wit, I said to him: "Well, now, Mr. Hass, you think I am a friend of yours, and I think I am in some respects; let me advise you as a friend, if you have any money now, put it where you can keep it; for in less than twenty years the temperance men will have abolished the liquor traffic in every State north of Mason and Dixon's line."

He laughed and said: "You can't bass dot amentment."

I said: "Why?"

He answered: "We haf cot $150,000 to put is dis fight."

I said: "Bless the Lord."

"Vat you mean?" he asked.

"I am glad you are going to make a square fight."

"Vat you mean by a square fight?"

"You say we are fools, and what we are talking about is nonsense. Do you think the people of this State are fools?"

He said, "No."

"You would be perfectly willing to let them try a case in which you had money involved?"

"Yaw."

"If we are wrong, why do you not hire the ablest lawyers and ministers, the best and purest women in this land, put them on the platform with us, and let them convince the people that we are wrong, let them show the people we are fools? Do this, and you have dug a grave for this temperance nonsense so deep that a grave robber would not waste time in hunting for it. Send a man to meet me to-morrow night, and send a good one."

"No," he said, in language I will not imitate; "we know a better way than that. The people up in the frontier counties are starving. We have money enough to divide up and put $10,000 in every frontier county in Kansas! Do you think you can talk against such arguments?"

He said that—the old criminal!

His only defence upon the trial of the case before the jury of the people was his power to corrupt men and buy them when they were starving. He did not dare to meet the charges. He did not dare to make an honest fight; but simply boasted of his power to corrupt and debase men.

Last spring a convention of liquor-dealers was called to meet at Lincoln, Neb. They met, and a committee was appointed to formulate a plan of organization. During the time the committee was deliberating, a member moved that the organization be called the Liquor-Dealers' Alliance of Nebraska. One liquor-dealer said, "Such a name would kill it."

The matter was referred to the committee, and the committee reported in favor of calling it the "Merchants' and Traders' Union,"—ashamed to own its true character, or, rather, wishing at least that the child should come out with decent clothes, although its name would make it illegitimate. So at the present time in Nebraska we have no liquor association—we have the Merchants' and Traders' Union. Printers organize printers' unions; farmers organize farmers' clubs. All decent trades organize under their own names; but the drunkard-makers organize "Merchants' and Traders' Unions." Think of a business so vile that men in it are ashamed of its name!

At the opening of the struggle for a prohibitory law last year, S. H. King, D.S., of Lincoln, formulated an indictment, and published a circular addressed to the President of this "Merchants' and Traders' Union," in which he said:

"The temperance leaders wish to try this case fairly before the people. They will hire the halls, pay every expense connected with the meetings, except the expense of your speakers, if you will send men with our speakers to try this question before the people of the State."

The temperance men waited three weeks, and the drunkard-makers made no reply. Then Mr. King offered to pay the expenses of their speakers (all but their whiskey bills) if they would discuss the question.

I met the leader of the dealers some weeks after this, and shook hands with him. I said to him: "When are you going to accept that offer of Dr. King's; when are you going to send a man to discuss the charges against the liquor trade before the people?"

Turning around to me, with a bitter oath, he said: "You don't think I'm a fool, do you? I would rather give $20,000 to prevent you from submitting the question to the people, than to try to beat you if you succeed in having it submitted."

They came to Lincoln, put their money into the banks, and they found men in the Legislature who were dishonest enough to accept it. Drunkard-making had twenty-eight votes; prohibition forty-nine. Prohibition needed fifty-one, as it takes three-fifths of all members elected to the Legislature to submit a constitutional amendment to the voters. In this way, ladies and gentlemen, this criminal traffic meets the charges of crime; by corrupting men, buying men, and destroying the very foundation of the American system of government—the purity of the individual voter.

Did you ever hear of a liquor-dealer taking the platform to defend his business on its merits as a social institution?

Two years ago the editor of a leading paper, a genial, courteous gentleman, came to Lincoln in favor of high license. His talk occupied two hours, and I talked half an hour in reply. In opening his argument he said:

"Ladies and gentlemen of Nebraska, I do not come to deny that intemperance is the curse of the State, that it is sapping and undermining our social, civil, and political institutions. All this is admitted." That was his starting-point, and he went on to say that the liquor business was bad, all bad, not a good thing in it, but it could not be prohibited; people would sell, and it was better to restrain, and get a little money out of it.

The logic of such a plea is: the Government has not stopped men from stealing by laws prohibiting stealing, so it had better license them to steal if they will divide the proceeds with the city.

A few weeks later, Judge Isaac Haskell, in the Academy of Music, in Omaha, advocated license, and I spoke for prohibition. He said at the beginning, "I despise drunkards; I hate drunkenness! It is the curse of this country." He went on to say: "People always have drank; they always will drink. You cannot prohibit the sale, you had better license and regulate it and get some money out of it to help pay taxes." By the same logic, because the Church cannot exterminate the devil, it had better go into partnership with him, and divide up the souls of men.

In Wisconsin a gentleman by the name of Wooster, an attorney, was once discussing the license question. He said, "I believe, just as honestly as my friend Finch does, that alcoholic liquor is a damnable beverage." Then he went on to say that people always had drank and always would drink. During my reply I said, if alcoholic liquor is a damnable beverage, then it follows that the traffic in a damnable beverage must be a damnable traffic, and a man who will advocate a damnable traffic in a damnable beverage must be—and there I left the audience to infer what the conclusion must be, and the man was mad.

Attack the Methodist Church and a Methodist defends; attack the Catholic Church and your opponent is proud of being a Catholic; but attack the liquor business and the liquor apologist is: "Just as good a temperance man as you are." Whenever you force the advocates of the dram-shop in this country to first principles, they always disavow their connection with the fruits of the traffic, and preface their statement with, "I am a temperance man." Why do they not say, "I am a beer man; I would rather have a boy who would get drunk; I would rather have a wife who would get drunk"? One is led to ask, if there is a redeeming feature about their accursed trade, why they do not stand by their business instead of sneaking and crawling like cowards. I would go half around the earth once, and pay my own fare, to hear a man, with cheek hard enough, and impudence great enough, to stand on the public platform, and claim that the grog-shop, judged by its record as a social institution, was fit to live.

Comparisons bring out colors. Compare the traffic with other trades. The liquor men will admit that a minister is as good as a liquor-seller as long as he behaves himself as well. Then write with the propositions already stated, the principle of political economy taught us when we were boys at school: that there are but three ways of getting money or wealth—make it, have it donated to you, or steal it. Some would say find it; the chances are too slim, and you cannot base a principle of political economy on chance. Change the form, and it is in this shape: "Without making it, inheriting it, or having it donated to him, any man who obtains wealth is a thief." In honest business every man is bound to trade in an honest manner. Although it may be unpopular doctrine in this country, I say I have no sympathy for the accursed practice called sharpness, which is held to justify lying to a man in a trade and then laughing about the trick; it is no better than stealing. I would respect a man who would steal twenty-five cents from my pocket-book as much as I would a man who would lie to me in a trade and get it in that way. When I have taken a man's word it hurts my faith in humanity to find my trust betrayed, and I lose both faith and money, while the thief simply takes money or value.

You hire a minister, you pay him money (that is, I suppose you do). The man is hired just as any other man is hired, and you expect he will give you value received for the money that he gets. I hire a minister, or help to hire one, on the same basis that I hire a man to dig a ditch. I expect he will do good work; if he does not, I will help to turn him off, and get a new one as soon as I can. But when he is hired, I am us much bound, in honor, to pay him what I agree to pay him as I am bound to pay a man who undertakes any other labor for me. You hire a minister and pay him, if you are honest; a man who will cheat a minister is as big a knave as a man who will cheat any laborer. I suppose you always pay your ministers. People do not in my State—unless it is in promises to pay. One curse of moral reform in the States is the large number of persons who are trying to dead-beat their way into Heaven on the coat-tails of a starved ministry.

I call a clergyman up here and say to him, "You receive money; now, sir, tell the people what you give them for the money they pay you; show them what you give them. Mr. Clergyman, they do not pay you alone for preaching, although it is pleasant and instructive to listen, but a preacher is a teacher, and must be judged by results to be shown by the future as well as the present. They do not pay you to run revivals, though it is a good thing to take the minds of the people away from this world to the future—and let me digress here to say, it has been my experience as a lawyer, that you can collect debts after a revival that were not worth ten cents on the dollar before. The religion of Jesus Christ does make men honest. If a professing Christian is not honest, it is good evidence that he is a religious fraud. A town could afford, for the sake of business alone, to run a revival once a year. But, Mr. Clergyman, you are not living for to-day, for to-morrow, for next week, for next year; will you come up here now, and defend your work? We do not want you to defend it by young converts or by middle-aged Christians; we want you to come here by the death-bed of the Christian and tell us, sir, if you will defend your faith there." He would come and say, "That is the test I want. I do not want you to try Christianity by the sunshine Christians, who work for the Lord on Sunday and the devil the rest of the week, nor by the people who are in the Church as an insurance society, to keep them from burning after they get on the other side; but I desire that Christianity shall be judged by the record and life-work of people who have loved God and kept His commandments. By that test I am willing the religion of the Master shall be judged." My friends, it matters not how far you may have drifted upon the sea of doubt and unbelief, you must accept such a test, and say to the man of God: "Any person whose teachings make men more honest, develop intelligence and morality, and smooth the pathway to the grave, thereby lighting up the dark future, is entitled to a world's gratitude. You earn your money, stand aside."

We want to examine another profession, and we call the school teacher. "What do you give the people for what you receive? They pay you and they expect that you will return value received. What do you give back?" The teacher would come, and calling up the merchant, doctor, lawyer, and tradesman he had taught, would say, "This is the result of my work." "Universal education is the foundation of liberty." Then reaching his hand to the teacher of morals—the minister—he would say: "Educated conscientiousness and educated intellect—a dual unit—is the only safe foundation for a government of the people, by the people, and for the people." Let me say to you, if I may say it in a temperance talk, that I believe, in this country, any system of education that does not develop the morals as well as the intellect, is a fraud and a failure. Come with me to the frontier, and I will show you men who are graduates of Eastern colleges, who have fled there to avoid the effect of crimes committed in their former homes. They are vile and devilish. To make a symmetrical man or woman, the moral nature must be developed, side by side with the intellectual, or the student becomes an intellectual monstrosity.

Therefore we say to the teacher, "Take your place with the world's workers, who fairly earn the compensation they receive."

We want to test another trade, and we shout out to the blacksmith. We say: "You get money, come up here and bring specimens of your work." He would come, and, holding up a horse-shoe, would say: "Here is my work. Every time I put a shoe on a horse the owner is better off, and I am better off, if he pays me." Placing him beside the minister and teacher, we call a milliner to represent the ladies, and say to her: "You get money, and it is an important question to us married men what you give back." She comes up, and holding a finished hat or bonnet, says: "I made that—is it not well done?" Although men make sport of hats and bonnets, yet we are free to confess that our wives look prettier when they have them on, and when we take the thing and look at it, almost trembling, fearful lest we crush it, we realize that we can earn the money to buy it in a day, and with our clumsy fingers we could never make it; so we make up our minds it is a necessity, and give the milliner a place with the others who render fair return for the money they receive.

Now having tested these, we want to test the keeper of the dram-shop in this State by the same standards. "Come up, sir. You said a minute ago the minister was as good as the liquor-seller, if he behaved himself as well. If the minister is your equal you must get into the same scales of political economy in which we have weighed him. Do not plead the baby act, but come. *You dare not come?* Do you hesitate? You toil not, neither do you spin, yet you make more money with less brains and capital than any other tradesman. Few workmen can wear such clothes as you do. What are you giving in return for what you get? Come up here, sir; bring a finished specimen of your work; hold it up here for the crowd to see, and show us its fine points!" Would he come? You could not drive him up here if you put a shotgun behind him. What should he bring? What does the dram-shop manufacture? What has it always manufactured? It has manufactured drunkards, first, last, and all the time. A dram-shop keeper is as distinctly a drunkard-maker as a man that makes shoes is a shoemaker. That is all he ever did make, that is all he ever will make.

Show us a first-class sample of dram-shop work. Do not show us a specimen of raw material from which you make your finished product. We know where and how it was raised. We know how the father gave the best years of his life and the mother her girlhood bloom to develop the bright, brave boy. We know how he entered your trap with good muscle, nerve, brain, character. Do not bring such a specimen, bring a finished job and show us how you have improved the raw material. Could you induce a liquor-dealer to come up here and hold up the specimen? What is the drunkard-maker's defence? You say to him, "You make drunkards." His very first defence is, "I do not sell liquor to drunkards; I do not have them hanging around me." If it is a good thing to make a drunkard, a drunkard must be a good thing after he is made. Suppose, ladies and gentlemen, the minister should come here and give you as a reason why his church should be endorsed, that he did not have any old Christians hanging around his prayer-meetings. Suppose he should say to the young men: "Follow Christ; attend church, Sunday-school, and prayer-meeting regularly for thirty years. By that time it will have made you such a wretch that we will kick you out when you come to church." Would that be a good advertisement for the Christian religion?

I recently saw by the papers that at a camp-meeting at Des Plaines, Illinois, they called together on the platform all the old men and women who had been in Christian work fifty years, and there was a crowd gathered in the auditorium to hear their testimony; the papers stated that as these old veterans in the service of Christ gave in their testimony of the wonderful love and goodness of God, the feeling pervading the meeting was wonderful. Why do not the drunkard-makers come here and call up a number of their veterans—a number of men they have worked on for ten, fifteen, and twenty years, with red noses, bleared eyes, ragged clothes, worn-out shoes? Bring them up here and exhibit them to prove the beautiful effects of liquor-drinking on the individual, and through the individual upon the State of which the individual is a unit. Let the liquor-seller now act as interlocutor—open the Bible and read: "No drunkard shall inherit the kingdom of heaven," and then call on them to testify. Upon their evidence we would be willing to rest the whole case against the vile traffic. Why will not the drunkard-makers do it? Is their business so mean, so low, so devilish, that when they have finished their work with a man who has stood by them through thick and thin, giving them his money, character—everything, they kick him out and say: "He is a dirty, drunken dead-beat." "We do not want any old drunkards around us!" The representatives of the business are ashamed of its results. Such is the evidence in the case.

Go down the street; a new wagon is standing by the curb; you stop to admire it, and at last say: "I wonder who made it." "I did, sir," answers the wagon-maker. "Will you please examine the wagon closely, because we challenge examination of our work." Look at the man. He is dressed in poor clothes, but see how proud he is as he contemplates his finished work. Last year while visiting a country fair, together with a friend, I was standing by one of the stock-pens, looking at a calf. "I wonder who raised the calf?" said my friend. "I did," answered a farmer standing near by. As the farmer spoke, he straightened up, as much as to say, "I am proud of my work." As you pass along the streets of our cities you frequently see other work nearly finished, sitting on the curb or wallowing in the gutter. Stop and ask: "Whose job is this?" Will the drunkard-maker run out of his factory and say: "I did that work! Look at that nose, face, and mouth. That man once had a face like yours, but I fixed him." The reason why the drunkard-makers will not defend their work is, it is indefensible. Can you separate a workman from his chips? If the liquor business is respectable, its products must be respectable. The liquor business has its own record and social crimes to meet and defend; this much, no more. These crimes have not been committed in moments of sudden anger and passion, but coolly, deliberately, and wilfully. The cost has been counted, the profits estimated, and the sanction of Government bought by men who know right from wrong, men who are responsible for their acts. They must now receive justice.

The advocates of the home will continue to press the charges against the traffic, and labor to perfect their plan of prosecution against such a wilful, malicious, cold-blooded, social criminal. The object of the prosecution is to protect the home, the wife, the baby against a traffic conducted by men who spare neither age, sex, nor condition. If the people find a verdict of guilty it will save drunkards and prevent drunkenness.

The civilized people believe in reaching down into the depths of debauchery and getting hold of the victims of this traffic; reaching with tears and prayers, and lifting and holding them up, but after they have helped them out, they believe in closing the factory itself so other men will not be tempted to ruin. Save the drunkard and prevent drunkenness.

Such, ladies and gentlemen, is the indictment against the liquor traffic, and the methods of the prosecution and defence. Firm in the belief in the righteousness of their cause, the home advocates will move for a verdict of guilty, and demand that sentence be passed on this vile hoary-headed criminal; and then, when the people have settled the question, and settled it right, we may say in reality, as we now say in theory, "Vox populi, vox Dei."

III.

WHY THE INDICTMENT IS PRESSED.

An Address delivered in the Opera-House at Waukesha, Wisconsin, Thursday, Oct. 12, 1882.

LADIES AND GENTLEMEN: Early in September, while visiting in the city of Madison, I received an invitation from temperance friends to return to the State, and talk on the subject of the prohibition of the alcoholic liquor traffic. I was willing to accept this invitation for two reasons.

1st. I was in your State four years ago, and when I returned to my Western home I carried with me the memory of many pleasant places, which I had a sincere desire to revisit that I might meet old friends.

2d. I wished to know if the people of this State were keeping pace with other States in the great work of outlawing the drunkard-makers of this country. Although the newspapers almost always tell the truth, yet sometimes you cannot depend upon their telling all the facts about the prohibition movement, and I thought if I wanted to know the whole truth, the best way would be for me to come here and see and talk with you.

I am not here to deliver any lecture or set address. I was not asked to do that. I was invited to come here and talk to you, and that is what I intend to do—talk to you upon a question that involves your interests as much as it does mine, that should interest you as much as it does me—a question that you must desire to see settled as earnestly as I do—although you and I may differ in regard to the best methods of settlement.

I always wish, when I am discussing this question before an audience, that I could call up every man and woman and swear them as a jury, on the Bible, to render an honest verdict on all the facts in the case.

A great business—a great traffic—is on trial for its life before a jury of American citizens. The temperance men of this country have indicted the traffic as a social criminal. The counts of the indictment are as positive and plain as those that are preferred against any criminal, and the people are the jury who are to determine the truth or falsity of the charges as they are stated. Therefore, I always feel that what I may say will do no good unless it shall lead the people to act—perhaps first to think, and then to act.

When I leave the platform to-night I shall be no better temperance man than I am now. If I accomplish any good it will be because I appeal to your reason and your judgment; thus leading you to act up to the full measure of your convictions. If I could, by any trick of sophistry, or any power of personal magnetism, lead every man and woman in this house to shout for prohibition, I would not do it unless your judgment, reason, and intelligence told you to do so. The battle is to death; no compromise will be accepted. Christian civilization must abolish the liquor traffic, or the liquor traffic will abolish Christian civilization. We are not in this conflict for a day, we are not in it for a week, we are not in it for a year, but we have enlisted in this campaign to stay until the close of the war.

The purpose of the temperance men of this country has been for years well defined, and they have not changed it, and will not change it, until victory shall come. They demand the complete outlawry of drunkard-making, and they will accept no compromise that allows it to exist in any form.

There is no doubt about the object of the temperance movement. The temperance men intend to destroy the drunkard-making system of America, root and branch. There is no such thing as compromise upon the issue. In the end, the liquor traffic of this country will abolish temperance, or temperance will abolish the liquor traffic. The issue is squarely made and squarely joined before the people; hence I say, I would not lead any man into the temperance ranks unless he comes because he believes it is right, and comes to stay. I would have you take the facts to your home, to your office, to your store or place of business; and when you are alone, and away from all exciting influences, sit down calmly and honestly, and, after having examined the liquor side and the temperance side of the question with equal care, make up your verdict in accordance with your honest judgment. If I should succeed in convincing you that I am right, if your judgment, reason, intelligence lead you to that conclusion, and then you refuse to work up to the full measure of your convictions, you are guilty of injustice, or cowardice, of which I would not believe you capable.

The whole issue involved is simply a question of fact. If the dram-shop of this country is a blessing; if it makes honest voters, honest citizens, kind husbands, and loving fathers; if it leads to an observance of the Christian Sabbath; if it leads to morality, manhood, and intelligence; if it discourages crime, vice, pauperism, illegal voting, and false swearing, then there can be but one position for you and me to take on the question. If the liquor traffic is a blessing, every patriotic American, every man who loves his country, owes it to his citizenship, to his own sense of honor, to stand by that traffic, talk for it, work for it, vote for it; if he is a praying man, to pray for it; if he is a preacher, he is a humbug if he will not preach for it.

If the reverse is true—if the liquor traffic of this country makes drunkards, cruel husbands, and unkind fathers; if it breaks women's hearts and degrades children; if it fills our penitentiaries, our almshouses, and our jails; if it stimulates riot in our great cities; if it stands and laughs at the stuffing of the ballot-box; if it causes men to swear falsely on the witness-stand or in the jury-box; in other words, if it is an enemy to this Government; if it is an enemy of law, and order, and civilization, then will you give me a single reason why you and I, as honest men, should vote "not guilty," and sustain it, in the face of such a record?

We are not to settle this question as individuals. The institution is a public one. If it be destroyed, that must be done by the State and National Governments. The part that you will take, the part that I shall take, in destroying it, must be that of citizens of the State and of the Republic. The question then is, not how it will affect me individually, but "What is for the best good of the whole State?"

You should weigh honestly every argument that liquor men may bring, before making up your verdict. You should weigh just as honestly the arguments of the temperance men.

A man asked me some time ago: "Would you advise a temperance man to read whiskey papers?"

I answered: "I would not give much for a temperance man if he would not do it. You are not to settle this question as an individual. You are a citizen of the State, and when you vote on this question, your vote does not alone affect yourself, but the whole State as well. You must forget your individuality, and remember your position as the patriot and citizen. If there are any arguments in favor of the liquor traffic, you owe it to your honor, manhood, and truth to weigh carefully every inducement the liquor men may bring to influence you in making up your verdict. Take the liquor traffic and all the good it has done, and put it on one side of your scales of judgment. Do not leave out anything. If there is any doubt give the criminal the benefit of it. That is the rule of law we want applied in this case. After putting all the good it has done on one side of the scale, put all the evil it has done on the other side. Take its record in this country, weigh it honestly and well, and if you believe, after an investigation of this kind, that the liquor traffic has done more good than it has done injury; that it is a blessing to the country; that it tends to perpetuate the Government, then it is your duty, beyond all question, to stand by and support the business. If the dram-shop of this country is an enemy to the State, an enemy of our institutions, I cannot see how any honest man dare stand and defend it—defend an institution that is opposed to the highest interests of his country. A man who will give aid or comfort to an enemy of his country, and thereby help to injure it, is a traitor."

Let us now examine the case. Every person who reads will be satisfied that this question must be settled in this country. The question, "What shall the Government do with the alcoholic liquor traffic?" is one that cannot fail to command attention.

As surely as this American people is a nation of freemen who govern themselves, just as certainly they will render a verdict in this case, even though that verdict destroys every political party that has an existence in this Republic.

Go home to-night, and when you reach there you find your boy in bed; he has been indisposed for several days; you see he is sick; you put your hand on his head; it is burning hot; put your fingers on his pulse; you find it running above a hundred; speak to him; he answers in broken sentences. You at once send for the physician. When he comes you ask:

"What is the matter with Willie?"

The physician makes an examination of the boy's body, asks how he has been feeling for the past few days, and tells you that Willie has a fever.

You might ask your physician, "What is fever?"

He would reply, "The child has taken, through the nose and lungs, malarial poison. The fever and the increase of pulse are simply nature's efforts to expel the poison and save the child's life. This increased activity of the vital forces is nature's way of defending herself against the poison which would destroy the organism unless expelled."

You ask: "What shall we do for Willie?"

The medical man will answer: "I shall leave medicine to help nature to do its work, and instruct you how to nurse him. Willie will get well."

Then you ask: "Doctor, how long before he can recover?"

The doctor will answer you: "Never, until the poison, the cause of the heat, the cause of the increased pulsation, is driven out of the system."

He will tell you that you can do nothing more than to help nature expel the poison, and when the poison is gone, the heat of the body will become normal, the pulse will go down, and the child will live.

To-day the political pulse is feverish. Men are talking, women are working and praying. Organizations are being formed, conventions are being held. What is the cause of this agitation? It is the poison of the liquor traffic in the political system. The temperance movement is a social power which will cease when the poison is expelled. Until that time there is no hope of political or social health.

In past ages governments born of a higher civilization developed rapidly for a few years and then died, thereby destroying the hopes of the people. Such governments sickened and died because social poison in their political systems was not expelled by rational treatment. This is the history of the world, and the only hope for long life of the American Government is the destruction of false notions of dealing with social, political disease. The hope that this Republic will live longer than other governments have, is based upon the increasing intelligence of the masses in regard to matters of social rule.

When a man says Americans should follow any custom, because people follow it in another land, he talks nonsense. Take the history of the world, and you find that, after a few years, or at most a few centuries, governments created with every prospect of success have died of diseases generated in their own systems by neglect of the ordinary rules of political hygiene. They have become things of the past, because they have allowed the poison of social and political vices to remain in their organisms.

The only hope for this Government is, that the statesmen who have charge of the life and health of the Republic shall profit by the lessons of past ages. One thing I fear is the tendency to cling to customs and habits of other lands. The attempt to develop here the customs and practices that have destroyed liberty in other lands will be national suicide.

This Government is largely like the people; it is widely different from most European forms of rule. Take this thought into your minds, and keep it there. I have never heard a gentleman talking against prohibition and defending the liquor traffic in this country who used this word "government" in its American sense. Liquor men always use the old or despotic sense of the word. Daylight and midnight are not more opposite. In this country the Government is made *by* the people; in Europe it is made *for* the people. Here it comes up *from* the people; there it comes *down* from the king. Here it is the people's power delegated to official representatives; there it is Divine (?) power delegated to the ruler. Here it is intelligent common-sense; there a superstitious clinging to old forms. Once, while I was speaking in Iowa, a gentleman interrupted me, saying: "Mr. Finch, if this Government should pass a prohibitory liquor law, it would become a tyranny."

I said to him, "Please say that again, and say it slowly so I can catch it."

He repeated it: "If the Government passes a prohibitory liquor bill, the law becomes a tyranny."

I asked, "Sir, who is the Government?"

He answered, "The people."

"The Government being the people, if a prohibitory liquor law is made by its authority, it must be either an organic law ordered by a direct vote of the people, or a statutory or functional law, enacted by the people, through their delegated representatives?"

"Yes, sir."

"If the operation of such a law is tyrannical, then the people are the tyrants?"

"Yes."

"Over whom are the people going to tyrannize?"

"The people."

I asked him if that would not be a good deal like a man sitting down on himself.

It is the grossest kind of ignorance to say that in this country, where all political power is inherent in the people, any despotism can ever exist until the people place themselves in a position where they cannot govern themselves. When a man talks about the popular will in a government of the people, being tyranny, he talks nonsense. In this country the Government is a government of the people, by the people, and for the people. This *should* be the fact, whether it is or not. Consequently, the people are the units of Government.

In a building of brick or of stone, the unit which makes up the structure is the single brick or stone in the wall. If I ask upon what the strength of this opera-house depends, you would answer me, that its shape has something to do with it; that the work upon it has something to do with it; but its strength primarily depends upon the stone in the wall. If the stone is rotten, I care not how good the work, I care not how good the plan, the building will be unstable—it will not be strong. The strength of the building is the combination of the strength of the units of the structure. In this Government the unit is the man, the woman, the child. Each man and each woman who sits before me is a part of the American Republic. The strength of the Government may depend somewhat upon its form, somewhat upon the Constitution, yet primarily it must of necessity depend upon the character of the individual citizen. Anything that debauches the citizen will injure the Government. Anything that elevates the citizen will elevate the Government. To ruin a republic is simply to ruin its citizens. To strengthen a republic, you have but to build up the intelligence, morality, and character of its units.

As the Government partakes of the nature of its citizens, so it is subject to disease, like the people who compose it. Whenever you see a moral, social, or political fever sweep over the country—when the political pulse runs up, every thinking man must perceive that somewhere in the organism of the Government there is a poison to cause the fever. Especially is this true if the fever is not temporary. Let us examine this temperance fever. It is as well marked a type of social or political fever as any country ever had. It commenced almost with the birth of the Republic. It swept over the States, increasing in force until about 1856, when suddenly in the political organism another fever broke out. It was acute in form, and yet the strange fact in regard to these two national diseases is that inherited poison is the primary cause of both. The poison of slavery was transmitted to the child from the parent, and for long years it caused local irritation; a breaking out in certain limbs of the body ensued, until in 1856 it assumed an acute form. In 1860 the question was fairly raised, "Shall the Government die or live?" As soon as that question came up, the temperance men and religious men of the nation said, "This question of the continuance of the nation's life must be settled at once. If the Government be killed, then our reform will die with it. Let us save the nation's life."

But no sooner was that fever broken up, no sooner was the poison which caused it eliminated from the body of the Government, and risk of its return avoided by the adoption of the amendments to the Constitution of the United States, than from the north to the south, from the east to the west of this nation, the temperance fever broke out anew, until to-day you can hardly ride upon a railroad train but you hear people talking about it; in the post-office they are discussing it; the newspapers are full of it; in the churches the ministers preach about it; in the prayer-meetings the Christians pray about it; in political conventions the politicians swear about it. There is not a section of this land where it is not felt to-day. What does it tell you? No matter whether you drink liquor or abstain, what does it show you? It must tell you that somewhere in the political organism of this nation there is a cause. It will not do to say that this excitement is caused by a few fanatics and a few old women. To say that, is to say the American people are fools. If the American nation, for more than seventy years, has been excited and nervous over the stories of fanatics and old women, the American people are bigger fools than anybody ever supposed them to be.

You know that the best men of to-day are talking about this question. You know that there is something, somewhere in the political organization of this country, that causes this fever. You ask me how long before it will cease. I answer, as the physician answered in regard to your boy, "Never, until the grog-shop poison, the cause of this disease, is forever eliminated from the political organism of this country." This question you must settle. You cannot nominate a man for Congress; you cannot nominate a man for the Legislature,—from this time forward—you will never even nominate a man for President where this issue will not be forced upon him.

The liquor oligarchy crack the whip of political corruption over the political parties of this country, and cry, " Do our bidding or perish." You may talk about postponing it, but the drunkard-makers demand of every candidate for office that he get down in the dirt of political subserviency. If he wants a nomination he must come into convention with the token of his own defilement on him, so that the delegates who are tools of the grog-shops may smell it. If he will not do that, he must keep his mouth closed and his principles to himself.

When the temperance agitation started in this country, there were two classes of men, just as there are now. One class said, " If the liquor traffic is a good thing, let it go free;—do not hamper it with law; do not shackle it; give it a fair chance for existence; do not put any more chains on it than you would on a grocery or a dry-goods store. If the liquor business is a friend of the Republic, the Republic ought to be a friend to the liquor business and should leave it free and unfettered. On the contrary, if it tends to loosen the bands of the young Republic, and break down our institutions, kill it, and kill it at once."

The other class of men said, " Hold on; that will not do; the people are not educated up to prohibition."— Did you ever hear anybody say, "the people are not educated *up* to prohibition"? I always feel like thanking a liquor man when he uses the expression. You never heard him say, "the people are not educated *down* to prohibition." By his own language he admits that prohibition is on a higher moral, social, and political level than the license compromise with evil.—This other class of men went on to say, " There is no use in making a law until the people are educated up to the point of obeying it." And when they said that, they said God Almighty made a mistake. You ask me what I mean? I mean this: That if God had not passed His prohibitory commandments until the people were educated up to the point of obeying them, He never would have ordained them. He said, " Thou shalt not steal." They were stealing then in the wilderness, and there is stealing in America to-day. He said, "Thou shalt not bear false witness." I presume they were doing it then, and it is certainly being done to-day. If you do not think so, indict a liquor-seller, and bring him into court, and ask some of his customers to swear against him. While God amid the thunders of the mountains was saying, "Thou shalt have no other God," His high-priest, at the foot of the mountain, was setting up a calf for the people to worship.

There is a class of men, and we have a great many of them, claiming to be leaders of public opinion, who are incessantly preaching that there is no use in making a law until the people are educated up to the point of obeying it, while they know, if they know anything of the principles of government and law, that it is the thinnest twaddle ever used by demagogues to catch fools.

Law is not passed for men who will obey,—it is passed for the men who are not educated up to the point of doing so. If all the people of this country were educated up to the point where they would not steal, would you want any law against stealing? If they were educated up to the point where they would not murder, would you want any law against murder? What do you want any law against stealing for? Not for the men who are educated up to the point where they will not steal. You want a law against stealing for those who are not educated up to the belief that it is particularly wrong to take your horse. You do not want a law against murder for men who are educated up to the point where they will not kill, but you want a law against murder for men who are not educated up to the point of regarding human life as sacred. The whole theory of law is, to deal with the law-breaker, and not the man who will obey. It is for the men on a degraded plane, and not for the men on an exalted plane. Law is the educator.

This is true throughout all of God's universe. Go home to-night and take your baby boy in your arms. Baby knows nothing about law. He can say a few words— nouns, the names of things with which he is familiar.

If you tell him to say law, he will say it, but he does not know the difference between law and a turnip or a cabbage. There is a fire in the stove and it is hot. Baby is attracted by the red color. He places his little hand on the stove and is burned. Baby is punished by the law, even more than an old man who knew all about it, because the man's hand is hard and baby's is soft. The law is there as an educator, and baby will not be as apt to put his fingers out in that way again. A mother goes up-stairs with her little one. There is a chair by the window and the window is open. The mother is busy; baby creeps to the chair and climbs upon it—tumbles out of the window and breaks his neck. What killed him? The law of gravitation; yet baby did not know of the law. The law was passed upon correct principles, and it has existed in nature since the foundation of the universe. You gray-haired men can almost remember the time when Sir Isaac Newton discovered the law of gravitation. Before that, there was not a man in the world who could tell why he fell down. They did not know why they did not fall off the earth instead of towards it. Every step that science takes, every step that the medical profession takes, is simply digging out laws that have existed since the earth was formed.

God said it is wrong to steal: "Thou shalt not." The law lay along the principle. God said it was wrong to bear false witness: "Thou shalt not." The law lay along the principle. God said it was wrong to kill: "Thou shalt not." The law lay along the principle. That is God's plan. I presume that we have men in this country, who, if God had invited them into the Garden of Eden, would have told Him He was making blunders, and advised Him to change His plans.

In my own State, in the cattle counties, for several years, the law against murder was practically a dead letter. Public sentiment was very low. It was really considered a mark of honor to have killed a man. If a man told another he lied, a revolver would be drawn, and life lost. The people said: "Served him right." A man going along the street was pointed out as having killed two men. Several times I have been touched on the shoulder by a friend who said: "That person has killed a man." Public sentiment justified it. For a long time it was impossible to indict a man for murder and convict him on trial. Perhaps there was not a man on the jury but had committed a murder himself. The result was "not guilty," or "killed the man in self-defence." But the Government did not pass laws on the level with the moral sense of the people. The Government did not say: "We cannot prohibit you from shooting, so we will pass a license law and allow you to shoot, if you will give us $500; we will keep the penalties down until you are educated up to the point of thinking it is wrong to kill." The Government said, "It is wrong to kill," and it held the law over these counties, till the people came up, *up*, UP to the law, and to-day there is no portion of the United States where the law is better enforced. It is better enforced in the counties of Nebraska than in the cities of Chicago and Milwaukee. The State acted on the correct principle: the law was used as an educator.

The talk of the license men is that the Government shall pass a law on the level of the worst element of the people, and then educate the people up *through* and *above* it. This is utter nonsense. The license idea has heretofore prevailed. License laws have been passed. For more than seventy years, in this country, we have been trying to regulate and restrain the liquor business with license laws, and what has been the result?

A gentleman said to me the other day: "Prohibition does not prohibit."

I said: "That is not the question. The question for you as a license man to answer is, 'Does regulation regulate?'"

When prohibition has been tried as long as license has been, backed by the State and National Governments, if it prove as big a fizzle as license now is, we will consent to the adoption of a new plan. We are not particular about the plan; it is simply the *result* we wish to achieve. For more than seventy years we have tried this license system. The liquor business was weak when the license plan was adopted; but under the fostering care of this accursed fraud it has become the autocrat of politics; and you know this to be the fact.

That license laws are a dead letter, no man will dare to deny. In your own State the law says the dramshops shall not sell liquor to minors. They do sell to minors. The law says they shall not sell liquor to drunkards. They do sell to drunkards. The law says they shall not sell liquor on Sunday. They do sell on Sunday. The law says they shall not sell adulterated liquors. They do sell poisoned liquors. For more than seventy years in different States in this Union the people have tried to make this old license fizzle work. The temperance people during this time have done all that they could to secure obedience to the law, and to save men from the pernicious influence of the licensed liquor traffic. They have used the pledge. They have gone down into the gutter and lifted out the victims of this devilish system. And when they have lifted them out of the pitfall, the license men vote to keep the pitfall open, so that other men may fall in; thus temperance men have a job on hand all the time. Temperance workers have established temperance lodges. They have built Friendly inns. They have built coffee-houses. They have established reading-rooms, and put lecturers on the platform and paid them. They have circulated books and arguments; and *they have gone into towns and cities and organized leagues to enforce this law and try to make it work.* Now, after seventy years of earnest trial, after seventy years of tears and prayer and hard work, and money-giving and struggling, I stand here to say, what no man dares challenge, that this work has demonstrated the license system of this country to be the most unmitigated humbug that was ever invented by bad men to fool an ignorant people. But the license man springs up, ready to raise an objection:

"You have laws enough now, if you would only enforce them."

"Sir, we have tried to enforce them, though they are not laws of our making. We have no faith in them; have you?"

WHY THE INDICTMENT IS PRESSED.   49

"Yes," he answers.
"You are in favor of license?"
"Yes."
"You voted for license?"
"Yes."
"You believe it will work?"
"Yes."

"Why, then, do you not make it work? If you are a license man, are you not ashamed to come and ask the prohibitionist, 'Why do you not enforce our law?' Why do you not enforce it yourselves? We do not believe in the system. We have worked for its enforcement, because it was the best thing we could do. We never believed in it."

Before the high license law was passed in Nebraska two years ago, I was talking with a gentleman, a member of the State Senate. He asked:

"What are you going to do about this high license law?"

I answered, "Nothing."
"Are you in favor of it?"
"No, sir."
"Why not?"

"I believe if whiskey-selling is a good thing, the poor man has as much right to sell as the rich man. If it is a good thing, let everybody sell it. If it is a curse, LET NO ONE SELL IT."

He said: "That is theory."
I replied: "It is fact."
He said: "A prohibitory law cannot be passed, and could not be enforced if it was passed."
"Yes, a prohibitory law could be enforced."
"But who will do it?"
"The prohibitionists. Give them the law, and if they do not make it operate then repeal it."
He said: "This license law will be enforced."

I answered: "You know, and every man in this country knows, that a license law never was enforced and that it never will be. License law means, let the liquor man pay so much money for license; then let him do as he pleases. You support license because it is as near free whiskey as you can get. If this license law is passed it will be a dead letter because your men will not do anything, and the prohibitionists do not believe in it."

Said he: "If it be passed, it will be enforced."

"Who is to see that it will be enforced?"

"The license men."

The law was passed. When it came into effect last June it was universally disobeyed over the State. The liquor men would not even pay the license. The prohibitionists waited to see what the license men would do. They wanted to see if men who talked and voted license were honest. The license men did not lift a finger! At last an editor, in a long article, declared that I was the leader of the strongest political temperance organization in the country, and that it was my duty to enforce that law! The same man had been in the Legislature and had voted for the law. A few days after I met him, and he inquired:

"Did you see that editorial of mine?"

"Yes; and I laughed."

"Why did you laugh?"

"To think what a fool you are."

"What do you mean?"

I asked: "Whose law is it; your law or mine?"

"It is our law."

"You believe in it; I do not. You voted for it; I did not. You say regulation will regulate; I say it will not. Is not such the fact?"

"Yes."

"Then take care of your own babies, please. Do not come around to me to have me take care of them."

In not a single instance in the State did the license men lift a finger to enforce the law; and when at last the rebellion had become general, the prohibitionists of Nebraska stepped out to say: "Drunkard-makers, you must pay this license." And after one of the bitterest fights ever made in our State, they were compelled to pay over the money, in all sections of the State, though the law was and is a dead letter in all other respects.

As well try to regulate a rattlesnake by holding it by the tail, as to permit and then attempt to regulate saloons. The way to regulate a rattlesnake is to kill it, smash its head—its tail may live until sundown, but it cannot bite. The way to regulate the liquor business, is to kill its head, the licensed grog-shop, the school of vice, crime, and political corruption. Its tail may live in cellars and dark places during the twilight of ignorance and superstition, but when its head is destroyed it is powerless to resist—to bulldoze officers or breed assassins.

In the city of Omaha, Neb., there was living, a little more than a year ago, a gentleman by the name of Watson B. Smith, clerk of the United States Court, one of the finest gentlemen ever in the State—a leading politician, an earnest Christian, a prominent layman in the Baptist Church; a man who had done as much for Nebraska Sabbath-schools and Nebraska civilization as any other man. Mr. Smith was an honest man. He said: "The liquor-sellers must obey the law in this State." Some business men rallied round him. They tried to make the liquor-sellers take out licenses in accordance with the laws of the State. They commenced their prosecutions in July, and in October Col. Watson B. Smith, at the hour of midnight, was shot down by assassins, at his office door, in the United States Government building, for no other reason than that he was working to make liquor cut-throats obey law.

In all parts of this land the liquor business to-day is an outlaw, and there is nothing too vile or too mean for it to do. When a man says, "I am a license man," the only thing I desire to ask of him is to be an honest believer; that is, to try to enforce the law in which he believes.

If you think license ever was, or ever can be made to work, suppose you try it to-morrow morning. Go down and swear out warrants against liquor-dealers who are selling liquors to minors; arrest those who are selling adulterated liquors; keep it up for six months, and if at the end of that time you are not a prohibitionist, I will buy you the best suit of clothes to be found in this town. You know, my friends—I care not how much you talk in favor of license—that you do not try to make license work. You know that if you did, the liquor men would endeavor to injure your business and smirch your character; that they would hire bullies to come up behind you and club you on the head. In Milwaukee, simply because some of the citizens asked that the law might be enforced so far as closing disreputable places on Sunday, the liquor men organized and boycotted every man who dared ask the enforcement.

After seventy years' trial every man must be convinced that to talk regulation, to talk license, is to advocate the most contemptible nonsense.

The question which comes up as we proceed to look for a remedy is: What is the nature of the dram-shop —what is its relation to the Government? I said a few moments ago—and I wish to repeat it, because it is the turning-point of this discussion—that this Government is not like European Governments. That men drink liquor in Germany and Russia is no reason why the liquor traffic should be authorized by American Governments. On the contrary, it is the reverse of a reason. The difference in the forms of government must be remembered.

Suppose the people of Russia become drunken, debauched, riotous, and violent, who will control them? "The Government." Who is the Government? "The Czar with his army." He can control them, because the Government is distinct from, and independent of the subject in his empire. There is an immense standing army at the command of the Czar ready to suppress any uprising of a drunken, an ignorant, and a riotous populace. Suppose the people of this country become drunken, debauched, and riotous—who is going to control them? "The Government." Who is the Government? "The people." Then the people are to govern themselves? "Yes." But the people being the rioters, and at the same time being the governing power, the Government becomes anarchy. You see the difference at once.

The only safety of this country is the intelligence of its voters; intelligence on the farms and in the workshops; intelligence so widely diffused that high and low, rich and poor, shall be alike educated. To say that, because an institution can safely exist where there is a standing army to control it, it can exist without danger in a republic, where the citizen is the controlling power, is foolish.

Ever since I have lived in Nebraska, men have come to me and said: "Your taxes amount to so many dollars." "For what?" "In part for school purposes."

Why do they tax me? I have no child old enough to go to school. Why do they require me to pay for schools? Because the very basis of this Government is the intelligence of its citizens. When you educate the boys you strengthen the Government, and by strengthening the Government you insure your property, because property can only exist while Government stands. There can be no property without law, and law is the child of government. I never in my life paid a cent into a school fund that I did not regard it as just so much insurance on my life and property. It costs less money to educate a boy and make a man of him, than to let him go to the bad and take care of him afterward.

Take the instance of the James boys. The twenty thousand dollars that Governor Crittenden gave to have Jesse James assassinated would have educated twenty boys in the path of manhood. The James boys at an early age were thrown into the society of bushwhackers and renegades, and grew up in that terrible school of outlawry and crime. For twenty years the State of Missouri trembled in their power. Their training with cut-throat bands made them criminals. It is cheaper for the Government to educate the children than to take care of the criminals.

The foundation of this Government rests on four things: the Church—and I do not speak of any particular Church, but of the Church universal—the school, the press, and the home. Take these four institutions from America, drive them out so they will not come back, and you can dig the grave of this Republic, and the corpse will soon be ready.

When the people tax me to maintain schools, on the theory that the intelligence and virtue of the people are the only true safeguards of a republic, I have a right to ask, "Does the liquor traffic develop or destroy intelligence and virtue?" You say that the common school has a wonderful influence. What influence has the dram-shop? It must have some kind.

Four years ago I received a challenge from Judge Isaac S. Haskell, of Omaha, to come to that city and discuss with him the question of prohibition. The judge was a license man, and I very gladly accepted the invitation to meet him. I thought he would defend the liquor traffic, and I prosecute it; consequently I desired to get the evidence against his old client in the town where the discussion was to take place. I went to Omaha after facts. The first place I visited was the office of the superintendent of city schools. I asked the superintendent, "How many schools have you here?"

He answered, "Seven: six ward schools and a high-school; also, a college and some private schools."

"How many teachers have you in the city institutions?"

"Eighty-four."

"How many graduated last year?"

"One hundred and eight."

I then went to look up the record of the other schools, the dram-shops. I went to their superintendent, the police judge, and asked him:

"How are your schools getting along?"

He said, "Are you drunk?"

I said, "You should not think I am drunk because most of the men brought here are."

He inquired what I meant. I explained. He laughed. "So you think I am the superintendent of the grog-shops."

"Are you not?"

"Well," said he, "I do not know but I might be so termed."

"Well, judge," said I, "how many schools of this kind have you in the city?"

"One hundred and fifty-five that are licensed."

"How many teachers in those schools?"

"Including cappers, bar-tenders, and owners, about four hundred."

"How many scholars did you have up for graduation during the year?"

Opening his commitment-book, he rapidly separated the criminal entries into classes, and after adding, said: "I gave diplomas to the rock-pile, county jail, and fined about twelve hundred. Some graduated three or four times over; but it is perfectly safe to assume that there were six hundred different graduates."

Now, my friends, as thinking people, I want to ask you if the social effect of this system of education is not a question of importance. You say that these free schools with seven buildings, eighty-four teachers, and one hundred and eight graduates, have a wonderful influence — what kind of an influence have the dram-shops? There are seven schools to one hundred and fifty-five drinking-places, eighty-four teachers to four hundred cappers, bar-tenders, and owners; one hundred and eight graduates in learning, against six hundred graduates in crime. Now I submit that it is a question that every man who loves his country must ask himself, "What is the nature of the educational influence of the grog-shops on our voters and people?" If the dram-shop education is good, then take the dram-shop, and place it beside the school, and we shall have the home, the church, the school, the newspaper, and the dram-shop as the bulwark of our liberties. If its education is all bad, if it tears down the work of the other institutions, then let the dram-shop be abolished. What sense is there in educating a boy until he is twenty-one years of age, and then opening a drinking-hell to send him to a drunkard's grave, to prison, or to the gallows? What sense is there in running these two systems of education? The dram-shop destroys the work your common schools are doing, debauches and rots the very foundations of this Government, by corrupting the individual character of the men and women who compose the Government.

You may ask what is the influence of the liquor traffic. I do not need to insult your intelligence by going into details to show you. You all know. Suppose you open twenty-five drinking-places in Waukesha for the first time in the history of this town.

Suppose you never had them here before. When you have opened them and they are in good running order, what other building will you have to erect in this town? Suppose you open twenty-five dry-goods stores; they would take care of themselves. With twenty-five groceries, it is the same; but with twenty-five grog-shops you must have a prison. You can no more run a grog-shop without a prison as a tail, and officers as strings, than you can fly a kite without the same requisites. Why do you need a police force in a city like this? How often are your policemen called upon to go to a church and arrest old Christians coming from prayer-meeting under the influence of Christ's spirit, to keep them from fighting? How many knock-down fights did you ever know to occur in this town under the intoxicating influence of pork and beans bought in a grocery store? How many men did you ever know in this town to go home at night under the influence of new boots bought in a boot store and kick their wives out into the snow? How many assaults and batteries and riots were ever caused in this town by the stimulating effect of beefsteak bought in a butcher-shop? What other institution in the world is there that necessitates officers to arrest its products, and prisons in which to lock them up?

I was in Illinois City last winter when a gentleman asked me to ride through the place with him. In riding through the city I was astonished to see how their dram-shops were located—three in a bunch—the bunches being in different parts of the city. I said to the gentleman, "These liquor-dealers must be fools; why do they open their grog-shops so near each other?"

He said, "We compel them to locate together, or we will not license them."

"Why so?"

He answered, "If three of them are together one policeman can watch the three. If they were scattered all over town we should require a larger police force."

Speaking with the chief of police of one of the largest cities of this country, a man who drinks liquor and who is a license man, I asked, "If you abolish every drinking-place in this city, how many policemen would be required?" He replied, "Five hundred night watchmen could do our work." They have at the present time more than twenty-five hundred armed, disciplined, and uniformed policemen.

No honest man can doubt that the liquor-shops of this country are primary schools of crime.

At a fair, sometime since, I addressed a very large audience in the forenoon; in the afternoon I was walking about the grounds looking at the exhibition, when a man came to me and said:

"Are you the man who talked temperance this forenoon?"

"Yes, prohibition and temperance."

He said, "Well, it all means the same thing."

I told him some people thought so.

"Now," said he, "I do not want to insult you."

I felt it was exceedingly fortunate both for him and for me,—it might save unpleasantness.

He said, "I am a liquor-dealer, and the managers of this fair did a dirty mean thing to get you here. This fair represents all industries, and mine is a legitimate business. For them to get anybody here, at a public fair, to bring into disrepute one of the industries of the country, is mean."

I said, "It does look as though there was a reason for your complaint. My friend, I believe you have been insulted, and, if I was in your place, I would go over to the president's office, and kick up the biggest row they ever had on this ground. You say this is for all the industries of the country." I took out of my pocket a premium list, and said, "Here is a premium for the nicest horses, the nicest cows, the best calves; for chickens, ducks, turkeys, and geese; for all kinds of ladies' work; for cheese and butter. The managers of this fair seem to have offered a premium to encourage every industry but yours. Now I would raise a row."

He asked, "What do you mean?"

I replied, "You do a legitimate business. You are manufacturing and turning out your products all the time. They ought to offer a premium on some of your finished jobs. They ought to put down $25 for the best specimen of a bummer made in a grog-shop in this country; $15 for the next, and $10 for the next, and a red ribbon for the fourth. If you will go with me to the president we will ask his reasons for not doing it."

The liquor-dealer straightened up, and said I was an infernal fool.

Drunkard-makers say temperance men talk gush and nonsense. But, I answer, the liquor business can no longer plead the baby act in this country. It must stand on the same plane of political economy with every other trade. It must be judged by its results.

In the West, since I have lived here—and I have been here some years—I have heard some men say that in New York City the Democrats stuffed the ballot-boxes and hired repeaters to vote "early and often." You ask me if they did this. Undoubtedly they did. Up and down the land we have heard men talking about the purity of the ballot-box. People say, "Does not corruption exist in New York?" Of course it does. If it exists, what is the cause of it? Did you ever stop to think? There is no such corruption in the country districts. You cannot corrupt the farmers, you cannot corrupt the sober men. If corruption exists at the ballot-box there must be a cause for it. What is the cause?

There stands a workman; he does not drink; he has money in his pocket; he has a good job; his brain is clear; his wife and family are happy. For the first time he goes to a drinking-place and drinks. During four or five years he goes down and down, and by and by he gets reckless, loses his business, and his family have to beg. He is an outcast on the street. On an election morning this man stands on a street corner, ragged, dirty, sick; craving for something to drink; such a craving for the poison, that he would sell his soul for a drink of liquor. The only thing that man possesses which will bring money, is his vote. Do you suppose that man, with morals gone, reputation gone—starving, ragged, and hungry—will vote like an American citizen, according to his convictions, if he can get money for voting otherwise? Sad to confess, no.

The dram-shop is the cause of most of the corruption in our great centres of population. Talk about purifying the ballot-box in our great cities! The ballot-box never will be purified until the voters are purified. You may pass election laws and fence around the ballot-box, but the only hope of its integrity lies in a pure citizenship.

What is true of New York is true of every great city. The debauchery of the voter, the corruption of the ballot-box is an effect; and the cause is the American dram-shop. The tendency of the liquor interest in this country is to degrade men; to debauch voters; to stuff ballot-boxes; to elect bad men to office, and, in every way, to tear down and ruin American institutions; consequently, it is a question in this country whether the American system of government shall live, or whether this curse shall destroy it.

Now, as to the remedies. One man asks, "Has the Government the right to destroy this business?" A friend interrupted me once to say: "I have a natural right to sell liquor."

"What do you mean by a natural right?"

He did not answer.

"I suppose you mean, if you mean anything, that in a state of nature you had a right to sell it; that is, when you were a wild man you had a right to do so. And to whom would you sell whiskey in a state of nature? You cannot sell whiskey unless you have somebody to sell to, and that would be a state of association. You could not trade unless men come together to trade, and that would be the formation of society. All trade is the child of society. If trade is the child of society, society has the same right as any parent. If trade will not behave itself, society may take it across its knee. If that will not do, it may do more."

Suppose a man comes here with a club to kill me; probably under the laws of this State I would be compelled to retire as far as I could with safety, but when the issue is between his life and mine he must die, because every man has the right to defend himself. I am a man, I have a right to be a man. I exist, I have a right to exist, and the right to exist takes with it the right to defend that existence. This is the foundation of social and political ethics.

A story is told of a muscular preacher who believed in using all the powers the Lord had given him, fists as well as tongue. Some of his flock thought he was too much inclined to use his fists, so they sent him this text: "If a man smite thee on thy right cheek, turn to him the other also." They thought they would puzzle the old man to harmonize the text with his conduct. He said he would preach from it the next Sabbath; and on that day he opened with the usual services, took his text, and went ahead. He went on to say that the Bible was distinguished from all other books by appealing to the God-man and not to the brute-man, by teaching man to use reason and judgment, not passion or lust. "If a man should strike you on the right cheek he might do it through mistake, or might do it through a feeling of mischief, and if you turned on him without asking any questions and struck back, that would be acting like a brute. You should use your reason and judgment; be certain before you act. You should turn the other cheek. If he strike you on that, you know that he means it; then go for him."

That may not be very good Bible interpretation, but it is a very good interpretation of the law of this country.

The right that is inherent in every individual, self-defence, is the safety of the State, of which the individual forms a part. The Government has a right to defend its own life, and we have seen in this country to what extent it may defend it. You remember, and so do I, when more troops were necessary and a conscription act was passed to draft men into the army, how many men fled to Canada to avoid the result. Why was the draft ordered? On this same principle, the right of the Republic to defend its own existence. That right is so sacred that the Government can take men from their homes, dress them in its army blue, put guns in their hands and place them on battle-fields to be shot to death to save its life. The right of the Government to defend its own life must remain as it is, or the Union is good for nothing. The Government has the right to destroy any business, any custom, or any trade that tends to destroy the Republic by debauching the character of the citizens who compose its society. The highest courts of the nation have again and again affirmed this right and power. A government which has the right to take its free citizens from their homes against their will, and place them on a battle-field to save its life, certainly has the right to kill a vile drunkard-factory that is threatening its existence.

The Government has the right, through its police power, to protect its own life.

If there exists this right, the question is how to use it. As I have said, this Government is not like European dynasties. They do not recognize the fact that the civilization evolves, develops. This Government does recognize that fact. I do not know when I have laughed as much as I did the other day, as I read a Democratic platform adopted in one of the States. The reason I laughed was because I was once a Democrat myself, and used to believe such foolishness. What they said was, " We are in favor of returning to the primitive government of our forefathers." That was their declaration. I laughed. You ask me why, and I tell you. Since the sunrise of creation's morning humanity has moved on, on—up the hill of progress. There have been eddies in the great tide of advance that have made it seem almost as though humanity was moving backward; but I stand here unhesitatingly to affirm that, as a whole, humanity has never retrograded. As society has advanced, government has advanced. First, the patriarchal form, then as the people progressed others were adopted.

Fifty years ago, in the days of our forefathers, we did not need any legislation to look after railroads, because then there were no railroads. As mankind went forward, inventive genius developed railroads. As soon as they were developed, the Government had to meet the railroad problem; and to-day, in that question, this Republic has as mighty a problem of legislation to deal with as our forefathers ever had.

Fifty years ago we did not need a government to look after the telegraph wires; to-day we require it.

Ten years ago we did not need a government to look after telephones; to-day it is necessary.

Thirty years from this time our civilization will be far in advance of to-day. New social problems are constantly arising, and as these are forcing themselves to the front, the Government must meet and solve them, or die.

In Europe they have never provided for this growth. There the governments are like iron bands. Take Russia to-day; it is a despotism because the Empire has no provision for development. The people have developed until the Government holds them like bands. The people have tried to break one with the dagger, with the bomb, and by social revolution, but they have not succeeded. But as sure as God's people go up to the point He has ordained them to reach, just so sure that Government will go to pieces and let the people advance. There can be no doubt about it.

In much of Europe the only avenue for mankind's advance is the pathway of bloodshed. Every advance made has been with the bayonet or the dagger.

The men who laid the foundations of this Government did more wisely than that. They said, "This nation will grow."

The prudent mother who has a little girl who is growing very rapidly, when she buys a dress of durable material, puts in tucks, so that when the child grows the dress can be let out to fit her.

The wisest thing ever said by an American statesman was: "Unless we provide for the peaceable future development of the people, some day they will develop through bloodshed and assassination. The founders of the nation gave us a Constitution under which the people can develop without fighting and without revolution. In the Constitution of every State they put an adjustable line, providing that the people may, when they wish, amend their organic law and develop their government, without riot, without revolution, and without bloodshed." In other words, if there was a revolution, it should be a revolution by votes, not by bayonets.

The temperance men say the remedy for this evil of

intemperance is simply that the Government shall develop. For years, long years, in the State of Wisconsin they have gone, with tears in their eyes, to the Legislature of this State and said: "Grant us—the people, in a government of the people, by the people, and for the people—the right to rule ourselves. Give us the privilege of amending our organic law. Not YOUR organic law, Mr. Legislator, but OUR law. Give us—the people—the right that belongs to us, to govern ourselves." They have gone up there in thousands, by their names, and have begged the party machines in this State to recognize one of the first principles of this Government, by submitting an amendment to the Constitution in accordance with the genius of American institutions. But the liquor men have said, "If you submit it, the people will pass it. You must not submit it; if you do, we will beat your party." And the party men, whipped down by the liquor-sellers, said it would not do to submit it.

You say Russia is a despotism. Why? Because the Czar says, "You shall not make a constitution for yourselves." In Wisconsin the party machine sits on the neck of the people and says, "You shall not make a constitution for yourselves." Can you tell me the difference between the despotism of the Czar and a despotism of political demagogues?

You say in Wisconsin you have a government of the people and for the people, and you know that for years and years the statement has been made a lie by the political machines of this State. The people begged for the right to vote on a primary principle of government, but, because some men feared it would knock a cog off the wheel of the old party machine, they denied the right of the citizens to govern themselves.

Thus, ladies and gentlemen, under the license system the liquor oligarchy has grown until it impudently defies law and seeks to overturn the very foundations of the Government. Its character as a political assassin is so well known that politicians ask—not, "What will the people do?" but, "What do the liquor men want? how will the dram-sellers regard our action?"

In view of all the facts, it seems to be the plain duty

of every patriot and every citizen to rally to the defence of American liberties, and by crushing the grogshop oligarchy, strengthen the foundations of our civil and political institutions. I have faith to believe that the jury of America's voters will condemn the traffic, and that the Republic will execute the sentence. Then, indeed, may the patriot poet sing:

> " Columbia, Columbia, to glory arise,
> The queen of the world and the child of the skies!
> Thy genius commands thee; with rapture behold,
> While ages on ages thy splendors unfold.
> Thy reign is the last and the noblest of time,
> Most fruitful thy soil, most inviting thy clime.
> *Let the crimes of the East ne'er encrimson thy name;*
> *Be freedom, and science, and virtue, thy fame.*"

IV.

AN EXAMINATION OF THE ISSUES.

An Address delivered at Lewis' Opera-House, Des Moines, Iowa, April 22, 1882.

Ladies and Gentlemen: I have come to your State, by request of the Grand Lodge of Good Templars, to discuss the necessity, feasibility, and practicability of the outlawry or inhibition of the alcoholic liquor traffic. This traffic having been indicted by the legislative grand jury, is now in the court, to be tried by the grandest jury of a republic—the people.* Your legislators have indicted the alcoholic liquor traffic for social crime; the case is in your hands to investigate, consider, and determine. The law-making power being the one to pass on the question, the issue involved is not one of law, but of fact. I enter this investigation with misgivings in regard to my own abilities to materially assist you. I come as an assistant, not as a teacher, and hope if I do anything, I may assist you to reach a just, righteous verdict. In view of the great interests involved, I would not, as an American citizen, dare to mislead you, but deem it my duty to counsel the fullest, fairest, and most complete investigation of all the facts in this case.

The advocates who are defending the criminal have, and probably will continue to exhaust every quibble before they will go to trial on the *real issue*. A celebrated lawyer once said to a graduating class, "If you have a client who is guilty, and who has no defence, never let him be tried." "How will you prevent it?" asked one of the students. "If they force you into

---

* The Legislature the previous winter had submitted a prohibitory amendment to the State Constitution. The amendment was to be voted on at a special election the following June.

court, try the opposing attorney, try the witnesses, try the judge, and if nothing else will win, try the jury, but never try your client." This advice has been and will be adopted by the defence, and it may be best for us at the commencement of this investigation to determine by whom and how the case is to be tried, and what issues are, and what are not involved in the case.

This question is to be tried by you voters, not as Germans, Irishmen, Englishmen, Scotchmen, New Yorkers, or Illinoisans, but as citizen voters of Iowa, bound by your honor as voters to do what in your honest judgment is best for the State. It is to be deprecated that the advocates defending the liquor traffic have thought it necessary to appeal to class, clan, and national prejudices, thereby disintegrating society for selfish ends. Although such demagoguery will not influence sensible men, it shows how utterly reckless and unscrupulous are the advocates on the other side.

See what interests they jeopardize to secure an acquittal. A republic must be homogeneous if it hopes to live and prosper. An individual cannot take into his stomach pine-knots, sticks, stones, tacks, and nails, allow them to remain there unassimilated and undigested, and live; so Iowa cannot take into her political organism New Yorkers, Illinoisans, Germans, Irishmen, and persons from other nations and States, allow them to remain in the political organism banded together as clans and nationalities, unassimilated and undigested, and politically or socially prosper. Anything that prevents the assimilation or digestion of food in the physical organism is an enemy of the body. Any man or class of men who try to induce Germans to band together in this country as Germans, or Irishmen as Irishmen, is a traitor to the Government and its liberties. All such work and talk is unrepublican, undemocratic, and un-American, as well as an insult to the nationality thus sought to be used as tools.

The term "German vote," which, during the last few years, has become a power in certain political circles, originated in this vile demagoguery. All voters in this country are Americans, native and foreign born. No man has a right to vote in Iowa as a New Yorker or a German. If he votes, it is as a citizen of Iowa. Any man who does not love this country more than any other had better emigrate. American know-nothingism was a curse to this nation, because it acted as a disintegrating force on society. German know-nothingism, as now developed by tricksters and liquor-sellers, is of the same class of political heresies. If it continue it will undoubtedly develop American know-nothingism as its antidote, when the Germans who have been led into this movement will be the ones to suffer, as five American votes will count more than one German vote. But it is to be hoped that this accursed political trickery may die before such a remedy will be necessary. No greater insult could be offered to the German-American voters of Iowa than to insinuate that they are controlled by their stomachs instead of their brains, and that with a swill-pail full of beer they can be led up to the polls and voted either way. The grass on Southern battle-fields, growing green over the graves of noble Americans born in Germany, who died for this country, hurls the lie in the teeth of the men who claim that Germans are controlled by appetite and by liquor demagogues, not by principle.

These men who appeal to German ideas, theories, and practices, do so to subserve selfish interests, and I submit that such practices are enough to cast doubt on the merit of their defence. Anything that excites race-feeling instead of intelligence, appetite instead of reason, passion instead of conscience, self-interest instead of duty, should be shut out of a case involving grave questions of the functions and duties of government.

The voters should investigate the arguments and facts brought forward by both sides, and on these, and these alone, as explained by their own experience and observation, render their verdict.

Among the issues not involved in this case at present is that of political partisanship. I stand before you to-night a Democrat, with my reason and intelligence endorsing the principles of American democracy. Not as it is represented in some of the State platforms written by political tricksters to catch traitors; I have no sympathy with this gerrymandering of political platforms to catch soreheads from other parties, believing, as I do, that a man who leaves his own party for spite and votes with another party for revenge is an unsafe and unreliable man, and not worth purchasing at such a price—but believing in the principles as laid down when the party passed seven prohibitory laws in as many different States.

My friend Senator Kimball is a tried, true Republican. On the conclusions to be deduced from certain political data we differ broadly, but on this issue we agree. Love of home, country, civilization, and liberty are as equally dear to the Democratic as to the Republican father, and if these mutual interests are endangered by the liquor traffic, partisanship is forgotten in the struggle with the common enemy. "For home and native land" is the war-cry that makes us brothers.

Neither is the issue of the use, nor abstinence from the use of alcoholic liquors involved in this campaign. The prohibitory constitutional amendment no more prohibits the USE of intoxicating liquors than section 4035 of the statutes of Iowa prohibits the USE of adulterated foods. That section reads: "*If any person knowingly sell any kind of diseased or corrupted or unwholesome provisions, whether for meat or drink, without making the same fully known to the buyer, he shall be punished by imprisonment in the county jail not more than thirty days, or by a fine not exceeding one hundred dollars.*"

The section does not prohibit the *use*. If you want to eat diseased meat you injure yourself and, indirectly, society; but if you sell the meat, the sale is a social act, you injure another, and society interferes to protect its units from imposition and injury. This section deals with the traffic, not with the use. Trade being a social institution, society has a right to destroy it if its effects are deleterious. Use is an individual matter over which society has no control as long as the individual does not injure it by the practice.

Section 4041 of Iowa statutes reads: "*If any person throw, or cause to be thrown, any dead animal into any river, well, spring, cistern, reservoir, stream, or pond, he shall be punished by imprisonment in the county jail not less than ten nor more than thirty days, or by fine not less than five nor more than one hundred dollars."*

This deals with the public act of poisoning the water, not with the individual use of the poisoned water. It does not say you shall not drink, but it says you shall not poison the water. The one act directly affects society, the other affects the individual, and indirectly disturbs society, and the former is prohibited.

Society will never undertake to say that an individual shall not read obscene literature, but it does say individuals' shall not print and circulate such literature, to corrupt the elements of which society is composed, thereby endangering its life, prosperity, usefulness, and peace. Self-preservation is the first law of life, with States as well as individuals. Trade, traffic, business depends largely upon society—the State—for its existence. Anything that affects deleteriously the health, morality, order, or safety of the public by its presence or conduct, the State must destroy as far as in its power, to preserve its own life. The State must guard against those social diseases that tend to break down its system, or it will die. The thing which every trade and traffic must show is that it strengthens and builds up the health of society. If it fails to show this; if it generates disease in the political system; if it acts as an ulcer on the body politic, society—the State—must, to maintain its own existence, destroy as best it can; and no rights are violated thereby, the traffic having forfeited all right to demand legal protection, by its indirect attacks on the life, prosperity, and order of the State.

The friends of the amendment, recognizing the fact that society is made up of individuals, and that the health and character of the unit of society, the individual, affects to a very large degree the health, prosperity, and usefulness of the political system, believe it to be for the best interest, and, in short, the duty of society, to make everything as favorable as possible for the development of those traits and characteristics of the race which tend to build up and strengthen its power for good, and to destroy as far as possible all institutions, customs, and practices which tend to develop those viler characteristics of the race, which endanger its life, and weaken its power to bless the people. In short, they believe with the great English statesman that it is the duty of Government to make it as easy as possible for the individual to do right, and as difficult as possible for him to do wrong.

The anti-amendment advocates claim, on the contrary, that it is the duty of society to take into its system those institutions which generate corruption and disease of the elements of its own life, in order to test what elements can stand the strain and be stronger by it. In other words, that an individual had better take corruption or poison, in order to generate a fever to purify his system. Would not the learned materiamedicist say, "It is better never to poison the system and subject its elements to such a test"?

The issue in this campaign is not a question of total abstinence. In Nebraska there are thousands of total abstainers who are prohibitionists. There are also hundreds of prohibitionists who are drinkers.

The ex-chief justice of my own State, one of the ablest criminal lawyers on this continent—learned, logical, and eloquent—whose hatred for the dram-shop is so intense he can hardly find language to express it, is a man who used to drink wine, and I think he does yet. When you talk to him in regard to total abstinence, he says, "That is an individual matter." When you talk to him in regard to the American dram-shop, he says, "It is a social nuisance that must be suppressed."

The man who drinks liquor may love his home; the man who uses liquor may love his wife; the man who uses liquor may love his child; and the man who abstains may do the same thing. In this campaign, and on this issue of home and family, they are one; and if the liquor traffic is proved to be the enemy of home and family, there is no reason why the drinker should not stand with the abstainer in favor of this amendment.

This question of the prohibition of the alcoholic liquor traffic is in no sense a question of individual abstinence any more than the prohibition of the sale of rotten beef is a question of the prohibition of eating it, or the prohibition of the sale of bad milk a question of drinking it. The one implies the protection extended by a State to society as a whole, the other implies the individual action based on a man's judgment.

It may be best for us to look for a moment at this proposition, because the opposition will almost surely endeavor to drag these two distinct lines of work together, and endeavor to whip out of the prohibition ranks all men who drink alcoholic liquors. On the principles underlying the temperance reform in this country all men are agreed.

There has hardly been a session of the Brewers' Congress or the Distillers' Union in the last twenty years that has not resolved against the evils of intemperance. On the primary proposition that these exist all classes agree. The only question is the question of remedy.

The theory of the prohibitionist is that it is the duty of the State to make it as easy as possible to do right, and just as difficult to do wrong; that it is the duty of the State to make the road up to manhood and honor as smooth as possible; to plant along the side of the road the flowers of hope, of promise, and of public approbation. Into the road down to licentiousness, and vice, and crime, and infamy, and death, roll the rocks of law, hedge it with the brambles of public opinion, the briars of public condemnation, and then place the citizen at the beginning of the two ways and say to him, " Take your choice." The State can never enter there and say you must go this way and shall not go the other. It will simply make the road to manhood pleasant and the road to disgrace disagreeable, and allow the young man standing at the entrance of the two paths to choose along which he will journey. He can go to Heaven if he will, or he can go down to ruin if he will. In the way of his free moral agency the State can never come, until by his individual action he injures others. At this starting-point the moral suasion organizations come, to persuade, to convince that it is best for him to go the better way. The State simply steps in to prevent temptation, leaving the free will of the individual untrammeled, while the work of the moral suasion society is to show the individual what is right and what is wrong.

Take another view: Intemperance, as it is known to the people of this State, is known to the scientific world as alcoholism, or dipsomania. Better known to the American physician, the English physician, the French physician than any other form of chronic poisoning. The prohibitionist says: "The same rules of common-sense should be applied in the treatment of this disease that are applied in the treatment of other diseases." The only cure for the man who has the small-pox—you know something of this disease from the terrible scare which swept over the country last winter—is the treatment of kindness, nursing, and doctoring. It does no good to pound a man on the head with a club who has the small-pox. It would do him no good to put him in the "cooler," or to set him at work breaking stone. The only way to treat a sick man is to treat him with care and scientific treatment. The people use common-sense rules for treatment of small-pox—treatment for the sick, vaccination for the well, quarantine for the disease. In the temperance movement the temperance societies adopt the same methods. The pledge is vaccination. If it does not take the first time they vaccinate over again, and keep on vaccinating until it works. Last spring, when it was reported that small-pox was spreading from every part of the country, there was heard a universal demand for the interference of Government, not with the idea that its interposition could cure those men who were sick, but with the idea that the hand of Government through that agency known as the police power of the State, could keep the disease within certain limits and protect those who were well.

The State of Iowa has adopted this theory.

Section 4039 of your statutes reads:

"*If any person inoculate himself or any other person or suffer himself to be inoculated with small-pox within this State with intent to cause the spread of the disease or come within this State with the intent to cause the prevalence or spread, etc., he shall be imprisoned and fined.*"

The State does not say people shall not catch the small-pox, but the State will make it as difficult to catch it as possible. The love, care, and kindness shown to the patients sick with contagious disease is moral suasion; the red flag out in front of the house, the strong hand of quarantine, is prohibition. This prohibition is of the State. If this system is sensible with other diseases, the same system should be applied to this wide-spread disease of intemperance.

Yellow fever swept up the Mississippi and located at Memphis. The second year, within twenty-four hours after the time it appeared in Memphis, every place which had communication with that city had quarantined against it; they stopped the passage of merchandise, and even stopped the passage of United States mails from the city until disinfected. Why did they do this? They could not legislate the poor fellows who had the yellow fever back to health, but they could legislate them into a quarantine to prevent other people from catching it.

Twenty-one thousand three hundred and eighty-four people in this country died from yellow fever in the last ten years. Take that number, think of it—21,384! Does any man say it was wrong to quarantine Memphis, though it destroyed merchandise, though it destroyed business, though it wrecked the whole city? No; it was right! The disease of alcoholism, during the same time, has killed more than 650,000 American citizens. This is not the statement of a temperance lecturer—it is the statement of Willard Parker, the first surgeon of this country. It is the statement of N. S. Davis, the celebrated physician of Chicago, and it is the statement of every doctor in this country who is tall enough in his profession to be seen over three counties. And yet the drunkard-makers object to quarantine. Alcoholism has killed 650,000, and there are men in this audience, I presume, with these facts before them, who have been so mistaken that they have voted to license a man to take the seeds of this terrible disease in his hands and sow them among the boys and girls of this country. Yellow fever has ruined less men, less women, and less children in Memphis than alcoholism has in the State of Iowa. The one is prohibited, the other licensed.

While the churches and the moral suasion organizations go down to the gutter after the poor drunkard, while they endeavor to cure his sick body by scientific treatment, and his sick soul by the grace of God, it is the duty of the State to do away with the places, to destroy the trade which incessantly turns out these sick men and keeps the supply constant, and forces this work through the years and on through the ages.

The question in regard to State action is not the question of what the treatment of the individual shall be. It is simply the question of what is the duty of the State, what is the power of the State, to restrain, or to prevent the spread of this fearfully contagious disease.

The question before the people of Iowa during the next sixty days is not: "Are you a Democrat? Are you a Republican? Are you a Presbyterian? Are you a drinker or an abstainer? What is your individual convictions in regard to the use of liquors?" but, "*What is the effect of the American dram-shop on the best interests of the State?*" This is the sole issue in this campaign. Everything else is subterfuge,—is thrown in to deceive, and every person who endeavors to prevent the people from considering this primary question is working in the interests of the liquor men.

I was through the canvass in Kansas. The same issue was presented there, and from the beginning to the end of the fight, I never heard the liquor men meet the issue squarely and fairly on its merits.

The whole question to be tried is simply, What is the relation of the liquor traffic to society in this State? That much and no more. I am well aware that when you have reached this point, when you have arraigned the liquor interest on its record, and insist it shall come into court and plead to the indictment, that it will at once move to quash the indictment on certain specious sophistries. One will be this: that this business is an old institution; that the State is composed of people who have come from different countries and different nationalities; that the German having come from his Fatherland has the right to bring here its customs; that the Irishman coming from the Evergreen Isle has the right to bring the customs of that country here.

Let us look at this position for a moment, the position that is everywhere held and urged by the liquor men of this country. Let us examine whether this idea is in harmony with the primary principles of government.

Political institutions are the outgrowth of social customs, not social customs the outgrowth of political institutions. Society is built from the bottom, not from the top. The home comes first; then families assemble and you have a village; villages and you have a township; townships and you have a county; counties and you have a State; and, in this country, States and you have a nation. All political customs grow out of social life. The political customs of this country are the legitimate children of the social customs and life of the founders of the Government, of the men who made our liberties and our institutions possible.

If I ever get indignant in my life, it is when I hear men born in other countries, together with dirty, dough-faced American demagogues, sneering at the Pilgrims, and ridiculing Puritanical morals and ideas. No man has greater respect for the good traits of our foreign-born citizens than myself, but I believe that a native-born American is as good as a foreign-born American, as long as his life and his conduct are as good; and I most earnestly protest, in free America, against the beer smut-mill being turned on the men who planted our liberties, and suffered and died to perpetuate them. A few American sneaks, in order to catch the beer vote, enter the cemetery where America's noblest dead are buried, desecrate the graves, and attempt to defile the memory of those who built the Government and established the liberties under which these ghouls live. Who were these Pilgrims who are now made a by-word and jest by the beer-guzzlers of this country? What did they come to America for? What kind of a country did they find? Britain's poetess answers:

> "The breaking waves dashed high
>   On a stern and rock-bound coast,
> And the woods against a stormy sky
>   Their giant branches tossed ;
> And the heavy night hung dark
>   The hills and waters o'er,
> When a band of exiles moored their bark
>   On the wild New England shore.
> Not as the conqueror comes,
>   They, the true-hearted, came ;
> Not with the roll of the stirring drums,
>   And the trumpet that sings of fame :
> Not as the flying come,
>   In silence and in fear ;—
> They shook the depths of the desert gloom
>   With their hymns of lofty cheer.
> Amidst the storm they sang,
>   And the stars heard, and the sea ;
> And the sounding aisles of the dim woods rang
>   To the anthems of the free.
> The ocean eagle soared
>   From his nest by the white wave's foam,
> And the rocking pines of the forest roared—
>   This was their welcome home.
> There were men with hoary hair
>   Amidst that Pilgrim-band :
> Why had they come to wither there,
>   Away from their childhood's land?
> There was woman's fearless eye,
>   Lit by her deep love's truth ;
> There was manhood's brow serenely high,
>   And the fiery heart of youth.
> What sought they thus afar?
>   Bright jewels of the mine?
> The wealth of seas, the spoils of war ?—
>   They sought a faith's pure shrine !
> Ay, call it holy ground,
>   The soil where first they trod ;
> They have left unstained what there they found,—
>   Freedom to worship God."

Such was their coming, and such the motives which led them to leave the Old World and its comforts for the unknown New. By struggle and toil, through disease and suffering, they developed the land and planted the ideas of liberty in their descendants. Their theories of liberty and morals were developed by their children.

Who died at Lexington? Whose blood wet the

AN EXAMINATION OF THE ISSUES. 77

ground at Bunker Hill? Whose breast was in front of British bullets at Brandywine and Germantown? Who starved at Valley Forge?

Through blood the land was made free. What was then done? Did Americans close the doors of the Republic and say, "We are free; let the world take care of itself"? No! They welcomed the down-trodden of all nations. Immigrants have not been asked to come as alien paupers. They have been received as brothers, and made members of the family. After all this, for these refugees from the despotisms of Europe to attempt to destroy American customs by traducing American dead is disgraceful. If they came here to be Americans, they are welcome; but if they prefer European ideas and customs, and the governments which those ideas and customs have produced, a ticket from New York to Europe will cost little more than a ticket from Europe to New York, and they are free to go. Americans are satisfied with American institutions and American liberties.

This Government is the child of that morality, that theory of religious liberty, that theory of governmental life which was taught by the men who settled and developed the Colonies; while, on the contrary, the German despotism of to-day is the legitimate child of the German social life and German social customs. Whenever the people in this country destroy American social customs and American social life; whenever the people drift away from the rocks on which their forefathers founded this Government, into the seas where despotisms have floated; whenever American customs cease and the customs of despotic Europe take their place, this Government had better order its graveclothes, and invite in the mourners. America, as a republic, can only live while the customs that made it a republic live. This theory of government can only continue while the social life that developed it continues. When a different form of social life, a different form of social thought, a different form of social teaching, a different form of moral training come in, I have no hope for the Government.

Suppose I could to-night take a hundred thousand

native-born Americans, and, with a motion of the hand, plant them over in the German Empire, would not Von Bismarck have a lively time governing them? Why? Because their training in their mothers' arms, their training in the cradle, their training in the primary school, in the graded school, in the academy, in the university, have all developed a different line of thought, a different theory of government, a different theory of responsibility, from that developed by the German social life, the German social customs, and the German schools. The idea that because customs have lived in another country, and have been developed in another form of government, that they must of right be allowed to continue here, is utterly fallacious.

Suppose before the missionaries went to the Fiji Islands, a man from that island had drifted over and located in the city of Des Moines. (You know that the Fiji Islanders were cannibals.) Suppose this Fiji Islander had come. Now, he is a different man from the American. His teeth are different, his head is especially different. He has different passions, different appetites, different ideas. For a time he restrains his inclinations, but at last, the old appetite in him being aroused, he makes a raid on your home, catches your fat baby boy, kills him, dresses him, cooks him, and puts him on the table for a meal. You get your shotgun and go up to interview him. Don't kill him on sight. When you see what he is about, you say: "What have you done?"

"Why," he says, "nothing, only killed a boy."

"But you have committed murder."

He says, "I do not understand."

"Why, you have killed this child. You had no right to kill him. You have no right to do what you are doing."

"I thought this was a free country!" he exclaims.

"It is a free country, but it is not a free country to commit murder in."

"But," he says, "I used to eat babies over in the Fiji Islands. Have not I got the right to eat them here?"

What would be the answer? "Sir, the Government of the United States is not the Government of the

Fiji Islands. Your social customs have developed your form of government, our social customs have developed our form of government. When you leave that Government you must leave every custom that is inimical to this Government or destructive to its institutions, for we have no desire to have introduced here the customs that propagated the governments of your native island."

Suppose the ex-Khedive of Egypt, when he was deposed, instead of moving to Italy, had come over here with his wives and children and gone to housekeeping in Des Moines. An officer takes him by the shoulder, and says, "Hold on, sir! What are you doing?"

"I am keeping house."

"You are my prisoner."

"What for?"

"Bigamy."

"What is bigamy?"

"Having more than one wife."

"I thought this was a free country!"

"It is."

"I used to have these wives in Egypt. Have not I the right to have them here?"

What would you say to him? "Sir, this Republic is a different Government from the Despotism of Egypt. This Government is a product of our social institutions. Consequently, when you come to this country you must leave every custom that would be injurious to the welfare of this country and the perpetuity of this Government." The idea that American freedom means universal license is the dangerous idea in this country.

In my State a young woman recently from Europe was brought into a court charged with the murder of her infant child. When the indictment was read, and she was asked, through an interpreter, to plead, her answer was: "I thought this was a free country."

The idea that this country has no form, no customs, no laws, no institutions, which immigrants are bound to respect; that men have the right to come here and follow any customs, any ideas, any theories, and any practices, is an idea utterly antagonistic to American institutions, and if carried out will ultimately build on the chaos of our liberties the worst despotism that the world ever saw.

At the birth of this Government, the institutions of the Colonies were the institutions of a monarchy in a modified form. The men who settled at Plymouth Rock were men who had given up, in a measure, their old ideas and theories, and a new social system had been slowly developing. This change ultimately developed a social life that would not endure even the limited monarchy of Great Britain. When the United States came into existence as a nation, they were a long way from having republican institutions. The American leaders were not destructionists, they were reformers.

The difference between the French and American Revolutions was this—the Americans simply wished to tearn down the building of a monarchy, to take out of it all the material they could use in another form of government, while the French endeavored to destroy and build wholly new.

The work of American statesmen for the first hundred years of this Republic has been the work of changing, adjusting, and trying. Look! see what changes have been made. Examine the law; you could hardly recognize it as the child of the law in existence when the Colonies became free. The old theory was that the king received his authority from God, that he stood in the relation of God to the people; with the destruction of that idea, the individual became the sovereign, and the ruler the representative of the people. The result of this was a change in the law in accordance with the change in ideas. The old theory of the divine right of kings to rule the people developed the theory of the divine right of the husband to rule the wife. The old marriage forms—every one of them—contained a clause stipulating that the wife should obey the husband. If I had been young at that time, and one of the ladies here had also been living, worth fifty thousand dollars in bonds, notes, and real estate, and married me, by the act of marriage (unless her property had been entailed upon her and her children) every dollar would have become mine. I could have spent it or gambled it away, and she could not have prevented me by other means than love or the broomstick. The old law has been changed, and shaped, and polished until to-day, in my State, if I wanted my wife's money, the only way I could get it would be to persuade her to give it to me. She can buy and sell property, and transact business in her own name; and next November many of Nebraska's voters will say that the women of the State have the same right to a voice in the Government under which they live that the men have. This is the legitimate result of a change of customs from a monarchy to the broader idea of a democracy, founded upon the morality and intelligence of the people.

The founders of the Republic recognized the fact that the foundation of universal liberty must be universal education. At the birth of this Government the schools of America were private schools, but the necessity of making the citizen-sovereign intelligent, developed our free-school system. All the institutions that America inherited have been moulded, shaped, and developed. Among these inherited institutions was the accursed drinking-place. The dram-shop is not a child of American customs, liberty, ideas, schools, or theories. It was inherited from the despotic governments of Europe. At the laying of the foundation of the Government there were men who openly denied that it should continue to be in the new structure.

Those who favored a compromise were in a majority. They said: "It will not be fair to reject the liquor traffic until it has been tried in the new form of government." They prevailed and it has been tried.

Its results have been the same as in Europe—drunkenness, debauchery, vice, crime, riot, communism. In the rich soil and genial climate of our Government it bore fruit early, and in 1676 the Government of Virginia found it necessary to protect the people from the multitude of evils resultant from the traffic and the conditions favorable to its development. As increasing population, seconded by wise statesmanship, has enlarged the nation's borders, it has grown with our growth and increased with our strength; it has been crippled only where persistent prohibitory efforts have made the conditions for its development unfavorable. The evil has long been admitted by all, and a persistent effort to remedy it has been made by a few. Compromise has followed compromise, the unrestrained sale, license, high license, civil damage, local option; and I wish to assert in the light of history that all these compromises have been failures to just the extent that principle has been sacrificed; and successes just to the extent that right has been recognized, and prohibitory features incorporated into their text. Thus this institution has been tested and found unworthy of a place in a free republic. It is an enemy of American liberties, and must be destroyed. Then:

> "There shall be sung another golden age:
> The rise of empire and of arts,
> The good and great inspiring epic rage,
> The wisest heads and noblest hearts—
> NOT SUCH AS EUROPE BREEDS IN HER DECAY,
> Such as she bred when fresh and young,
> When heavenly flame did animate her clay,
> By future poets shall be sung.
> Westward the course of Empire takes its way,
> The first four acts already past,
> The fifth shall close the drama with the day :
> Time's noblest offspring is the last."

V.

EXAMINATION OF THE ISSUES AND DEFENCE.

An Address delivered at Moore's Opera-House, Des Moines, Iowa, April 23, 1882.

LADIES AND GENTLEMEN OF DES MOINES: I came to your State at the request of the old prohibition corps of the temperance army, the Good Templars, who have fought on this line since 1851, to discuss with you the question of what is the best thing for the people to do with the alcoholic liquor traffic of your State. Your Legislature has submitted this question to you. I would have preferred that the question could have been submitted to every one who suffers from the accursed influence and effects of the drink traffic, or whose heart is bleeding from its direful effects; but the provisions of our American Constitution are such that men above the age of twenty-one years must settle this question, while the great class who suffer most from the evil influences of the liquor traffic—the women of the country —are debarred from expressing their opinion in making the final verdict. I would that this were not so; but as it is submitted to the voters of this Commonwealth, you, as voters, must settle the question. The day has passed when a man can afford to laugh, to sneer, or to jeer at this question. As citizens of the State, bound by the highest obligations of a Christian civilization— home and love of country—you are to take the question without passion, without prejudice. without bitterness, and fully consider it in all its phases. This question is one that must be settled calmly and dispassionately. The drunkard-factory of this State must be weighed in the balance of political economy, of social life. It must be weighed, not by prejudiced men, not by bitter men, not by unfair men, but by jurors willing to consider each of the counts in the indictment against it, and then to render their verdict according to the facts.

To-night let us examine the relations of the liquor traffic in this country to society and its interests; then, as you go from this hall, weigh the evidence, and if your judgment tells you it is conclusive against the traffic, if your judgment tells you my statements are correct, act upon them. If your judgment tells you my reasoning is incorrect, reject it. I would not think much of you if you would accept something as true, because I said it was true. I would not think much of you if you would reject what I said, simply because a temperance man said it. You are moral, responsible, intelligent, cultured men, and you must take the statements and weigh them in the scales of your own judgment, your own experience, your own intelligence, and then make up your minds whether they are true or false. The power of the liquor traffic to do great good or great evil to the Commonwealth cannot be doubted. The immense number of these retail shops, the large number of men engaged in the business of selling liquor, the great capital invested in the manufacture and in the buildings where liquor is sold, make the business capable of doing great good or great evil to any city, county, state, or nation where it is permitted to exist.

That this capacity is always exercised in the direction of evil is scarcely deniable. No man dares dispute the pernicious influence of the grog-shops of this country.

A few weeks ago the Chicago *Inter-Ocean* described a certain section in the city of Chicago, which is called "the Black Hole." Many of you saw the description. It declared that in that section of the city the vicious elements upholding vice and crime, licentiousness, debauchery, and lewdness were the governing factors and the controlling interests. A few days later the same newspaper published a diagram of the streets of the city where the "Black Hole" was located. Suppose that to-night I should draw on this curtain the same diagram. Suppose, further, that you had not seen the *Inter-Ocean* article. After I have drawn this diagram I take the *Inter-Ocean* in my hands, and, standing before you, I read the description of the locality, studiously omitting the names of the places, the kind of business carried on there, and only speaking of the moral and social condition of the people. After I have read the description, my license friend, if you are in the house, I want you to tell me what kind of institutions are located along those streets; what institutions will produce such a condition of things.

Suppose I told you that on the first corner is a Methodist church, then from there down to the next corner it was blocked solidly with dry-goods houses. At the end of the street the Presbyterian church is located, and across the other side are retail houses. Then there is a Baptist church, and on the other side are manufactories—in other words, I tell you that that section of the city is filled with churches, with schools, and with business places. My license friend, would not you say my statement could not be true? Is it possible for such a state of things to exist where any respectable business exists? Then let me ask *you* to tell me what kind of business you think is transacted along these streets? Why, you would answer in a minute, if you were honest, "Grog-shops and their children, gambling hells and houses of ill-fame." The last two—the children of the first—infest the streets. That is the kind of institutions the *Inter-Ocean* says are there.

A few years ago—the older men among the ministers here will remember—the metropolitan press of New York turned the public gaze upon a section of that city controlled by vice, crime, and immorality, and when the public looked at the streets where this horrible state of things existed, what did they see? Did they see churches, schools, and business to produce these results? No! The centre of Five Points was an old brewery, and every street radiating from that brewery was crowded with grog-shops and their attendant institutions, where liquor was sold and humanity debased. When the Christian element of the city wished to elevate the social and moral condition of Five Points, the very first thing they did was to buy the old brewery and change it into a city mission.

When Christianity came, the devil packed up his pet institution, to a certain extent, and moved over to Water Street, and then Water Street became the worst section of the city. The vicious element followed the dram-shop.

Last September, one of the great newspapers of the city of Chicago arraigned Mayor Carter Harrison for not revoking the license of a certain liquor-dealer. The paper charged that this man had repeatedly violated the law, and insisted that the mayor should have revoked the license, and that his failure to act was his fear of injuring his political interests. Mayor Harrison, talking to a reporter, said that the accusation of the paper, regarding the guilt of the liquor-seller and the failure to revoke the license, was true; but he said he allowed that dram-shop to continue because it was a resort of thieves—it was a trap where the policemen could find criminals and catch them, and he allowed it to remain simply for this reason. Would he keep a church open as a trap for criminals? I think not.

I was born in the State of New York, where the farmers plough the land on three sides—top and two sides. One time, while a boy, an old gentleman in our neighborhood came to me and said, "See here! Do you want to go and hunt foxes with me to-morrow?" I said, "Yes." The next morning he came with the hounds. I had my gun ready, and we started out across the hills. We went up one hill, down on the other side, across the valley, up the second hill. About half-way up the hill we came across a fox-track in the snow. It was what we were looking for. The old hunter brought the dogs, put them on the track, and away they started, along the range to the north. I shouldered my gun and started after them. The old man said, "Where are you going?" "Going after the foxes." He said, with a laugh, "You follow me"; and he started across the hill to the southwest. The dogs had gone north; he went southwest; and I, without a word, followed him over the top of the hill and part of the way down the other side. He said, "You wait behind that stump." He went and sat down behind a tree. For a whole hour I sat there in the snow. The thought commenced to come into my mind that the old gentleman had brought me there to freeze. Just as this thought was taking definite shape, on the wings of the wind from the north was borne the baying of the hounds. They came nearer and nearer. The fox was shot in front. After the fox was shot the old hunter came up, and I asked, "How did you know the fox would come here?" "Why," he answered, "this is his runaway. I have known over three hundred foxes killed on this range, and I never knew one to run on this side of the hill in any place but between this stump and that tree."

Every hunter will tell you such is the habit of many kinds of game, and it is equally true of the criminals of this country. Suppose a man should break into a store here to-night, and leave for Chicago to-morrow—your police get a description of the man, and telegraph to the chief of police at Chicago to arrest him. Where would the Chicago police first search for him? Would they go to the prayer-meeting? Would they go to the stores? No! they would go to the grog-shops, or to the progeny of grog-shops—houses of ill-fame, gambling hells—because this kind of game always seeks this runaway, its old familiar grounds. Take the records of the courts of this country, and they sustain this charge so thoroughly that no one will dare challenge it. And, gentlemen, before the license men of this State can hope to defeat the amendment, they must show that this charge is false. If the liquor traffic of this country stimulates crime, if it stimulates and produces vice, if it upholds it and sustains it, there is no argument that will justify a man in voting to continue the business.

Again, the dram-shop of this country is a school of perjury. From the very day it is opened it makes liars of men. You may say this is a strong charge. Indict a liquor-seller in this town for violation of your liquor law. Your detectives tell you that he has persistently violated it. Bring him into court and put him on trial. Subpœna from their houses in this city twenty-five men, young and old, who have patronized him. They come into court. You reach out the Bible they will swear, on God's Holy Word, to tell the truth, the whole truth, and nothing but the truth. Try to prove by them facts which they know to be true. Nineteen out of the twenty-five will swear to a lie to defend the man who sold them the liquor.

One of these witnesses is on the stand:

"Were you in that liquor-shop?"

"I was."

"Did you buy something there?"

"I did."

"What was it?"

"I don't know."

"What did you call for?"

"I didn't call."

"Well, what did you get?"

"I don't know."

"You drank something. What was it?"

"Well, it might have been tea, it might have been coffee, it might have been lemonade; I don't know."

Lie? Of course he lies.

Suppose he had gone into the saloon and asked for beer, and the bar-keeper had set up lemonade, would he not have known the difference?

Suppose he had asked for whiskey, and the bar-tender had set up tea, would he not have known the difference?

And yet that man comes into court, and, after taking his oath on God's Truth, deliberately and wilfully perjures his soul, degrades his manhood, dishonors his citizenship, to defend the man who will take his last dollar, make him a drunkard, and then kick him into the street and call him a drunken dead-beat! Have you ever tried to enforce the law against liquor-sellers? If so, you know this to be true.

They everywhere try to corrupt judges, to suborn witnesses, to defeat the ends of justice, and prevent an honest, fair, and full enforcement of the law.

The liquor traffic of this country is a parasite on legitimate business life. The dealers and their advocates will tell you, before this amendment fight is over, that the dram-shop (in some way, they will be careful not to specify how) conduces to the general prosperity and the business interests of this State. If this statement is true, then certainly they have a good defence with which to meet the indictment against them.

Let us for a few moments examine the theory of State building, in order to fully understand the causes of city, state, and national prosperity.

A king from Asia Minor was one time visiting a king of Sparta. In Asia, in the early days of the world, all cities were walled, as a defence against enemies. When this king came to Sparta and discovered the absence of walls, he was astonished, and asked the king of Sparta, "Where are the walls of your cities?" The Spartan ruler answered, "I will show you to-morrow." The next day he ordered the armies of Sparta to pass before his guest in review. As these proud freemen marched by, the king, touching his visitor on the shoulder and pointing with pride to his soldiers, said, "These be the walls of Sparta; every man is a brick.". Ladies and gentlemen, the morality, intelligence, and virtue of the people is the foundation of city, of county, of state, and of government building.

The unity of society is the individual. If you wish good society you must build up the units of society, cultivate the institutions and customs whose influence and effects tend to improve and elevate the individual. If Iowa has institutions that only develop health, strength, morality, and intelligence, her future prosperity is assured; but if she sanctions and enters into partnership with institutions which debauch public morals, destroy public health, impair individual credit, stimulate vice and crime, the day will come when, with a political system destroyed by social debauchery, Iowa, as a Republican State, will be a thing of the past. The laws of social and political health are fixed; to violate them is to invite disease and death.

"What constitutes a State?
  Not high-raised battlement or labored mound,
    Thick wall, or moated gate;
  Not cities proud with spires and turrets crowned;
    Not bays and broad-armed ports,
  Where, laughing at the storm, rich navies ride;
    Not starred and spangled courts,
  Where low-browed baseness wafts perfume to pride.

> No: MEN, high-minded men,
>   With powers as far above dull brutes endued
> In forest, brake, or den,
>   As beasts excel cold rocks and brambles rude,—
> Men, who their duties know,—
>   But know their rights, and, knowing, dare maintain,
> Prevent the long-aimed blow,
>   And crush the tyrant, while they rend the chain;
> *These constitute a State;*
>   And sovereign law, *that State's* collected will,
> O'er thrones and globes elate
>   Sits empress, *crowning good, repressing ill.*"

The defendants in this case have only to prove that the liquor traffic builds up the State by building up the individuals who constitute it. If it builds up its patrons socially, financially, intellectually, and morally, the case of the people against the traffic must fail. If, on the contrary, they fail to show that their business benefits directly their customers, then their business must go. Let us see if it does.

Our Greenback friends, during the past four years, have told us a great many things that are true. One of the principles of political economy which they have been teaching persistently, or rather developing, is that there can be but two types of men in our social organism,—the first the producing class—those who, by their work, add to the material wealth of the State, or at least produce enough to take care of themselves. That class have a right to a place as long as their production does not injuriously affect the society in which they live; consequently they are dismissed from consideration. The other class, the non-producers, are the men who must show to the satisfaction of society that they are entitled to a place outside the almshouse. All political economists group this second class into two sub-classes—assistant producers, and parasitic non-producers.

Let me illustrate. Call up here a merchant and a doctor; two of one class. Place here a saloon-keeper and a thief; two of the other class. Do not say I am making my point too strong; this is the teaching of every man whoever wrote a work on political economy, and I am simply stating what has been affirmed by men who advocate and believe in license. I will show you the difference between these classes. I turn to the merchant and say to him: "You receive money from the producers of this country. You must show what you do for society, and what you do for the producer for the money you receive. What do you give in return for the producer's money?" He answers: "I am simply the agent of producers. I act as their hired man, to a certain extent. The producers manufacture or grow certain commodities; in another country other producers provide other commodities. I take the commodities which these men produce, ship to other producers, and bring their products back for others." Although our farmers tried to abolish the merchant a few years ago, they learned that the conduct of commerce is a science, and that the men who were novices in the matter were illy fitted to carry it on. When we have examined the merchant, we find he returns equal value for the money he gets.

We turn to the doctor and say: "Doctor, you receive money from the producers while you produce nothing yourself. Tell us what return you make for the money received." He answers: "The producers of this country do not take care of themselves. In the first place, many of them do not understand the laws of hygiene. They become sick, and I am simply the one who repairs the machinery." One time, on the Chicago, Milwaukee, and St. Paul Railroad, I was talking with an honored friend, Mr. Quick, and I asked him: "What is your business?" He said: "I am pump-doctor." He was the hydraulic engineer. He was the man who had charge of the sick pumps of this road. When a pump would not work, he doctored it. Now, the physician stands in the same relation to society in which that man stands to the railroad; he is the one who repairs the physical machinery of the producers. When we have examined him closely in regard to the money he has received, and the work he has done; when we think how we have seen him standing by the sick-bed of loved ones, as hope was dying out, and the only ray of light was the thought that God gave and God was taking away, and heard him saying, to comfort the breaking heart: "While there is life there is hope"; when the loved one came back to health and strength, we took the money from our pocket and willingly paid the bill for services rendered. The physician assists the producer for the money he receives.

Next, examine the others. "Mr. Liquor-dealer, you get the money, what do you give back for it?" "Whiskey and beer." "Well, sir, let me put a hypothetical question to you. Suppose a man comes into your saloon to-morrow, and drinks. During the next week, the next month, the next year, he patronizes you. For ten years he is your best customer, giving you the larger part of his earnings and the greater part of his time. At the end of the time what will you have done for the man in return for the money he has given you?" If the liquor-seller is honest he will have to answer: "He would have been better off if he had never come into my place. I have not only taken his money, but I have cursed him in the taking."

Try it again. "Mr. Liquor-dealer, suppose a man with a family comes into your place and becomes your patron. At the end of five or six years he dies in front of your bar under the influence of liquor. What will you have done for his wife and babies in return for the money you have received from him?" Again the answer must be: "It would have been better for that wife and child if he had never traded with me." Do you see the difference? The merchant says: "I benefit him, and you see the benefit." The drink-vender has to admit that he curses him, and everybody sees the effect of the curse.

If I put the same question to the thief. "I give peace of mind." What do you mean? "If a man has money he worries for fear it will be stolen; after I steal it he soon stops worrying—I do not injure his brain, nerves, or muscle."

Suppose four farmers come into Des Moines, each with fifty dollars in his pocket. One goes to a dry-goods store, one to a hardware store, one to a boot and shoe store, and the other to a dram-shop, and each spends his money in the place he visits.

After two weeks I come to you and say: "Let us go and see those producers; see what they received for the money they gave those non-producers." We drive to the home of the man who spent his money at the dry-goods store. "What did you get?" "Do you see that dress which Nellie is wearing and that coat that Tom has on? Well, I gave the merchant fifty dollars, and he gave me in exchange these things. He is better off; we are better off." Exchange of values; both are benefited.

We go to the man who traded at the hardware store, and we say: "What did you receive?" "Do you see the stove, and the axe, and those kettles?" "Yes." "Well, I gave him fifty dollars; he gave me these. We are better off; he is better off."

We go to the man who spent his money at the boot and shoe store. "What did you receive for the money you paid?" "You see these boots which I am wearing, and the shoes Nellie has on, and the boots that Will, Dick, and Harry and the rest are wearing? I gave that merchant fifty dollars for them. We needed the boots and shoes, he needed the money, and we traded." An exchange of values; both are benefited.

Now we go to the man who spent the fifty dollars in the dram-shop, and say to him: "Sir, you paid that non-producer fifty dollars. What did you get back?" "Come here and I will show you." Will he say that? No; he will hang his head and say: "I got this flaming nose, these bleared eyes, and have been sick ever since."

"My farmer friend, would you not have been better off if you had put the fifty dollars in the lamp and burned it, and never have gone to the drinking-place at all? Yes; because you would have had a clear head, hard muscles, and could have gone to work at once and produced more wealth to take the place of that destroyed. The liquor-dealer took your money and unfitted your brain and muscles for the production of more wealth."

In the Southern States you will see, in different places, clinging to the trees, the plant known to botanists as the mistletoe. You will say it is a beautiful plant, and yet the botanist will tell you that it is a base plant. You ask why? Climb up the tree and see. What will you find? The plant putting its roots down into the earth to suck its life from inorganic matter? No. It is thrusting its rootlets into the bark of the tree, sucking its life from other life, living by the destruction of organic life. Botanists call it a parasite. Among insects you have the same class. Go out along the old California trail in my own State or in Wyoming, anywhere between the Missouri River and the coast, stop in one of the old sod ranches and tell the keeper of it that you want a bed. Stipulate that it shall be unoccupied, and labor under the delusion that you will be given such a bed. When the time comes, you disrobe, retire, and start for dreamland. You will have to start pretty quick to get there. Just as you are passing over the border, something starts from your foot along up the leg. It stops, and you know where it lingers. You have a very urgent desire to put your hand down and interview it. By the time you reach down, there is something on your back and something on your side. You roll, and kick, and strike;—it will be fortunate for you if you said your prayers before you went to bed; it may keep you from saying something worse before you get up. At last you can endure it no longer; you spring out, light a lamp, and throw down the covering. See them run! the flat-headed cowards!

Oh, how humanity loathes them! The whole family—mosquitoes, gnats, jiggers, cockroaches, bed-bugs; ugh!

Come up higher, to the highest order God created on earth, and you have the same type. Every gambler in this country is a parasite on social and business life. He is a man who, through the meshes of his games, entraps other men, and grows rich by the ruin of his victims; a man who takes value without returning an equivalent. Every dram-shop in this country bears the same relation to society. The liquor-seller comes into your town, locates, commences his business, and sells his wares. What is the result? As the shingles go on his house, they tumble off the houses of his patrons. As he wears broadcloth, his victims come to rags. As he drives up the street with his nice team, his victims plod, with hods on their shoulders, earning money to buy the liquor man another team.

As you meet the liquor-seller's wife, with her silks and satins, tripping down the street, you meet the victim's wife, scantily clad, carrying a basket of clothes she has washed to earn money to buy food for her babies. You meet the liquor-dealer's boy flying his kite, while his victim's boy meets you with: "Mister, won't you give me just one penny to buy bread? I am starving."

The license man objects: "But the liquor-dealers do not get rich, or their wives wear silks or satins." True: the picture is what *would really be* the condition of the liquor-seller's family, but for the fact that blood-money always curses the receiver. Money made from the sale of liquor is like money made from gambling—hard to keep. But, my license friend, is not my point strengthened by your objection, for, it being true, the liquor traffic curses even the families of those who engage in it? It is a universal curse, without a redeeming trait.

The liquor-seller lives by ruining his customers. The dram-shop of this country, worse than the devil-fish of Victor Hugo, not only wraps its arms around its victim directly, but thrusts those insatiate arms into their homes, taking the carpets, pictures, books—everything that makes home pleasant for wife and children, and drawing into its maw the very element that civilizes and Christianizes the country.

Suppose that I could take all the money which the producing community of the State of Iowa could make —I am not speaking of the money you could borrow in the Eastern States—but all the money you can make in a year. Pile it here on the table. This money must build the homes and fences; lay down the carpets and buy the books; it must run the stores, run the manufactories, carry on the newspapers, and build up all other kinds of trade. It is the life-blood of commerce. When you have it piled up here, the lawyers, doctors, ministers, merchants, newspaper men, and manufacturers gather around. Five thousand liquor-sellers step forward and say, "More than nine million dollars of that is ours." You say, "No"; but they say, "Gentlemen, we bought the privilege of the first grab at it, and that grab we are going to have."

My friend, are you in business in Des Moines? Do you not know this to be true: If a farmer who drinks liquor comes into this city with one dollar in his pocket he will spend it for grog, and ask you to trust him for a dress for his wife. Do you not know that the saloons of this city and other cities are located on your principal business streets, and that they sell their liquors for cash, while you trust for the necessaries of life? Do you sell jewelry? If you do, do you sell the best of your jewelry to the man who spends his money in grog-shops? Do you sell nice clothing? How much do you sell to the man who spends the greater part of his money in a drinking-place? Do you sell silk dresses, my friend? Are the patrons of the dram-shop your customers? Do you not know, business men, as a matter of fact, that the dram-shop unfits its patrons for you, and takes the money which would buy nice things to beautify the home—buy nice clothes and good food—leaving the home without these blessings?

"But," says one, "the liquor-dealer buys these things." "Oh, yes, gentlemen; but he is one where his patrons are a hundred. Where you sell him one suit of clothes you lose the sale of a hundred suits to his customers. Where you sell him one picture to go into his home to beautify it, you fail to sell his customers a hundred pictures to make their homes pleasant for their children and families."

Take a leech: press all the blood out of it. Now I will show you a trick of license economy. I take a lancet, draw a scratch on my arm, and say to the leech, "Suck." It does. Just look at it. It is growing respectable—it is getting sleek, and smooth, and fat. When it is full, it will let go. There is this difference between insect leeches and human leeches: an insect leech ceases sucking when he is full, while a human leech will continue to suck as long as there is any money in the pockets of the victims or until he is choked off.

I want to show you the statesmanship of license advocates.

I take the leech and squeeze it; two or three drops of blood come from its mouth and I swallow them, and say I have gained so much blood. Some boy in this house cries out, "You are foolish. Every drop of that blood was in your body—the leech sucked it out of you. You have only got part of it back, and that part in a way that will do you more injury than good." Liquor men come into your State, and the law draws a scratch on your business life and sticks them on, and says, "Suck." See them change their clothes! See them grow fat as they live on the business life of the city and the country! When the year rolls around, the city council inverts them, and squeezes out of them five hundred, one thousand, or fifteen hundred dollars, and says, "Ha! ha! we have saved so much money to the city." But where did the liquor-dealer get the money? He did not have it when he came here. He came into our State, and without giving a single thing of value—without building up society, without helping society, he has sucked from it thousands of dollars. He keeps the largest part, and gives you a pittance to be allowed to continue. You take it, and congratulate yourselves that you are dividing up with the spoiler of your homes, your prosperity, and your civilization.

Build up a city, gentlemen? Just as well build up a man by putting lice on his head as to hope to build up the material interests of a city by opening dram-shops! In every business relation the liquor traffic of the country is an institution which receives value without returning it. It lives on society as parasites live on other bodies.

A saloon bears the same relation to legitimate business that a bed-bug does to a man who sleeps in the bed where the bug lives. Recently a lady said to me, "I wish you would not use such horrid comparisons." I did not ask her how she knew they were horrid. I simply said, "My dear madam, if I should catch a bed-bug and an ant, and place them here with microscopes over them, would you come and look at them?" "Yes." "Well, I submit the bed-bug is prettier than the ant —prettier body, prettier legs. If I had mentioned the ant, you would not have objected?" "No." "Then why object to my mentioning the better-looking insect? Is it not from simply the way it makes its living?"

Ladies and gentlemen, you would admire a louse as much as you do a honey-bee if it lived in the same way. It is not the anatomy of the insect. Some of the parasites are among the most beautiful of insects. It is the way they live—by sucking their life out of other life—that raises the feeling of disgust and leads to their destruction. It is not a liquor-seller's clothes or looks which causes society to detest him and his trade: it is the way he lives in society—a mere parasite on business life. As the shingles go on his house they fall off the house of his customer; as he and his family live easily, in idleness, his customer and his customer's family suffer in rags. For this crime of parasitism he is on trial.

I suppose I ought to say, in justice to myself, that I never like to compare things unfavorably. I do not like to drag anything into a position where it ought not to be, and I feel at this point like apologizing—to the bed-bug. You ask what I mean? I will tell you. I never knew one bed-bug mean enough to eat another bed-bug, or one louse mean enough to eat another louse. It remains for the last and highest order, which God created in His own image, to develop the type which will live on their own kind and off their own species; who will fasten the fangs of parasitic avarice in the pulsating flesh of their own kin, their own blood, their own sex, and their own race; and grow rich, not by the destruction of other species, not by the destruction of other orders, but by the destruction of individuals who feel the same, who enjoy the same, as they do. It is unfair to a parasite that lives on other forms of life to compare it with a class low enough, vile enough, to live on its own kind without a feeling of sympathy, without a pulsation of regret.

Again, the liquor traffic is the enemy of home life. The keystone to American civilization is the American home. I would I could take you to the frontier—to the cattle and mining towns of this country, where home life is comparatively unknown, and by ocular demonstration impress this fact upon your minds—show you how the words "mother" and "home" have the power to awaken the latent manhood in, and lead out to a grander and better life, men seemingly lost to all influences for good. You, especially you business men, know how great this influence is on public life. The opposition you meet, the trickery and fraud you see practiced, make you hard, uncharitable, cynical, and, when gone from home for months, bitter and selfish. You return to your home, and, in the presence of wife and children, hatred, selfishness, bitterness, cynicism vanish like the cold, clammy, poisonous March fog before the morning sun. Home life and love is the sun which fructifies all the nobler impulses of man's nature. Few men go from home with the kiss of wife upon their lips, and the soft touch of baby fingers lingering in pleasant memories on their neck, but feel more charity for their fellow-men, more love for humanity, and a renewed desire to build themselves up in all that pertains to true manhood. Home is the moral and political conservator of the nation, the antidote of communism, socialism, riot, vice, and bloodshed. A man who goes from home with the softening influences of womanhood's homage and childhood's love lingering about him, seldom goes to murder, rob, or incite riot.

Into this garden of American hope the breath of the liquor traffic comes like the hot winds of the desert. By the use of the things sold in the dram-shop, all the finer feelings of the husband and father are injured and his passions stimulated, and from being the head—the life of the home—he soon becomes a despot and a terror. The money which should be used to buy pictures, books, carpets, and other things to make home pleasant, is spent to still further lower and degrade him. A drunkard's "home"! Can there be any greater mockery of the sacred word? Any institution or custom which causes such results is a terrible enemy to American liberty and civilization.

Again, the liquor traffic is the enemy of an honest ballot and a fair count. The effect of the dram-shop is to destroy the intellectual force and moral character of its patrons, as well as to reduce them financially, often to beggary. The high moral sense which should govern every voter is lost when a diseased craving for stimulants controls a man. In such a condition he is open to corrupt influences, and comes to regard his vote as a merchantable commodity which ought to bring enough in the markets of corruption to minister to his appetite and supply his wants. The threat of the brewers in their late convention was based upon the knowledge that the traffic had placed thousands of men in such a moral, physical, and financial condition that they could be corrupted. The liquor men have always boasted of their political power obtained in this way; and many a candidate has felt it necessary to leave money with the liquor-seller to influence the bummer vote. Look at Chicago, New York, and other cities. An honest vote in some parts of those cities is impossible. "In what parts?" Those where the dram-shops are most plentiful. Unless the liquor traffic of the country is destroyed, it will do for the whole nation what it has done for the great centres of population; and as the life of this Government depends largely on the purity of the ballot-box, which can only be guaranteed by the morality and intelligence of the individual voter, the Government must destroy the dram-shops or they will destroy the Government.

This is, in part, the case for the people. The issue raised is one of simple fact. Guilty or not guilty? The traffic must plead to the indictment. If the charges made are false, the amendment should be defeated. If they are true, it must, for the good of the whole country, be carried. Standing on the street corners, blowing or bulldozing, does not meet the counts in the indictment against this villainous social criminal.

Does regulation regulate? These charges are made against *licensed dram-shops.* If the charges are true, license is a failure. The *license system* of grog-shops is on trial, and it will not benefit liquor-sellers to cry out "Stop thief!" with the idea of turning public attention from the real issue. Is the *licensed* traffic guilty of the crimes and misdemeanors alleged? If it is, then *license* is a failure. The condition of things cannot be worse. The defendants must meet the indictment and show its counts false, and that dram-shops are a blessing, that *license is a success*, that they obey law, that the liquor traffic purifies the ballot-box, discourages corruption, builds up society, and promotes law and order. If they can show this, their business is safe. Liquor men, the voters of Iowa are waiting for you to meet the facts. Will you do it, or dodge and cry, "Keep it out of politics"; "Prohibition is a failure"; "Beer is a temperance beverage"; "Moral suasion is the way to work"? These questions are *not involved* in the campaign. The license system of grog-shops is being tried by its record, and you must confine yourselves to the issues; any evasion, or failure to meet the charges fairly, honestly, and manfully will be a confession of guilt, and will be so regarded by the people.

But, ladies and gentlemen, the drunkard-makers cannot and will not try to explain away or justify, the record they themselves have made. Every charge made by the amendment advocates is true, and the defence, as outlined by the brewers of Iowa, is in keeping with the nature and character of the traffic, not only in Iowa, but elsewhere. A telegram from Dayton, Ohio, received to-day says: "The Dayton *Journal* is being boycotted by members of the liquor associations on account of its stand on the Pond and Smith bills."

The record of the liquor business, the creed of the brewers, the admissions of their advocates, show conclusively that the dram-shop is a bulldozer, a rebel, a defiant outlaw, which assassinates business, character, or life, as it may deem best, to intimidate opposition, and prevent investigation of its record and effects. These cowards are universal bulldozers. I never knew the liquor business to do a manly thing in the world. I never knew it to make a manly fight. I never knew it to stand squarely on an issue. Its whole defence is a show of defiance, a show of bravado, a show of bulldozing, a show of braggadocio; and when these fail, the defence is private, cowardly assassination. What is the first argument brought against the amendment in this State? "You cannot prohibit the sale of liquor." What does that mean? Rebellion!

If prohibition will not prohibit, what is the cause of

its failure? The women will obey the law, the decent men will obey the law, and if it fails it will be because the liquor outlaws refuse to obey the will of the people. They are self-confessed traitors to good government.

I tell the liquor men of this country that if they think they are greater than this Government, the same thought has been entertained by other men. There is one thing more certain than that—this Government is greater than any class of rebels: it can enforce any law which a majority of this people, through their legislatures, say shall be the supreme law of this State. This must be taken for granted—that the State of Iowa can enforce any law that may be passed by a majority in its Legislature. If the votes of the majority of citizens expressed in the statutes of Iowa cannot be enforced; if five thousand saloon-keepers could bulldoze and intimidate the Government of this commonwealth, then the sooner that Government goes into bankruptcy and you get one which is good for something, the better it will be for humanity, civilization, and liberty.

Through the canvass in Kansas the same thing was said. They did not say that the charges made against the dram-shop were false. They said: "If you pass the amendment you cannot enforce it"; and, armed with bottled beer, they tried to bulldoze the State. What was the result?

Coming from Topeka, recently, to Kansas City, I was sitting in the seat just behind the leader of the anti-prohibitionists of that State—I had the pleasure of meeting him on the public platform during the canvass and discussing the question with him—we were talking about other questions for a time. At last he turned to me, and, drawing his face down as long as Job's when he was in affliction, went on to say, "Finch, all I predicted at Bismarck Grove in regard to this accursed law has come true."

"Well, what is it?"

"Why," he said, "it is killing Kansas. Germans are leaving the State by hundreds. It is driving men out, and immigration will not come. The State is dead."

I said to him: "You have this consolation: if the prohibitory law has killed your State, if it has driven large numbers out of it, then if Kansas is not to be renowned for the number of its people, it will be renowned for the sobriety, intelligence, and the morality of those who remain."

"Hold on," said the gentleman; "there is more whiskey and beer sold in Kansas to-day than there ever was before. You can get it everywhere."

Looking closely at him I asked, "For what, then, are those men leaving Kansas?" He saw he was caught, and abandoned the conversation.

If I pick up a copy of one daily paper published in Chicago, or another from St. Louis, I frequently see an editorial saying, in substance, that "Kansas is dead"; "Immigration to Kansas has stopped"; "The prohibitory law has killed Kansas." Perhaps the very next day I pick up a copy of the same paper, and I see an editorial, or an article by an anonymous correspondent, saying, "Whiskey is being sold in every town in Kansas just as free as water"; "There are more drunkards in Kansas than when the law was passed."

If men will lie, they should be consistent liars. The liars who are fighting against prohibition lack intelligence, for their lies contradict each other. In Maine they have fought the prohibitory law by the same contradictory lying.

If the battle had been between the liquor rebels of Kansas and the moral citizens of Kansas, there would not have been an open grog-shop in the State three months after the law passed. No sooner had the law been passed to enforce the amendment, than the combined liquor power of this nation stood behind the outlaws to encourage them and help them to defy the supreme law of that State; and what is still meaner, men from other States went in to help the outlaws assassinate the morality and the character of Kansas.

I remember reading in one of the great newspapers of Chicago, a long article, saying that in the Southern States the constitutional amendments were defied and the Civil Rights bill was a dead letter. The editor appealed to the solid North to rise *en masse,* and at the ballot-box crush out this rebellion against the Constitution and the laws. It said: "When an article is in the Constitution, when statutes have been passed to enforce it, men are rebels who defy it." And yet this same newspaper, the Chicago *Tribune*, is down in the mud before the liquor power of this nation, and has become the apologist for, and the sympathizer with, the liquor rebels of Kansas. It advises them to defy the supreme law of that State, and the statutes made to enforce it. Kansas' grand Governor—St. John—it calls every mean name which it can find in the drunkard-maker's vocabulary. Oh! if there is any one thing that would make every drop of blood in my veins grow hot with indignation, it is the way that the opposition meet this issue. I know John P. St. John, of Kansas. I have seen him with his family, standing, as he does, the grandest Republican Governor of the country. The opposition have not met him like men; they have called him everything that was vile, attempted to assassinate his character, traduce him and continue to traduce him; and men who ought to be in a better business, have become tools of the liquor rebels to carry on this dirty work.

Can the liquor business be stopped? Men of Iowa, there is no need of asking that question here. When the saloon men stand up and say prohibition will not prohibit, and that the traffic cannot be stopped, I answer, "I know better." The idea of five thousand liquor-dealers being able to control this State is absurd. When I hear a man or find a newspaper whimpering and crying, "It ought to be stopped, but we cannot stop it; they will sell anyhow," I get disgusted, especially in this State, settled by old soldiers. Some of you men, a few years ago, left your State, your mothers, wives, and children, and went down to the Southern land, and there, in the face of cannon—and you knew that behind those guns were brave men fighting for what they believed to be right, as you were fighting for what you believed to be right—in face of the sheeted fire and leaden hail, where death was on every breeze, you fought, suffered, and bled. For what? Just simply to say this Government was able to hold itself together, to enforce its laws, and to live.

The idea that in this State, filled with men who wear the scars of honorable battle—scars which were obtained in strife that makes them honored throughout the world—the idea of these men getting down to whimper and say, "The State cannot enforce the law!"

A Union general was riding up to the rear of his forces at the battle of Antietam, when he saw from the front ranks a tall soldier start, and, in double-quick time, make his way to the rear. The general was astonished, and, looking at him for a moment, said, "Halt, sir. Go back to your regiment."

The fellow stopped, commenced to cry, and said, "General, I can't; I am a coward, and I told them I was a coward when they drafted me into the army."

"Well," said the general, "if I was a coward I would not be a great baby. Go back, sir."

"Well, I wish I was a baby, and a gal baby at that."

Ridiculous! Yes; but is it half as ridiculous as for men, who are the Commonwealth of Iowa, to go whimpering around, "It ought to be stopped, but we cannot stop it. They will sell anyhow"? "Mr. Liquor-seller, you are in a mighty mean business—you are ruining homes—you are making criminals—you are filling jails—you are crowding almshouses—you are breaking the Sabbath—you are damning souls; but we cannot stop you—you will sell anyhow. Please give us five hundred dollars with which to build sidewalks in our cities."

Ladies and gentlemen, this Government is greater than any of its vices. When any of its vices become greater in force, the Government will die. When any class of men is able to defy the Government successfully, then it becomes the autocrat. If you grant that the liquor-dealers of this State are greater in power in the State, then you grant that Iowa has ceased to exist as a commonwealth, and has become an oligarchy of the liquor traffic. The supreme power of the State is the Government, and if the dram-shops have power greater than it exerts, the State is merely a puppet in the hands of a vital, aggressive, and active force. The threat of the Iowa brewers, the threat of the Iowa distillers, is an open declaration that the State of Iowa is not able to control them, and that they propose to control the State. The question, as it comes to you, is simply, "Will you be men; will you assert your power to consider the question on its merits and settle it, or will you be bulldozed—will you be intimidated—will you be corrupted, and sell your birthright for a mess of pottage?"

This, ladies and gentlemen, is the case as I wish to present it to you; take it to your homes; think over it fairly, fully, honestly; and when you render your verdict, have these two things in mind: 1st. Your obligations to your own homes—your own families. 2d. Your obligations as citizens of a State, to protect all homes, all families, all citizens.

The temperance question was never so dear to me—the cause never seemed so much my own, although I always loved it—as it was after the little bright-eyed boy came into my home. When he comes and climbs on my knee, puts his chubby little arms around my neck, and calls me "papa," the thought comes to me: "Will there ever be the time when my boy will reel along the street a drunkard, wear the chains of a criminal, or die in the almshouse, as the result of drink?" And so, if I could vote in your State in June, I should just ask what would be the relation of the grog-shop to that boy of mine.

You may say, "I have no boys; I have girls."

A gentleman, some years ago, came into my office and said to me, "What are the divorce laws of this State?"

I said, "I hope you are not going to apply for a divorce. It is an exceedingly disagreeable kind of litigation."

A couple of ladies had come in with him. I saw one was an old lady with gray hair, the other young, with care lines visible in her face, and a look of mental misery and suffering there.

"I have one girl," the man said, and he introduced me to her, "the light of our home; and if she *is* here,

I want to say to you she is just as good a girl as God ever gave a father. She was always kind to her mother. There never was a time when it was necessary to punish her in our home; if she did wrong, she was ready to come and ask forgiveness. She married a man I thought to be worthy of her. We did not know he drank, but it was so. Five years ago they were married. God has given them one child. The father drank more and more. My daughter did not tell me for a long time; she would not let us know how she was suffering. One night her husband went home, and in a drunken rage knocked her down with a chair." The old man stepped forward, raised the hair from her forehead, and showed the scar. "Struck her," continued the father, "struck her like a brute, the man who had sworn to love and honor her. He took her—the light of our home—from our arms, and then abused her like a dog."

Gentlemen voters, such may be your story some day. The little girl who will come to you to-night with bright eyes and loving smile, who will run and bring the slippers to papa, may some day return to you with a broken heart, her life ruined by a man who has been wrecked in the saloons, if you vote to continue them. When you make up your verdict, take into consideration your home interests and heart interests.

There is one thing, however, important as are these interests, that is still higher: the thought of how God would have you act. Dare you go to the polls on the 27th of June and cast a vote that you cannot ask God to bless? My friends, as you go there and vote, think if you in the silence of your chamber can ask God to bless the vote. If you vote to continue the drunkard-factories, of course you are willing to pray God to prosper them, to ask that their customers may increase.

So, if I were on the jury, I would take into consideration my home interests, the interests of my country, the approval of my God, and then, examining the facts, I would vote either to shut the saloons or to continue them, as my judgment and conscience dictated.

Gentlemen, when you have written your verdict on the 27th of June, it will either roll Iowa up to the plane of the civilization of Kansas and Maine, or allow her to remain down in the old darkness of compromise and partnership with wrong. God grant that Iowa may lead the way through which my State and the other parts of this Republic may follow, until in all the galaxy of American States there shall not be one that will license a business to ruin its citizens, to debauch its morality, or to break down its institutions.

" The crisis is upon us ! face to face with us it stands,
With solemn lips of questioning, like the Sphinx in Egypt sands.
This day we fashion destiny, the web of life we spin,
This day for all hereafter choose we holiness or sin.
Even now from misty Gerizim, or Ebal's cloudy crown,
Call we the dews of blessing or the bolts of cursing down."

VI.

THE DEFENCE REVIEWED.

An Address delivered at the Opera-House, Iowa City, Sunday evening, May 7, 1882.

Ladies and Gentlemen: Never was a more fully and fairly defined issue submitted to any people than the one now pending in this State. The case is entitled, "The People *vs.* Drunkard-factories, *alias* sample-rooms, *alias* grog-shops, *alias* dram-shops, *alias* saloons, *alias* hotels, *alias* bar-rooms." No criminal ever appeared in a police court with more *aliases* than this criminal. The American drunkard-factory is on trial for high crimes against society and treason against the Government. The terrible charges against it are made by the people, openly, boldly, and emphatically. The criminal is in the court of the people and asked to plead to the indictment. "Guilty or not guilty?" is the question asked by the clerk, and it must be answered.

The charges must be disproved or the drunkard-factories must be destroyed. The position taken by the drunkard-makers and their friends is neither fair, honest, nor decent. Their first defence is personal slander, lying, and mud-throwing. They evidently hope thereby to turn the attention of the people from the real criminal in the case. It is the old dodge of the snatch-thief, who, when pursued by officers with the cry, "Stop thief!" joins in the cry, to turn public attention from himself.

Once, when a boy, my father told an elder brother that if he and I would take care of the ducks on the farm during the summer, we might have all the young ones we could raise. During the summer we took good care of the ducks, and had, I think, eighty-six in the fall. The visions of skates and sleds grew apace. The duck-pen was near the stream, and one night an intruder dug in and killed several of the ducks. A trap was set, but the next night he dug around it, and continued his depredations. At last, brother and I determined to sit up and watch. The gun was duly loaded, and we sat down near the pen. Soon after midnight the sound of alarm among the ducks told us the enemy was there. We rushed to the pen—blocked up the hole, and caught him; but, ladies and gentlemen, it has always been a question, which were the worse punished, the dead animal or the boys whose clothes he spoiled. That experience taught me never to fight skunks, whether quadruped or biped, unless I did it with a long pole; and in this contest I shall not change the rule, whether the animal be a victim of the drunkery, or an apostate minister, who, Judas-like, having sold his Master, is now scorned and despised even by those who bought him.

The temperance leaders will press the charges—simply seeking to force a fair, honest, and full trial of the case—and if the other side fail to meet the issues, or resort to mud-throwing, as their dirty tools are now doing, it will be an admission of the guilt of the traffic, and simply show how low, ignorant, vile, and mean, are its hirelings.

To thinking men, their present contortions, evasions, quibbles, foolish statements, and lying must be disgusting. The issue is plain; a child can understand; but

> "They wriggle in and wriggle out,
> Leaving the hunter still in doubt,
> Whether the snake that made the track
> Was going out or coming back."

By such a course they enter a plea of guilty to the charges, and their evasions are simply made in hopes of reducing the nature and force of the inevitable verdict. They are like the condemned murderer who is anxious to have his sentence commuted to imprisonment for life. Their boldest leaders are willing to enter a plea of guilty, if the people will make the verdict imprisonment in high-license pens, rather than the death penalty of prohibition.

In Nebraska we have tried high license. It is a fraud and a failure. The saloon-keepers do not try to enforce the law against illicit selling. There is more liquor sold as a beverage in the drug-stores of my State than in the drug-stores of your own. *It will take more force, more power to enforce a high-license law than complete and entire prohibition.* But, as this plea for reduction of penalty has been entered, let us to-night examine the quibbles on which it is asked.

Their first defence—the one urged more than all others—I wish to read from their own papers. It is as follows:

> "It is more than twenty-four years ago, that the people of Iowa solemnly enacted that the business of brewing beer should be thenceforth a legal industry. This was done with full understanding and knowledge that it necessarily implied the investment of capital in property devoted to that business, and that such legislation, in the nature of things, ought to be permanent, and not a trap set to catch the confiding.
>
> "We were justified in believing that this was to be the settled policy of the State; and we have, relying in good faith upon the fairness and honesty of the people, invested our means in this business."

These men say: "If this amendment passes, it will confiscate the saloons, breweries, and distilleries." An editor in your own city says: "It is an axe-and-torch amendment." "The Government has no right to destroy the drunkeries of Iowa," is the claim made. That the State has the right to destroy the business of liquor-selling, is settled. In the language of the Supreme Court of the United States: "It is the undoubted and reserved power of every State here, as a political body, to decide, independent of any provisions made by Congress, though subject not to conflict with any one of them when rightful, who shall compose its population, who become its residents, who its citizens, who enjoy the privileges of its laws, and be entitled to their protection and favor, and *what kind of property and business it will tolerate and protect.*"

The State having the right to destroy the drunkery, the question for you, citizens of Iowa, to determine is, would such action be right and just? The State is a society of right,—justice is its fundamental idea. In this case Iowa cannot afford to be unjust.

Investigation will show that the States have always claimed the power to prohibit, both directly and indirectly, the wrongful use of property, or the use which injured society and civilization.

There was a time when the State of New York allowed lotteries to exist in its great cities; but, after trial, it became evident that the business was debauching the morals and intelligence of its people; and its Legislature said to the lottery-dealers: "You have forfeited the right to conduct this business, and it must stop." The dealers had thousands of dollars invested in their great buildings, in their advertisements, and in tickets, and machinery. But as soon as it was demonstrated that the business of conducting lotteries was an enemy to public morals, the State, obeying the law of self-defence, killed the business, and that ended it.

Some years ago, another class of individuals — I will not call them men, they do not deserve the name — made money by printing obscene literature. Over this country they spread it, in schools, private homes, everywhere. This execrable business was allowed to continue for a long time, until the detectives in our great cities commenced to see the harvest of crime which was being reaped. Thousands of men and women were debauched and ruined through this traffic. The State saw that a great ulcer was located on its life, and it took the scalpel of law and cut it out. To-day it is a penitentiary offence to send such literature through the mails.

Years before railroads reached the State of Iowa, there were thousands of coaches carrying the mails and passengers across the State. I think Iowa City was one of the old stage-coach stations. Men had thousands of dollars invested in coaches and horses. The State had chartered these coach lines, but the day came when the State said: "It is for the best interest of Iowa that we have railroads." It chartered the **railroads and killed the stage-coach dead as a hammer.**

In examining the first defence, the most noticeable thing about it is its falsehoods. It says: "The people of Iowa solemnly enacted that the business of brewing should be henceforth a legal industry." "We were justified in believing that this was to be the settled policy of the State." Remember the rule of law— "False in one, false in all." What are the facts? The decision of the Supreme Court of the United States was given years ago. Every drunkard-maker in the State of Iowa at that time knew such decision had been made. Not a single man who is selling liquor to-day in the State was selling it then. A decision was made by the Supreme Court; the right of the people to destroy the traffic was affirmed; the people were inclined to assert that right; the liquor men knew it; they bet their money on the chances as a gambler bets his money on the cards in his hands; and now, beaten by their own games, they are pleading the baby act; like the school-boy, trying to trade back. Did anybody compel them to go into the business? They knew that the question of its being stopped was being agitated. They took the chances. The statement that they had reason to think license would be the settled policy is false.

But what about the people enacting that brewing should be a legal industry?

In the year 1855, the people of this State, by a vote of 25,555 for, and 22,645 against, prohibited the liquor traffic in this State. Notice now: the people did this; the liquor men then had no right in the State whatever. The people had decreed the end of the trade. A few years rolled away, and the drunkard-makers went to your Legislature—they did not come to you—they went to a few designing demagogues among your politicians, and said: "If you will destroy the people's law, in defiance of the people's verdict, we will guarantee to your political party a certain support."

Honest men, if they had thought the law had wronged them, would have gone to the people to ask for a rehearing of the case on its merits. This they did not do. They dared not go before them. They simply attempted to defraud the people of the State. The politicians entered into the coalition, and, in defiance of public opinion, the traffic was readmitted. The business to-day stands in Iowa as a thief who has broken into your house. The liquor men know their business is here by fraud—that they are trespassers on the people's domain. The drunkard-factories secured readmission to Iowa by contract with political demagogues. The liquor men ask justice—it shall be given them. Those who ask equity must show equity. A contract secured by fraudulent representations is void.

What representations did they make to secure the readmission of their business into this State?

They said: "We will only sell wine, beer, and cider."

They said: "We will not sell liquors to minors or drunkards, or on Sunday." Each of these agreements they have persistently violated.

They have violated every contract, betrayed every friend. The celebrated German, A. F. Hofer, says:

"The saloon-keeper has put the manacles on his own hands. He has forged the handcuffs that are put upon him by a hundred enactments of law. He has wrought the chain of statutes, link by link, that is slowly crushing the life out of his business. And now he has attached the heavy ball to that chain which will drag not only his business, but the manufacturer who supplies him, down to perdition. The Senate has passed the constitutional amendment which will forever banish the retail liquor business outside of the pale of tolerated occupations, and which forever brands it as contraband in our Commonwealth. It has culminated into a thunderbolt welded into our fundamental law.

"We say the saloon-keeper has brought upon himself the terrible forces and rigors of the law. He was not satisfied with the old Iowa law, which treated the sale of liquors as any other merchandise. He abused its leniency shamefully. He was not satisfied with the original Maine law, which enabled him to avoid dispensing the more poisonous alcoholic liquors, and relieved him of responsibility as to civil damage. He abused the law like a dog. He brought upon himself the law which made him responsible for all damages flowing out from the sale of what flowed in. He was not satisfied with that, but next involved the owner of property in which he kept saloon. Next he abused the liberality of the privileges so that the Two-Mile Act and the Election laws were forged and hung about his insubmissive neck."

The people answer the first defence by the following facts:

1st. The statements upon which the liquor traffic secured admission into this State were absolutely and wholly false.

2d. The traffic has violated every provision of the contract. It has never obeyed the law. It is an outlaw, and has by its own acts shown that it must be treated as such.

The law says: "It shall be unlawful for any person to sell or give away, by agent or otherwise, any spirituous or other intoxicating liquors, including wine or beer, to any minor for any purpose whatsoever, unless on the written order of his parent, guardian, or family physician." Have they obeyed this provision of the law, or have they violated it? Are they in a condition to come into the court of the people and plead a violation of contract? The law continues: "Or to sell the same to any intoxicated person, or any person in the habit of becoming intoxicated." Have they kept this provision of the law, or have they violated it? The law says, "It shall be unlawful for any person wilfully to sell or keep for sale intoxicating, malt, or vinous liquors which have been adulterated or drugged by admixture with any deleterious or poisonous substance." Have they kept this provision of the law, or have they violated it? The law provides, "It shall be unlawful to sell or buy property of any kind on the first day of the week, commonly called Sabbath." Have they kept this provision of the law, or have they violated it?

The rule of law is, that if I make a contract with you to do certain things and fail to fulfil my part of it, and by my failure cause you to cancel the contract, I have no right to plead injustice or to ask for damages. If the liquor men of this State have obtained admission here by fraudulent representations, they have no right in equity, in justice, or common honesty, to come before this people and demand that a system introduced by lies, and living in outlawry, shall longer continue to legally exist. They must come with clean hands into this court. This they cannot do. Their hands are not clean. With such a record, their cry of injustice and persecution reminds one of the young man who murdered his father and mother,—when placed on trial, he asked the judge to be merciful to him "because he was an orphan."

If the liquor business had not injured the State, it would not be on trial for its life to-day. It has only its own vile record to meet.

Certain of the liquor men, abandoning the contest, ask: "Are you not going to pay us for our business?" Certainly, the people would not let you go without settling; they want to force you to return to society what you have taken from it, or to in part repair the damage done by your business. If you made a contract with me to go upon my farm, and then after a while were ejected for violation of contract, and sued me for damage, I would set up the damage which you had done to the farm. My liquor friends, make up your bill. Charge up the saloon, brewery, distillery, every trapping and fixture you have, in one bill. All that the temperance men ask is, that you give them a chance to file against you a bill for the damage you have done Iowa in the past twenty-four years. They want you to indemnify every wife whose home you have ruined; every little boy you have cursed; return to the tax-payers every dollar they have paid out to maintain a police force, and to run asylums, prisons, and almshouses to take care of your products. Pour back into Iowa's treasury the money you have taken from it, and, after the balance is struck, if the people owe you anything, they will pay it. Will you do it? Put in your bill to-morrow, and let the WORLD see who is the debtor.

If the liquor men of this State were compelled to return to Iowa what they have taken from it, they would be beggared, and they know it. They had no money when they started a few years ago. Now look at their great distilleries, breweries, and palatial saloons. Where did they get the money to build them? By making drunkards of the people. They have taken it from the wife and the baby. They have ruined the home life of the State of Iowa; and now, when they have amassed their millions by beggaring the people, they turn around and whimper because they will not let them continue this accursed business. They ought to be content with the ill-gotten gains which the State has given them twenty-four years to take from the people. I do not doubt that they feel badly. It is pitiful, when men have been supported in idleness and grown rich by the ruin of others, to force them into honest callings and avocations, and compel them to benefit the world in return for the blessings it gives them. In their days of disconsolation and sorrow the old lady's Scripture may soothe them and keep up their rapidly failing spirits.

A minister once called on an old lady, who was a member of his congregation, and said to her:

"Aunt Sally, how are you getting along?"

She replied: "Not very well, sir. Sal's run off with the hired man; John is gettin' obstropulous, and the pigs have eaten up the garden truck. But in my trials and tribulations there's jest one passage o' Scripter that allus consoles my heart, nerves me for the trials to come, and brings me nearer the throne."

Said the minister, "Aunt Sally, what is that?"

"Well," she said, "I don't remember jest whether it's in Proverbs or in Psalms where it says, 'Grin and bear it.'"

This advice I commend to the drunkard-makers of this State in this hour of their approaching defeat.

The second defence urged is:

"Beer is comparatively a harmless beverage, containing only about four per cent. of alcohol, and experience has shown that its use tends to diminish the amount of distilled liquors required, and thereby decreases drunkenness and promotes temperance."

You see they are fighting for beer in this country. They tell you the people have no right to interfere with the social custom of the German, because he used to drink beer in Germany; but the poor Irishman who used to drink whiskey in Ireland cannot legally get a nip in Iowa. If I was an Irishman living in this State, if for no other reason than to show that I was as good as a German, I would vote for this amendment, and get even with them. I submit, as a matter of fact, if the German has a right to *his* national beverage, the Irishman has a right to *his*; and it is the worst kind of demagoguery that will refuse Pat a nip and give Hans all he wants.

I am glad I have so many students around me as I take up this beer issue, for a knowledge of history will help to impress the point. Saloon men say that distilled spirits are the primary cause of drunkenness. This statement is best answered by the history of the evil. The process of distillation of alcohol was, in rude forms, undoubtedly known to the early alchemists, but it was first taught by Albucasis, an Arabian chemist or alchemist, who lived eleven hundred years after the beginning of the Christian era. Distilled liquors were not used as beverages until after the thirteenth century. Brandy, whiskey, gin, rum, and other distilled liquors, have a history of less than eight hundred years. Standing before this audience of scholars and students, I wish to say, the worst forms of national drunkenness the world has ever seen existed before distilled beverages existed or the process of making them was known. The use of fermented liquors then, as now, created a desire, a craving for stronger stimulants. Distilled spirits not being known, fermented liquors were drugged and became the strong liquors of history. The drunkenness of Rome, Greece, Babylon, and other ancient empires was the drunkenness caused by the use of fermented liquors, and the cravings which such liquors caused which led to the use of drugged liquors. History says: "The use of fermented liquors is the by-way which leads down into the valley of drunkenness." The brewer-drunkard-makers must destroy the history of experience if they wish to maintain their second proposition. The graveyard of nations answers their foul lie.

The third defence urged is:

"It is an attempt to pass, or rather to create, a sumptuary law, which has for its object the restraint of individual rights, and is, therefore, contrary to the principles of our Republican institutions."

Webster defines sumptuary laws to be "such as restrain or limit the expenses of citizens in apparel, food, furniture, and the like." If laws prohibiting the manufacture and sale of liquors are sumptuary, then the laws pohibiting houses of prostitution, gambling hells, the sale of diseased meat, and quarantining small-pox and yellow-fever are sumptuary. I have no patience with men who presume on the ignorance of the people. A person who will speak of a law prohibiting the traffic in intoxicants as sumptuary, is either an illiterate ass, a self-confessed idiot, or a political trickster.

The fourth defence is:

"It is an invasion of natural desires."

There is no such thing as a natural desire to drink whiskey, because in nature such a thing as whiskey or beer is unknown. God never created alcoholic beverages. You may take corn and pile it up as high as heaven, and let it rot to earth—every hour of its decomposition test it with the most delicate chemical tests, and you will never find whiskey in the process of rotting. Place grapes on your office table and let them remain until the blue mold has eaten them up, and alcoholic wine will not appear in the process of decay. God does not rot things that way. Alcohol comes in when mechanical force is used to break the starch-cells and bring the starch in contact with the juice. You must have the starch in connection with the juice when this unnatural kind of fermentation takes place. "But," objects one, "if God did not create alcoholic beverages, He did make the laws that cause the formation of alcohol." Granted. God made iron. He made the laws of cohesion and adhesion, but God did not make butcher-knives; and what would you think of the intelligence of a man who would prate about a natural appetite for butcher-knives! God created the laws that govern the formation of gunpowder, but nowhere in God's universe can you find gunpowder existing as the result of nature's own work. What would you think of a man who would prate about a natural *appetite for gunpowder!* A natural appetite for something that is unnatural is a thing that no man can understand; hence, you can see, the desire is not a natural one.

Let us see what you mean by the terms natural appetite or desire. You say: "I have an appetite for liquor." Appetite is a demand for supplies. In the school, in the store, in the office, you use a certain amount of muscular force; then you become hungry. What is hunger? A demand for supplies. The body asks you to supply it something out of which it may make force to take the place of the force you have used up. You go to the table, eat slowly, masticate the food thoroughly, and when you get up and go away, where is your appetite? A demand for supplies, and when the supplies are furnished it is satisfied. Enter a drunkery; drink one glass. Do you not want the second, then the third, then the fourth, each glass more than the one which preceded it? My liquor friend, you grant me the proposition when you say, "I have *will*-power enough to stop!" You do not use will-power to stop eating pork and beans when you have enough. The difference is this: When you give a natural appetite what it asks for, it is satisfied; when you give a diseased craving what it asks for, it but craves the more.

If we follow out this thought it will meet another sophistry often urged by the liquor men, that the liquor business of this country is governed by the same laws of political economy that govern the sale of the necessaries of life. You ask what they mean. They answer: "You must do away with the demand and the supply will cease. It is the demand which creates the supply." Did you ever hear this statement? There is not a student before me but knows this statement of the law is not correct. The true rule of political economy is this: In the case of absolute necessaries the supply is sought after because of the demand, but in the case of created luxuries the supply causes the demand, or changes a general inclination or desire into a demand for the specific luxury which is tempting. Let me state it again. In the case of absolute necessaries, the supply is created by the demand, but in the case of created luxuries the supply creates the demand. There is a natural demand for food; you must have it or die. I met a man in Fort McPherson who had travelled for four days and eaten nothing but a raw rattlesnake. The demand for food is natural and must be satisfied. Food being an absolute necessity, the supply is sought as the result of the demand. In this climate clothes are absolutely necessary to protect the body from the inclemency of the weather. Demand for these creates the supply. You must have clothes of some kind, and if you fail to procure them, nature will supply them in part by causing hair to grow upon the body.

Diamonds are not necessary to man's existence. They are a created luxury. A man goes to New York, purchases diamonds, and brings them home. Does he lock them up in a safe until you come around and tell him you want them? No; he locks them up during the night, and in the daytime places them in the show-case, where persons who enter his place may see them. Some young ladies enter who have no thought of diamonds, and see the rings, pins, brooches, and necklaces. One exclaims, "Nell, come here! Those gems are lovely." They admire their colors—"I wish I had them." What caused that wish? The presence of the luxury.

What are you thinking about? Well, I am thinking about watermelons. Now, they are not necessaries of life. They are luxuries. You will be down here next summer. You are not thinking of watermelons. You hear the musical cry, "Watermelons!" As soon as you hear it, there will be a demand for the melons. "I want one of those watermelons." The demand is created by the presence of the melons. Even in a case where necessaries are combined with luxuries, this is the rule to some extent. Hats of some kind are necessary in this country. Suppose a milliner has received some new Spring hats. Would she place them in a closet and lock them up until some lady called and told her she wanted one? Not much; she would put them in the show-case where every lady would see them. Ladies are passing:

"Is it not a beauty?"

"That's a jewel of a bonnet."

"And the colors!—my colors,—I wonder how I would look with it on. Let's go and see."

They go in, and she puts it on and looks at herself; and then she says, "I wish I had it!" What created the wish? The presence of the bonnet.

The liquor business of this country comes under the same rule. Alcoholic liquor is not an absolute necessity. Give it the best position you can, and it is a dangerous luxury. Then the presence of it creates the demand for it.

You go down the street—you are not an abstainer, neither do you care for a drink. A saloon-keeper has a big sign across the street, "Ice-cool lager." The presence of the sign, together with the knowledge that the beer is there, leads you to go in and get it. If it was further away, you would not think of it. Said the general manager of the Union Pacific R.R. to a friend of mine: "By closing up the saloons near our workshops, drunkenness has diminished two-thirds among our men. When the men were passing the saloons on their way to and from work, they would get a drink. Now, when they have to go three or four blocks for it, they do not get it."

The fifth defence is:

"If you shut up the saloons they will sell in the drug-stores and in holes."

To meet this it will be necessary for us to examine the causes of drunkenness in this country. What makes drunkards?

A liquor man exclaims, "Treating." Yes, sir, that is one of the principal reasons. Boys go into a saloon to play billiards—when they are in Rome, they must do as Romans do. After playing for a time they go up to the bar, turn glasses full, and standing there, clink their glasses and drink to each other's health. Poets and novelists of old times have thrown around the custom of drinking to each other's health a tempting sheen of romance. Break up the saloon, and where is your treating? Where will liquor be sold? In a drug-store? Notice a man treating in a drug-store. He looks up and down the street, and then sneaks in behind the prescription case to get a drink. Is not that romantic?

But they say it will be sold in cellars. Yes! a man will sneak through an alley-way, down a back stairway, into a cellar, where there is a keg of whiskey. He finds a tin-cup rusty with the saliva of other men who have drunk from it. Is not that a high-toned way of drinking? Will it tempt and make drunkards of the boys?

Another says, "They will carry it in bottles." Yes; but treating with bottles is not specially romantic. A wink of the eye leads one into a stall in a barn or around behind some building out of sight, where the bottle is drawn from the pocket and passed over to the friend. He takes a drink and passes it back to the owner, who takes a suck off the same nose. Now, is not that tempting, especially if one drinker chews tobacco and the other does not?

No, gentlemen, when you have broken down the lighted bar, when you outlaw this trade, when you drive it into holes—old bummers may get it, but the boys of this country, bright, and brave, and manly, will never sneak after something for which they have not learned to care. Said a leading statesman of Maine to me, "Old bummers of Maine kept on drinking, but we have a generation of boys who have grown up since the Maine law, who know nothing of the use of liquor." Close the saloons, and treating is dead, and the boys are safe.

The sixth defence is:

"It will destroy personal liberty."

Liquor-dealers met in the city of Des Moines, and declared that they were the defenders of personal liberty in this country, and to-day the liquor interest is masquerading as the champion of liberty; and a more ridiculous masquerade I never saw.

Gentlemen, scholars, what is the foundation of liberty in this country? Your schools, your churches, and your universities. The foundation of liberty is intelligence and morality. A drunken and debauched people can never maintain a government of the people, for the people, and by the people. Liquor-dealers, before you step out as the champions of liberty, please tell us what you have done to perpetuate liberty in the land? How many schools have you erected? Where are your colleges? How many churches have you built? How many hospitals have you founded? Show me a thing you have ever done to make this nation better, and grander, and truer.

But they say: "We have paid taxes." How? The nation wrung it out of you by police officers and internal revenue officers. In South Carolina and Tennessee you shot them dead in their tracks, and you would do it in the North if you dared. Where has the American Brewers' Congress ever built a college, or the Distillers' Union founded a church? When have they done a thing for liberty in the world? And yet these men, who have only made drunkards and debauched the people, step out and claim to be the defenders of liberty! My friend, the Hon. John Sobieski, would say: "The Goddess of Liberty has always been a dear goddess to me. I used to read stories of the days of chivalry. All boys and girls love to read such books. Recall your boyish ideas of the old heroes. Tall, well-formed, brave—such is the ideal knight. As I think of these new knights of liberty, the thought comes—how are the mighty fallen! They are not tall, but they make up for height by breadth. To-night, ladies, your are to go home with your loved ones. Suppose the 'Goddess of Liberty' had been on the platform during the meeting. A beer-wagon drives up in front of the hall, and a typical beer knight waddles up to the platform, and says: 'If you (hic) please, you are (hic) to go home with me.'"

Think of it!

If Liberty has fallen so low that her defenders are the class of men who debauch the manhood, and womanhood, and civilization of this country, God pity such liberty. The idea of these men arrogating to themselves the position of the special champions of the liberties of this people is absurd, ridiculous, and nonsensical. It makes me think of an illiterate church-member by the name of Walker, in southern Illinois. During a revival where his spiritual strength had been renewed, the idea came into his mind that he must preach. He called upon the officers of the church, and told them that he believed God had given him a special call. They expressed some doubts, promised to consider his case, and sent him away. A few days later he returned, still more fully impressed that it was his divine mission to defend the religion of the Lord Jesus Christ, and to turn sinners from the path of death. The officers of the church asked him if he had received any evidences of a call. He responded: "I went home from this yer meetin' troubled an' perplexed, an' the nex' day I went ter visit neighbor Jones on the hill. Comin' back late in the evenin' 'cross the pastur, the thought come to me that ef God had really called me, he oughter make it manifest to me thar. So I jest knelt down in a clump of bushes, raised up my voice in prayer, and asked God to show me my dooty clear. Jest as I was a-prayin', on the stillness broke an awful voice, sayin': ' Go, W-a-alk-er, W-a-alk-er, Walker! —Go, Pr-e-e-a-cher, Pr-e-e-a-cher, P-r-e-a-a-ch-e-r-r-r!'" The officers of the church examined the source of call, and found that it was a jackass, which, alarmed at his praying, had commenced to bray. For the life of me I cannot get rid of the thought that this call of the liquor-dealers, as the defenders of liberty, must have come from some such source.

But what is their cry? They say, "personal liberty." In other words, they mean sensual or natural liberty. Lieber, the great political philosopher, says, in his celebrated work on political ethics, as revised by Theodore D. Woolsey (page 325):

"This untenable view is another misconception arising out of the primary error of a natural state of man and a natural liberty in which man is believed to be absolutely without any restraint, except his own conscience and understanding, which, however, it would appear, must yet be very weak. Civil liberty, therefore, is judged by a negative standard. That is, it is believed the less you are required to give up of that original and perfect natural liberty, the greater the amount of civil liberty. The idea is radically wrong. Liberty, like everything else of a political character, necessary and natural to man, and to be striven for, arises out of the development of society. Man, in that supposed state of natural liberty, which is nothing but a roving state, is, on the contrary, in a state of great submission He is a slave and servant of the elements. Matter masters his mind. He is exposed to the wrongs of every enemy from without, and dependent upon his own unregulated mind. This is not liberty. It is plain barbarism. Liberty is materially of a civil character."

Again on page 384:

"Where men of whatsoever condition — rulers or ruled, those that toil or those that enjoy, individually, or by entire classes or nations—claim, maintain or establish rights without acknowledging corresponding and parallel obligations, there is oppression, lawlessness, and disorder, and the very ground on which the idea of all right must forever rest—the ground of mutuality or reciprocity, whether considered in the light of ethics or natural law, must sink from under it. It is natural, therefore, that wherever there exists a greater knowledge of right or more intense attention to it than to concurrent and proportionate obligation, evil ensues. What may there be found *a priori* is pointed out by history as one of its gravest and greatest morals. The very condition of right is obligation. The only reasonable obligations consist in rights. Since, therefore, a greater degree of civil liberty implies the enjoyment of more extended acknowledged rights, man's obligations increase with man's liberty. Let us, then, call that freedom of action which is determined and limited by the acknowledgment of obligation, liberty; freedom of action without limitation by obligation, licentiousness. The greater the liberty, the more the duty."

Unrestrained natural liberty is the enemy of civil liberty. Let me illustrate: It was personal liberty that enabled Guiteau to send the bullet through the back of President Garfield. It was civil liberty which hanged him on the 30th of June. Do you see the difference? It is personal liberty that would let me meet you on the street and knock your brains out with a club; it is civil liberty that would punish me for the crime.

It is personal or natural liberty which would let a tramp outrage your wife or daughter. It is organized or civil liberty which would hang him if he did. Civil liberty is developed by the restrictions of natural liberty, and the development of higher intellectual liberty among intelligent men. Go among the barbarian tribes on the frontier. One of the tribes which I visited a few years ago has very limited civil government. Their chief is elected on account of his brute strength. He has the force, and he is elected. Property is only held by the physical force of the man holding it. They have a marriage relation after a fashion. An Indian marries a squaw, and she becomes his absolute property. He may whip her, knock her down, or kill her. There is no punishment. I asked one of their chiefs, Running Elk, if there was no punishment for wife murder, and he answered, " No, unless her father or brother should take it upon himself to avenge her death." " Do they ever do that?" I asked. He answered: " No; they might want to kill their wives, and their killing him would set a bad precedent."

Come further East, to some tribes of the Missouri

River, and you will find that civilization and civil liberty have advanced by the restraint of personal liberty. These tribes have property. The marriage relation has taken more stability. The Indian may whip his wife, but to put her off must go through regular forms. If he kill her, he is punished by death or banishment from the tribe. Go South where the Cherokees control the territory. You will find a class of people nearly as intelligent as the people before me. Their property is permanent. Civilization has taken the brute Indian—very nearly a brute—restrained his personal liberty, and compelled him to be a man. Civil liberty is developed by the restraint of personal liberty. The vulture that flies across our Western plains is individually free to steal chickens. The coyote wolf is a type of individual liberty. The buccaneer on the ocean is a representative of personal liberty. Jesse James, the Missouri outlaw, was the best type of the personal liberty asked by liquor men in this country. For twenty years he was personally free to rob trains. Finally he went down to death under the hand of civil government. It might have been a bad way to assassinate him, but out West the people are glad his personal liberty was destroyed. Personal liberty means individual or brute liberty. Civil liberty means the restraint of personal liberty. I have a legal right to fill my mouth with tobacco, and chew, and chew, and spit. I do not believe I have the physical and moral right. I have a right to chew and spit this way, or chew and spit the other way—it is none of your business. You will not deny I have that right if I am alone on the prairie. I go into a crowd of men and exercise the right. I chew and spit, the juice goes in one man's face, and in another man's ear. I would be knocked down in a minute. As a man hits me on the ear, I exclaim: "Is not this a free country?" "Yes." "Have not I a right to spit?" You would teach me that my right to spit ceased where your right not to be spit upon began. This arm is my arm (and my wife's), it is not yours. Up here I have a right to strike out with it as I please. I go over there with these gentlemen and swing my arm and exercise the natural right which you have granted; I hit one man on the nose, another under the ear, and as I go down the stairs on my head, I cry out:

"Is not this a free country?"

"Yes, sir."

"Have not I a right to swing my arm?"

"Yes, but your right to swing your arm leaves off where my right not to have my nose struck begins."

Here civil government comes in to prevent bloodshed, adjust rights, and settle disputes.

Ladies and gentlemen, the idea that any man in this community has a right to do wrong, would, if it became a controlling principle, destroy any government. When Alexander Selkirk was on the island of Juan Fernandez, the poet made him sing:

> "I am monarch of all I survey,
> My right there is none to dispute;
> From the centre all round to the sea,
> I am lord of the fowl and the brute."

He could stand on his head, go without clothes—do as he pleased. If he had tried to do the same thing after he had returned to London, he would have been in the police-station in ten minutes.

Liquor men say: "Government has no right to say what I shall eat, drink, or wear." Get up and forget to dress yourself some morning. How far would you get in this city before the Government would tell you to put on clothes? One of you ladies dress yourself in men's clothes. How long before the Government will tell you to wear appropriate apparel? It is the duty of Government to restrain animal passions, and the cry of liquor men for personal liberty is simply a cry of barbarism. Let me show you the outcome of their doctrines as enunciated by their great high-priest, the high-priest of personal liberty—John Stuart Mill. I read from his works, and I advise you to get them and read for yourself, and see what this damnable doctrine of the liquor interest of this country means. I read from page 58, of the English edition, published in London, by Longmans, Green, Reader & Dyer:

"Fornication, for example, must be tolerated; and

so must gambling; but should a person be free to be a pimp or to keep a gambling house? The case is one of those which lie on the exact boundary line between two principles, and it is not at once apparent to which of the two it properly belongs. There are arguments on both sides."

Then for a whole page he discusses whether the Government has a right to deal with these vices, and says: "There is considerable force in these arguments; I will not venture to decide." Think of a man whose system of morals does not enable him to determine whether Government has the right to stop such things. Such is the doctrine of the liquor traffic. They would have the State become the procurer or agent to gratify the lusts and passions of its citizens, even though such gratification, by ruining them, would destroy its own life. Despots and devils would laugh at such a theory of governmental functions. If such a theory is adopted in this country, on the chaos of American institutions will arise the worst despotism the world has ever seen. The doctrine of personal sensual liberty is the doctrine of free-lovism, and means the reinstatement of lust, passion, and brute force as the governing force of the world.

The remainder of their defence is best answered by its absurdity. From their declaration I read:

1. "These laws have been tried and abandoned as failures in many of the States, and to-day, out of thirty-eight States they are in force in but six, and are actually enforced in none.

2. "Adopt this amendment and immigration will shun our State, as it is already shunning the State of Kansas. The rapid development of Iowa will receive a sudden check, as no immigrants will wish to live under such a tyranny as this amendment imposes."

It is a failure, yet liquor will be freely sold! It will stop immigration because the immigrants cannot obtain liquor, and they will not submit to such an awful tyranny!

Again I read:

1. "We believe it is an established fact that the attempt of Government to prohibit the sale or purchase

of intoxicating drinks sharpens and excites the disposition of men to obtain them.

2. "The fact that the adoption of this prohibitory amendment is an act of bad faith on the part of the brewing interests—that it practically confiscates our property, and makes us bankrupts, seems to have the least weight with the leaders in this fanatical and reckless crusade."

It is going to bankrupt them because it sharpens men's appetites and excites the desire to obtain liquors!

Again I read:

1. "That experience in Maine and Kansas, under the prohibitory laws, shows that it does not decrease drunkenness nor drinking.

2. "If passed, it will confiscate a large amount of property which has been built up in the pursuit of a legitimate business, and provides for no compensation to the owners for the loss."

Prohibition is a complete and entire failure; yet it destroys the breweries and distilleries!

Again I read:

1. "Wherever tried, prohibition has failed to prohibit.

2. "If the amendment shall be voted into the Constitution, a subsequent law, bristling all over with pains and penalties, will inevitably be passed to carry into full effect the intent of the amendment."

It will not prohibit! It will prohibit!

These statements are taken from different parts of their platform and grouped. If I had a boy of ten years who would make such contradictory statements, I would send him to the asylum for weak-minded children.

Their last defence is bulldozing—rebellion. Citizens, I would not overdraw the picture! I read from the Des Moines declaration of the liquor men:

"*Resolved*, That we will use all honorable means to defeat said proposed amendments at the polls; and if we are unsuccessful, will resist its unjust and oppressive provisions by every method known to law.

"*Resolved*, That we will never knowingly support

for any office or place of trust any one who shall vote for this proposed outrage upon our property and rights.

"*Resolved*, That the recent election in Ohio, which followed the passage of the Pond bill, is only a forerunner of what will occur in this State, if the Republican party adheres to its policy of fanaticism as against the liberal element."

This declaration is fully explained by one of their ablest defenders among the press of this State, which says:

"Prohibition is the first step in the direction of despotism.

"If you want to check immigration, vote for the amendment.

"If you want to increase your taxes, vote for the amendment.

"Personal liberty must and shall be maintained in impartial Iowa.

"Imperial Iowa will kick this temperance tomfoolery into a cocked hat.

"If you want to be ruled and ruined by fools and fanatics, vote for the amendment.

"The Prohibition party is made up of grannies and gossips, who have never learned to mind their own business.

"The defeat of the amendment is demanded by common-sense.

"Yes; and its defeat is demanded by common honesty.

"IF THE DOLTS AND DEMAGOGUES SUCCEED IN SECURING THE PASSAGE OF THAT SUM OF ABOMINATIONS KNOWN AS THE PROHIBITORY AMENDMENT, THE FRIENDS AND DEFENDERS OF PERSONAL LIBERTY WILL DEFY THE ENFORCEMENT OF THE ENORMITY.

"MARK THAT!"—*Sioux City Tribune.*

I have not thought that such threats, intimidation, and bulldozing could influence you voters, and only mention the statements to show you the utter depravity of the liquor traffic and its defenders. The threat of political ostracism and assassination is the emptiest kind of buncombe. The dram-shop has no political power other than as agents to bribe its debauched victims. It is a political pimp and go-between of the vilest sort—ever ready to sell itself to the highest bidder.

The threat of rebellion is the only one of any moment, and it simply raises the issue whether less than five thousand bloated liquor-dealers govern this State, or whether the people govern it. This issue you must meet and settle. The man is a coward who does not meet the defiance of the liquor men, and demonstrate the fact that the people govern Iowa.

Who governs Iowa? is the issue raised by the opposition; and in making up your verdict you are told, if you fail to place Iowa in the hands of grog-shops, you shall die politically. "Are you men, and suffer such dishonor?" No! These men who live in the sores of the body politic, as parasites live in the neglected sores of the beggar, will be washed out by your votes on the 27th of June; then—and not till then—can we hope for a healing of these loathsome social and political sores, or for sound political health and strength in the country.

VII.

THE QUESTIONS ASKED BY THE JURY ANSWERED.

An Address delivered in the Opera-House at Marshalltown, Iowa, June 18, 1882.

LADIES AND GENTLEMEN: To-night, as I close the case of the people, I want to thank you for your earnest attention and evident desire to do justice.

It is no small matter to change the organic law of a State. The verbal change may be small, but the results will affect its whole social and business life. Weigh the matter calmly, dispassionately. The people have the right to amend their organic law. The founders of the Government provided for such governmental changes. I use the word people, because it is the common term, not because it is the correct one. This is not a Government of the people. It is a Government of male voters; but, as the word people is commonly used, I shall continue to use it, and you will understand what I mean by it.

Around the proposition to amend your organic law, the opposition have conjured a host of imaginary dangers to intimidate voters. They have told you that this amendment is a blow at the liberties of the people; that it will take from them certain rights. The exact reverse is the truth. It takes rights from the Legislature, or rather returns to the people rights which years ago they delegated to the Government. The citizens have the right to recover any powers they have delegated.

A great writer has said: "Constitutions are the assemblage of those principles which are deemed fundamental to the government of a people. They refer either to the relation in which the citizen stands to the State at large, and consequently to the Government, or to the proper delineation of the various spheres of authority." This amendment is a change in the delineation of the spheres of authority. It proposes to take the authority and power to deal with a certain trade from a branch of the Government, and return it to the people.

The rule of construction of the powers of the Government in the Federal courts is this: Congress may pass any law for which an express or implied warrant can be found in the written Constitution of the United States. If an act is passed by Congress, and you wish to ascertain whether it is constitutional or not, you must take the Constitution of the United States and find in that instrument an express warrant or an implied warrant for its enactment. If you do not find it there, the law is unconstitutional. The Constitution of the United States is a restriction on the powers of the General Government.

The rule of construction in State courts is exactly the reverse. If you wish to ascertain whether a law passed by the Legislature of a State is constitutional, you must examine the Constitution of that State and find if the Legislature is prohibited from passing it. The Constitution of the State simply guarantees to the people certain rights, and all power that is not expressly reserved to the people in the Constitution, is vested in the Legislature and other branches of government of the several States.

In past years the people of the State of Iowa, and most of the other States of this Union, have been willing to trust in the hands of the Legislature the right to control the question of the alcoholic liquor trade. The people delegated their right to the legislative and executive departments of the State. The right to deal with the traffic in your State is vested in the Legislature composed of representatives elected by the people. Years have passed since this grant was made. The people have tested the system of legislative control, and have become thoroughly satisfied that the Legislature of the State is not the place where this power should be vested; and now the proposition in this State is simply to revoke the power granted to the

Legislature, and reinvest it in the people. It is the people stepping out and saying to their representatives: "Gentlemen, you have not dealt with this question as your constituents desired, and consequently we propose to take the power to deal with it out of your hands, and hold it in our own." The constitutional amendment, instead of taking a right from the people, takes a right from the Legislature and vests it in the people. The people can at any time amend the Constitution; a Legislature can never do so. That is the difference.

You ask why the people of this State are not willing to leave this power in the hands of the Legislature? Why they demand that it shall be returned to them, that they alone may decide the question? In 1855 the Legislature of your State—a Democratic Legislature, by the way—thought it wise to submit to the voters of Iowa the question whether a statutory enactment prohibiting the manufacture and sale of alcoholic beverages should become a law. The vote of the people was to decide the question whether the statute should exist. Of course the vote of the people had no effect, and the Legislature knew it could not have when they passed the law. It was simply asking a popular opinion whether it was best to enact this law. After a bitterly contested campaign, the people, by an emphatic majority, said that the statutory prohibition should be a law. In obedience to the decision of the people, the Legislature passed a bill, and it became law throughout Iowa. Hardly had this been done when the liquor men went to the legislative Solons of Iowa, and said:

"We want to come back into this State and sell wine and beer and lighter drinks."

"But," said the men in the Legislature, "the people have said you shall not come back." The liquor men used arguments which were unfair and dishonest; they were not willing to allow the question to be resubmitted to the people for a new trial; they induced the Legislature to swindle the people out of the law after they had rendered their verdict. In accordance with a political coalition, unholy as any ever made in the depths of the bottomless pit, the traffic was readmitted to this

State by legislative enactment, in defiance of the people's verdict and vote.

Therefore, the people of Iowa say to the legislators: "Gentlemen, we propose to take from you the power to unsettle the question at every session of your body. We shall take the question wholly into our own hands. We shall give prohibition a full, fair, and an honest trial; and then, if we, the voters, believe it to be a failure, we shall repeal the constitutional enactment. But it shall remain until the voters see fit to repeal it."

The constitutional change is in favor of the people. It is simply the people demanding their right to determine this question, instead of allowing it to be determined by a few men in legislative halls.

The question of the guilt of the liquor traffic is now admitted. The liquor men do not attempt to justify or defend the drinking-places of the State. They admit its guilt. I hold in my hand a pamphlet on personal liberty, which is now being circulated by the anti-prohibitionists, and I read:

"Herein, the opponents and advocates of prohibitory amendments and prohibitory laws agree:

"1. 'They agree that drunkenness is an old and great crime, which brings with it other crimes—that it is the fruitful source of pain, misery, pauperism, and disease.

"2. 'They agree that drunkenness, when it produces disorder, is neither an excuse nor apology for crime, and should be promptly punished by law. They agree that the adulterators of all liquors should be severely punished by law.

"3. 'They agree that the law should punish all persons who keep drunken and disorderly resorts for drunkards, idlers, and criminals.'"

Remember, this is written by a liquor man. For fear you should doubt, I will show you what a villainous liar he is, by reading from the last page of his book. He says:

"The sincerity of the whole prohibitory movement may be readily measured by the honest comparison of the professions with the practices of its leaders and its champions. Only one instance will illustrate the hypocrisy of the prohibitory movement. During the last summer, when the late President had fallen by assassination, the whole land was filled with grief and stricken with sorrow. The President had been a minister of the gospel, and the stroke which had fallen with its deadly power upon the Government and the dead man's family, was even more keenly felt by the Christian Church. Every church in the land was draped in mourning; courts and schools were closed during the days of sorrow; whilst the benevolent societies and political parties of the country vied with each other in their expression of horror at the crime, and lamentation for the dead Chief of a free people. When the funeral cortege passed from the East to the West, thousands of broken-hearted mourners stood with uncovered heads to meet the funeral car at its passage, and reverently bow in submission to the cruel fate of the nation. Inside of the funeral train, following the illustrious dead to his final resting-place, were the chief mourners. In the brief period employed in the passage from the East to the West (it must have been in bacchanalian revelry) the intoxicating drinks consumed by the Government mourners, in a carefully itemized account, footed up $1,700, which has been presented to Congress for allowance, about $300 of which was for cocktails. These mourners were the chief leaders of the great National Prohibition party."

This money was spent by Democratic and Republican statesmen; no member of the National Prohibition party was with the funeral escort.

The first three confessions of the gentleman is the people's case. The people say that drunkenness in this country is a curse, and that drunkenness is generated by the A-B-C school of drunkenness—the licensed dramshop. The liquor men do not deny it. So, after two months of trial in your State, and when in about ten days the question is to be determined by the voters, the liquor men come into court and enter a plea of guilty, and only ask that, because of mitigating circumstances, the punishment imposed may be high license. The issue we are to discuss is not the question of their guilt or innocence, because they have pleaded guilty.

These objections of the liquor men have been listened to by the jury, and I am asked to mention them. The questions have been written and passed to me since I came on this platform; I shall read by number and answer. They are as follows:

1st Question. "If the amendment is adopted it will be two years before the Legislature will meet, and during that time (the present law having been made unconstitutional) there will be free whiskey throughout the State, as there will be no penalties to secure an enforcement of the amendment."

This is urged by the liquor men; and one would think, in listening to their talk, that these men are terribly alarmed for fear that during a period of two years they will have a right to sell whiskey without any law restraining them.

To console them, and that they may not be mistaken, I assure them that this will be the ruling of our courts, as it has been the ruling of all the higher courts in this country; viz., that the adoption of the constitutional amendment will simply make the license clauses of your present act unconstitutional. Your law is prohibitory. It was passed as a prohibitory law. The amendment will affect only the explanatory clauses. which allow the sale of wine and beer.

"What will be the result?" Just as soon as it is officially declared that the amendment is carried, you will have a prohibitory law in existence in this State that is better than the Kansas enactment, for the latter is fearfully weak. Your old law will be in force; your future legislators may amend the present prohibitory law, but it will stand as a law except its license features, until your legislators change it.

The effect of the amendment on the law will be the same as though it had been a part of the Constitution when the act was passed. The license features of your present law will be unconstitutional. The only question will be as to penalties for wine and beer.

2d Question. "Will the amendment be effective without penalties?"

I say, No. There is not a single provision of the Constitution that is effective without penalties.

3d Question. "Will not the life of the amendment exist only in the penalties?"

I answer to that, No; and I will show you why, when I have read the fourth question, which is:

4th Question. "Will not the penalties tend to fluctuate with each Legislature?" "It is claimed that constitutional law carries more force than legislative enactment; but if the penalties depend upon legislative enactment, why the greater force?"

These are pertinent questions. To the third question, "Will not the *life* of the amendment depend on its penalties?" I answer, "No"; because all law depends upon public sentiment for its enforcement. The gentleman who puts the question, asks whether the constitutional amendment will have greater force than statutory enactment. I answer "Yes," for this reason: If the Legislature should pass a statute, it might be the opinion simply of the members of the Legislature, instead of being the opinion of the people. It might be the opinion of one hundred and thirty or one hundred and forty men constituting the law-making body of your State. An amendment to the Constitution, on the contrary, can only be placed there by a majority of the people, representing a majority of the sentiment of this State; and when law-breakers know that prohibition is not a mere statutory enactment, and that a majority of the people of this State are opposed to their misdeeds, they will yield; because no man likes to fight majorities. A statutory enactment seems to have nobody behind it, except the courts. A constitutional enactment has the people of the whole State behind it. Hence, I answer, the life of the constitutional amendment is the popular will, not the penalties. The life of the amendment is the sentiment shown by the vote that adopts it. Consequently the constitutional amendment must be of greater force than a statutory enactment.

The people having adopted a constitutional amendment by majority vote, politicians will be exceedingly slow to pass any law with penalties which will not carry out the expressed will of the people. In Kansas, where the amendment was adopted by the people's vote, the Legislature passed a law to carry out the will of the people, not daring to defy that will. The tendency of all law carrying out constitutional provisions is to permanency, because politicians do not like to antagonize the people.

5th Question. "If there is a greater force in *constitutional* provision to combat evils or crimes, why is not murder or other high crimes prohibited by constitutional amendment instead of legislative enactment?"

I say to the friend who wrote this question that they are thus treated. The Constitution of your State guarantees the life and liberty of the citizen, and if your Legislature should pass a law licensing murder, it would be unconstitutional. Murder, arson, and theft are prohibited by constitutional provision, and an enactment made to license these things would be a direct violation of the property and life guarantees of the Constitution, and would be declared unconstitutional in any court of the United States. The crimes named are prohibited by the constitutional guarantee of life and property.

6th Question. "The text of the amendment makes it a crime to sell within the State, but cannot prohibit the sale outside the State. In other words, Iowa men must not poison their immediate neighbors, but can poison Kansas without penalty. Would not such a law as a fundamental principle of our Government be dishonorable, inconsistent, and un-Christian?"

The questioner makes an incorrect statement, and on the incorrect statement bases his question. The amendment prohibits the manufacture and sale of liquors. The statement is one being urged by liquor men in all parts of the State. One is reminded that

> "When the Devil was sick,
> The Devil a monk would be;
> When the Devil was well,
> The Devil a monk was he."

The statement, as I said, is false, but if it is true I would vote for the amendment. If a rattlesnake were to crawl into my house, and my boy was playing near it, if I could not kill it, but could drive it out of doors, I would drive it out. If he bit my neighbor's boy I should regret that he did so, but charity begins at home. I should protect my own home first; and when Iowa has protected her own homes, let the gigantic temperance sentiment of this State carry the reform to every State of this nation, until the Constitution of the United States prohibits the traffic in the entire republic.

7th Question. "Could our Government exceed its authority by any act of the majority of its voters?"

I answer: The Government is the people, or the voters. All political power is inherent in the people.

The Constitution of the United States reads: "We, the people." The Government has the right to do anything it is not prohibited by the Constitution from doing. In making the Constitution a majority of the people is supreme. They can do anything they please. They may establish a state, a church, or a despotism. Therefore, the Government does not exceed its authority in obeying any "act of a majority of voters" expressed in their Constitution. The only safety for our liberties is the intelligence and morality of the people. For this reason the drinking-place should be destroyed, on account of its power to corrupt and debauch the people.

8th Question. "If our Government cannot exceed its authority as represented by a majority of its voters, why may not the Government prescribe the form of religious worship as well as to say what a man shall eat or drink?"

If the people are ever foolish enough to do this, they can do it, and you cannot hinder them, because in this country the people are the Government. If this people shall determine that a certain kind of religion shall be the religion of the State, then that will be the established form of religious worship; and the only guarantee against such a policy is to educate the people so that they will not be foolish enough to adopt it. The only safety for the Government is the intelligence and morality of the individual citizen. The safety of the principles of liberty is to educate the people to do right, and destroy every institution that educates them to do wrong.

But this question is unfair, inasmuch as it supposes a falsehood as a premise. Prohibitory liquor laws in nowise say what a man shall eat or what he shall drink. They simply aim to protect society from the pernicious influence of trade, which is a social institution. In no respect do they aim to interfere with the private liberties of the individual until those private liberties create public nuisances. The rights inherent in the people to say what is, or what shall be, the form of government in this country, exist to-day, and will in nowise be altered or changed by the passage of this amendment. The aim of the prohibitionists is simply to destroy in this country all institutions which have a tendency to debauch the morality and the intelligence of the inhabitants, and thereby jeopardize our liberties by corrupting the fountain-head of our liberties—the people.

9th Question. "The educational methods and restrictive measures in promoting temperance should go hand in hand. The restrictive should not be at the expense of the educational, from which all true reforms must come."

The question states the theory of every prohibitionist; the only error being in leaving the inference that restrictive measure are not educational. All laws educate.

10th Question. "Will not the conflict of society produced by efforts to enforce extreme measures require so much attention that the *educational* forces of temperance, as well as of other social evils, will be lost sight of?"

The temperance organizations in this country that are paying the most money to push on the educational temperance work are fighting hardest for prohibition. The Good Templars, whom I have the honor to represent in my own State as their chief officer, and in the world as chairman of their literature committee, have always fought for prohibition, but with that work they have always pressed reformatory and educational effort. To-day they are paying many thousands of dollars to circulate literature among the freedmen of the South, and none of the literature is prohibition literature *per se*. The Good Templars pay men to go up and down among the colored people and teach them the A-B-C of temperance.

In this State to-day, this same order of practical reformers are seeking to put text-books into the schools to teach the principles of physiology and temperance; and they are circulating documents, not only upon the prohibitory phase, but every other phase of the reform. The moral suasionists who are fighting prohibition do not give a dollar for the educational work. Show me a moral-suasion, anti-prohibition organization in this State or in America that has given a thousand dollars in the past year to teach temperance to the people, and I will show you a white crow. The organizations that have done most to educate the people, the most to save our boys, the most to pick up the drunkards, are those that say: "We will step down in the gutter and with one hand lift out the drunkard, while with the other we vote to close the place that made him a drunkard."

If those who claim to work most for moral suasion ever did anything for educational temperance, then I would see sense in the question. Instead of working for temperance they remain idle during the year, and as soon as the fight begins, instead of combating the liquor traffic, they are out with clubs to fight temperance men. I have learned to doubt the temperance principles of a man who never does anything for the cause, but who is continually attacking its friends and lending aid and comfort to the enemy. In the late war men who gave aid and comfort to the enemy were called "Copperheads." I don't know what you would call these, for they are of a meaner and viler type. "By their works ye shall know them."

Who are the so-called moral-suasion temperance men working for and associating with to-day? Take the history of the ministerial apostates who are fighting prohibition in this State, and find what they have done for temperance within the past year. How many drinking men have they picked up? How many temperance meetings have they held? How many temperance text-books have they circulated? How many temperance papers have they supported? "By their fruits ye shall know them." A man who receives pay from the drunkard-makers for preaching a temperance doctrine which will make every liquor-seller and drunkard-maker shout "Amen" is a fraud, and had better own that he gets pay from the devil direct.

11th Question. "Can Temperance Organizations hope to legislate men into habits of sobriety?"

The only men who ever said you could, are the men who advocate license. Temperance men do not propose to legislate a man sober; they propose to legislate men out of the business of making men drunk. "License men to make drunkards, hire officers to arrest the drinkers, build prisons in which to instruct them not to drink," is the license advocate's plan.

A poor man goes into a dram-shop and gets drunk. In the State of Nebraska I have never known a rich man to get drunk. "Why," you say, "that is strange!" The statutes of Nebraska make drunkenness a misdemeanor. I have met men with silk hats and canes, who could not walk without staggering. I thought they were drunk. I looked in the police court record the next morning, and I saw they were not arrested. I have seen laboring men who could walk with little difficulty. I looked in the police court record the next morning, and found that they were drunk. I do not know how it works in Iowa, but in the State where I live, the young snobs, who never do an honest day's work, who live on their papas until they find a girl who is fool enough to marry them, and then live on her papa, never get drunk. If they are found in a condition resembling drunkenness, by the police, they are helped home. If they cannot be taken home, they will be helped to a hotel, and their heads sponged. If the man who works gets drunk, he is always punished. Do you suppose, as a matter of fact, that a policeman would arrest a man who has money? The workmen of this country have long enough stood by this system which makes it a crime for a poor man to do what a rich man may do with impunity. The poor man is arrested by the police officer, and put into the " cooler." The next morning he is brought before the police court, and what is the result? The saloon-keeper got half of his money, the police officer, through the police magistrate, gets the other half, and the poor devil has not a cent left, and the license people cry: "Served him right; he ought to have been punished."

Come with me to some wretched part of your cities, and I will show you the ragged form of that man's wife, show you his boy and girl with naked feet, and after you have seen them in their wickedness and poverty, tell me who is being punished.

One night I sat in my office, preparing a brief—it was

very late, about three o'clock in the morning—and there came a knock. I went to the door, and there stood one of our city policemen. I asked:

"What do you want?"

He said: "I went down to the coal-yards. I was sent down there to look after the coal. As I went out to the cars I heard some one moaning in one of those little wretched shanties, and when I was coming back I knocked at the door, and was admitted; and I tell you, Mr. Finch"—and the tears came into his eyes—"I think they are starving! I built a fire for them. Just think," said he, "of the poor things starving to death on this bitter cold night!" The words came direct from his big Irish heart.

I said to him: "Jim, where did you get the coal?"

He said it was none of my business. "I came up town, Mr. Finch," he said; "the restaurants are all closed; I saw a light in your window, and thought you would help me."

I said: "Certainly."

I went home and called my wife. A basket was packed. My wife dressed and went with me. It was a bitter night in December. We went down the streets of that city, out into that wretched section, and went into that home. You ladies have, perhaps, seen such homes. There was no need of words to tell that they were suffering. There sat the poor woman in her wretchedness. My wife asked what she could do for her. She straightened up and said:

"Mrs. Finch, I am not a beggar. I do not want you to give me anything. If you will just lend it to me I will pay it all back to you some time. If I had some clothes and shoes I could take care of my own babies. It is hard, oh, so hard, to be here with such clothes that I cannot go out in the street, and the baby dying in my arms!"

I thought so too. I asked her where her husband was. I knew him to be one of the best stone-masons in the city. I knew that, because he had done some work for me a short time before. She said he had been put in the city jail for eight days, to serve out a sentence for drunkenness. "Punish the man who gets drunk!" The law had done that, and left his wife and babies to starve and freeze in mid-winter.

Any system of law that punishes the wife and children for the sins of the father is a disgrace to a civilized people. If it is right to license a man to make men drunk, it is right to get drunk; and a nation that licenses the manufacturer of drunkards, and then punishes men for doing exactly what it has licensed a man to make them do, is a long way from civilization of the highest type.

Remove temptation by the police power of the State, and educational methods will begin to influence the individual. Moral suasion will never have a fair chance until the State has branded liquor-selling as a crime.

12th Question. "Men are like hogs. You can coax them, but you cannot drive them. Will not the amendment make men worse?"

I have always doubted the theory of evolution from monkeys, and am not inclined to admit that reasoning men are like unreasoning hogs. The only evidence of the truth of the statement is the character and habits of the liquor men. A traffic that estimates man, "created in the image of his Maker," as a hog, ought to die.

Men *can* be driven. The late war proves it. Men who are in the wrong, who know they are wrong, are the greatest cowards in the world.

The amendment is reasonable and right. The people of Iowa are a reading, thinking, reasonable people. They will see the justice of the action and sustain it. The amendment will close up the human hog-pens, and the "men like hogs" will go with them.

13th Question. "If you say a man shall not do a thing, he will desire to do it. Will not the tendency of the amendment be to lead men to desire to break it?"

This is practically the last question in another form. If the statement made is correct, statesmen have always been in error. No laws should be passed prohibiting theft, because if you say a man shall not steal, it will excite a desire in him to steal. No laws should be passed prohibiting crime, because if you say he shall not commit crime, he will desire to transgress. The correct way, according to this "hog theory," would be, to pass a law saying a man must steal, that he shall be fined if he does not steal. Such a law would excite the hoggish propensities of man, and he would not steal, simply because the law said he *must*. Laws should be passed saying men shall commit crime, with adequate penalties to force men to obey. Such laws would excite the hoggish propensity to disobey, and no crime would be committed. Not only have parents and statesmen blundered, but God himself was mistaken in thinking human beings reasonable beings instead of brutes, if this saloon theory is correct. I only wonder how any person dares so insult an audience. Man is not a hog. He thinks and reasons. He is eminently an ethical being. The question and statement are not founded on fact, but suppose a condition of things which never did and never can exist.

14th Question. "Is not temptation necessary to the development of moral character?"

The question implies that evil is an educator of the moral forces. If temptation develops character, the Government ought to license gambling hells, so that the boys, by being tempted to gamble, would become honest citizens. If temptation develops character, the Government ought to license houses of ill-fame, and libertines, so that your daughters, by being tempted, would become virtuous women. Would you wish to try so dangerous an experiment? The dual nature of man must always be taken into consideration in the discussion of such problems. The intellectual, God-nature is always at war with the passionate, brute-nature. The highest type of manhood is developed when the passionate or brute forces are held in check by the intellectual nature, and made to act as the motive power to accomplish grand deeds. The lowest type of manhood is developed when the intellectual forces are the slaves of the brute-nature, compelled to devise ways and means to gratify lust and passion.

The associations of childhood develop one or the other of these forces. Like produces like. Throw around a child influences which develop the intellectual nature, and the chances are in favor of his being a manly man. Throw around a child influences which develop the brute or passionate nature, and the chances are in favor of his being a bad man—a criminal. " Evil communications corrupt good manners" is an old saw, the truth of which no sane man will dispute. One might as well hope to develop a rare rose by taking it from the sunlight and placing it in the dark, damp cellar, as to expect to develop noble, pure manhood and womanhood by surrounding the child with the noxious atmosphere of vice and crime.

No man ever understood human nature as the Master who taught us to pray, "Lead us not into temptation, but deliver us from evil."

15th Question. "Will not the passage of the amendment make the temperance question a political question?"

Politics is the science of government. Politics is that division of ethics which deals with the government of a State; the preservation of its prosperity, safety, and peace; the protection of citizens; the preservation and improvement of their morals. Any institution, trade, or custom which affects the safety, prosperity, or peace of a State, or which injures the morals of the citizens, is political. In a government of the people, by the people, any trade which affects the people injuriously, affects the Government, composed of the people, injuriously, and its regulation or destruction belongs properly to the science of government—politics. The school and the church influence the unit of the political structure—the citizen; and to that extent are political institutions. Every sermon or lesson which influences the life and conduct of the citizen has a good or bad influence on the State, and to that extent is political. The old cry of political demagogues, "Keep temperance and religion out of politics," is a sample of stupid ignorance boiled down.

No other institution in America exerts the terrible influence on political action that is exerted by the liquor traffic. The questions, "What can the Government do with the traffic?" "How can the Government destroy the pernicious influence of this traffic?" are questions which must be determined by political action. The laws passed to regulate and restrain these influences are political measures devised to meet the issues presented by the liquor traffic. The question is a political question *now*, and it will remain so until it is settled by political action.

If the questioner means to ask whether it will become a partisan question, I answer, "It will." In a Government like ours, parties are political machines to work out political problems. The Government is a ruling by the party in power, and until the Government—the party in power—pronounces in favor of the enforcement of the law, it will be openly violated. With one political party openly opposed to the law, and the other political party a coward, prohibition will be between the "devil and the deep sea," and will remain largely a dead letter on your statute-books. Unless one of the present parties shall, in its State and National platform, declare in favor of passing and enforcing prohibition, a party will be formed which will carry the measure to victory. Boobies in the science of government may prate about settling this as a non-partisan question, but persons who have had experience in public life, who know what lever is necessary to move great dangers from the path of government, will not indulge in such idle fancies.

16th Question. "What is your opinion of the success of prohibition as tried in Maine?"

Prohibition has been a success wherever tried. It is truly a wonder that it has, for it has never had a fair trial. The State has branded the business of making drunkards as a crime. The influence of the General Government has always antagonized State action. The State has prohibited the manufacture and sale of liquor. The General Government has always, by its power to regulate inter-State commerce, licensed the importation of liquors into the State. The State has prohibited the sale of liquor. The General Government has said to liquor outlaws: "Pay into the treasury of the United States twenty-five dollars a year, and you may violate the State law by selling the liquors. Congress has licensed you to import, and the agents of the United States will remain silent, wink at your crime, and let the State punish you if it can." Prohibition will only be tested when the General Government ceases to be a partner, or rather beneficiary, of the liquor traffic; when the National Constitution shall prohibit the importation, manufacture, and sale of alcoholic liquors; when the political party controlling the nation is in favor of prohibition honestly enforced.

In the face of such disadvantages, prohibition has succeeded. Let us examine the evidence, to see if this is not true.

Remember the rule of law to be: "Hearsay evidence is uniformly held incompetent to establish any *specific fact*, which, in its nature, is susceptible of being proved by witnesses who can speak from their own knowledge." The learned author who lays down the rule says: "That this species of testimony supposes something better, which might be adduced in the particular case, is not the sole ground of its exclusion. Its extrinsic weakness, its incompetency to satisfy the mind as to the existence of the fact, and the frauds which may be practiced under its cover, combine to support the rule that hearsay evidence is totally inadmissible."

The prohibitory law of Maine is on trial. You are the jury. The evidence produced must be of a character that would be received in a court of justice. The enemies of the law open their side of the case with the statement that it is a failure. They are asked to produce their witnesses. They offer newspaper articles written by irresponsible, anonymous correspondents, and put men upon the stand to swear: "I heard it did not prohibit." Would such evidence be admissible to prove anything? In a court it would be rejected as hearsay.

Cross-examine one of these witnesses:

"You stated prohibition was a failure in Maine. Tell the jury what you know about it."

"I think I read about it in a paper."

"When?"

"This morning."

"What paper was it published in?"

"The Chicago *Tribune*."

"Was it an original article or a copied one?"

"It was copied from the New York *Sun*."

"From what source did the *Sun* get its information?"

"I do not know."

"Do you wish to swear that you know anything about the results of prohibition in Maine?"

"Only what I read."

"That is not an answer to the question. Do you know anything about it?"

"No."

The prohibitionists now call United States Senator Frye, of Maine.

"Mr. Frye, where do you reside?"

"In the State of Maine."

"Do you frequently visit different parts of the State?"

"I do."

"Are you familiar with the practice in your State courts?"

"I am."

"And know something of the moral and social condition of the people in Maine?"

"I do."

"Tell the jury how the prohibitory law has affected your State."

"I can, and do, from my own personal observation, unhesitatingly affirm that the consumption of intoxicating liquors is not to-day one-fourth so great as it was twenty years ago; that, in the country portions of the State, the sale and use have almost entirely ceased; that the law itself, under a vigorous enforcement of its provisions, has created a temperance sentiment which is marvellous, and to which opposition is powerless. In my opinion, our remarkable temperance reform of to-day is the legitimate child of that law."

Call the Hon. Hannibal Hamlin. Mr. Hamlin is asked the questions which qualify him as a witness, and testifies:

"I concur in the statements made by Mr. Frye. Of

the great good produced by the prohibitory liquor law of Maine, no man can doubt who has seen its results. It has been of immense value."

Call James G. Blaine. He is qualified as a witness, and testifies:

"The people of Maine are industrious and provident, and wise laws have aided them. They are sober, earnest, and thrifty. Intemperance has steadily decreased in the State, since the first enactment of the prohibitory law, until now it can be said with truth that there is no equal number of people in the Anglo-Saxon world, among whom so small an amount of intoxicating liquor is consumed, as among the six hundred and fifty thousand inhabitants of Maine."

The list is continued until every leading public man in Maine has testified, and each swears to the same thing. The records of the courts, prisons, and almshouses are offered to corroborate these witnesses and the case is given to you.

Suppose in a case involving five hundred dollars the same class of witnesses had been called—for whom would you give a verdict? Would you believe the newspaper clippings and idle stories by interested parties, or disinterested witnesses like Frye, Hamlin, and Blaine? A question of veracity is raised by the testimony. Either the stories offered by the liquor men are false, or Frye, Blaine, Hamlin, Perham, Dingley, and others, lie. In determining which evidence is to be believed, you must stop and see who has reason for lying. If prohibition is a success, it destroys the liquor business. If the people in your State can be made to believe prohibition a failure, and by such belief be led to defeat the amendment, the liquor will continue; hence the liquor-dealers have a financial reason for lying. What reason has Mr. Blaine for testifying falsely in this case? Will he gain anything financially by so doing? No. Will he advance his political interest by so doing? No. The same is true of the other witnesses called by the prohibitionists. If the evidence in that case is taken and considered as it would be in a court of justice, the verdict must be, "Prohibition is a success in Maine."

The evidence which the liquor men bring from Kansas is of the same character as that brought against the law in Maine. The prohibitionists bring St. John and other State officers who testify to the success of the law. In addition, I wish to call your attention to the admissions of the liquor men themselves. They are the parties in interest and their admissions may certainly be accepted as evidence. My talented friend, Col. Frank J. Sibley, wishing to ascertain from the liquor men themselves how the law was working, requested a friend to write, at his dictation, to a number of ex-liquor-sellers asking what were the chances to start a saloon in Kansas. Let me read one answer:

"CLAY CENTER, Kansas, *June* 10, 1882.

"DEAR FRIEND:—I write you a few lines to let you know that I received your letter a few days ago. You don't want to come to Kansas to start a saloon unless you want to get busted. Kansas is a hell of a country. I just laid out four weeks in jail for selling beer, and I got enough of it. Don't come to Kansas to start a saloon.
"JOE MONTEL."

Another, written in German, translated, reads:

"BELOIT, Kansas, *May* 21, 1882.

"Your letter I have received, and as you require me to let you know what the prospects for selling beer and wine,—answer, none at all to begin a saloon, because the temperance people will not let you sell anything. JOHN EBERLE."

I hold in my hand copies of letters received by Mr. Sibley from ex-liquor-sellers in eleven different towns and cities of Kansas, all making substantially the same statements.

In view of all the facts can I do other than answer, PROHIBITION IS A SUCCESS?

Gentlemen, voters, that is our case. Take it, and as a jury, bound by the most sacred obligation—your honor as citizens—pass upon the evidence and arguments. The evidence in regard to the guilt of the traffic is not contradicted. No attempt is made by the liquor advocates to explain. The evidence all says, "The liquor traffic is guilty"; and I have no doubt what will be your verdict.

To you, then, we submit our indictment. We submit their threats, and our evidence. We submit their blackguardism, false assertions, bulldozing, and defiance of law; our proofs uncontradicted and undeniable;—and we ask you, citizens, voters, to render a verdict which shall stay this foul curse. Prayers, tears, and persuasion have been tried; but the lecherous, licentious traffic still destroys the youth, manhood, and virtue of the land.

Richelieu, the French Cardinal, whose niece was pursued by like bold and shameless enemies, plucked from his breast a cross, and drawing the circle of the Church of Rome around her, hurled in their faces the defiance:

> "Mark where she stands!
> Around her form I draw the awful circle of our solemn Church.
> Step but a foot within that holy ground,
> And on thy head—yea, though it wore a crown—
> I launch the curse of Rome."

Gentlemen, all other remedies have failed. We ask you to draw the protecting circle of the Constitution around our homes, and say to this "black death," "Thou shalt not cross these thresholds."

VIII.

THE DEFENCE ANSWERED.

An Address delivered in Beecher's Hall, Detroit, Mich., March 26, 1887.*

LADIES AND GENTLEMEN: For years the question of what is the correct policy of Government in dealing with the alcoholic liquor traffic has agitated this State. It has been discussed in the pulpit and upon the platform, written about in the press, prayed about in the prayer-meeting, and sworn about in the political caucuses. At last the Legislature of Michigan in its wisdom has seen fit, by proposing an amendment to its organic law, to refer this whole question to the voters for their decision on the 4th day of April next. The question involved in this submission is the existence or non-existence of a great traffic. Last Monday night in the Opera-House in this city a mass meeting was addressed by prominent speakers in opposition to the proposed prohibitory amendment, and I have been asked by leading citizens to come here to-night and reply to the statements made by the learned gentlemen who addressed that meeting.

First, let me call your attention to the difference in the conditions under which the two meetings are held. As I have already stated, the issues involved in this campaign are questions affecting the existence of a great business—a business in which thousands of men are employed and in which millions of dollars are invested. I hardly need stand before an audience of this character and urge that questions involving such interests should be discussed calmly and investigated intelligently.

One of the speakers at the Monday night meeting, the Hon. Charles W. Jones, *from* the United States

---

* Mr. Finch had been laboring in Michigan, with other workers, for the Prohibitory Amendment. At an anti-prohibition meeting held in Detroit on Monday, March 21st, speeches in opposition to the Amendment were delivered by the Hon. D. Bethune Duffield, a leading lawyer of the city; Prof. Kent, of Ann Arbor University Law School, and United States Senator Jones, of Florida. Mr. Finch was requested by the Amendment Campaign Committee to reply. This he did on the following Saturday night, to an immense audience.—ED.

Senate, in his speech asserted: "This is not a sentimental age; this is eminently a practical age; and I am sure there are no more practical people in the world than the people of the State of Michigan." His experience along *sentimental* lines in this State will preclude me from challenging his judgment, and I am sure if he has reached this conclusion, the fair State of Florida will not long be without a second Representative in the Senate of the United States. If, by leaving his post in the Senate and devoting his time to sentiment in Detroit, he has failed to make the people of the State of Michigan sentimental, I am sure they are not a sentimental people, but are fully ready and duly competent to discuss and settle an issue of so great importance as the question of prohibiting the alcoholic liquor traffic. The advocates of the amendment simply ask for a full and fair investigation of all the facts which may be brought forward during this campaign. In a government of the people, by the people, and for the people, freedom of speech, freedom of investigation, and freedom of action is the only guarantee of wise and conservative legislation. With this thought I do not propose to challenge the intelligence, the motives, or the conscience of any man who votes against this amendment, and I only regret that the opposition have deemed it wise, by systematic organization, to threaten to ruin the business of any man who dares speak or write or vote for this amendment. Free America is reaching a dangerous point when the Strohs, the Ruoffs, the Goebels, before they can speak the American language, may say to American business men, "You shall not examine, discuss, or determine matters affecting the policy of the State."

The meeting on Monday night was held under the boycotting pressure of the saloons of this city. A prominent business man who signed the call for that meeting informed me to-day that at the time of the signing he did not read the call, had no knowledge of the statements that it contained, and really had little thought of what the meeting meant until he saw the call in print, and said, "I should not have signed it had not my business interests been threatened." I submit that any trade or institution whose only defence is boycotting, bulldozing, and intimidation is entitled to very little sympathy at the hands of intelligent men.

I regret very much that the gentlemen who addressed the meeting on Monday night saw fit to avoid the main issue involved in this contest because it must inevitably create the impression they could not or dare not meet it; and, in order that we may intelligently consider all the points raised by them, let me examine the real issue and state the object and the purpose of the prohibitionists of this State. This is made doubly necessary by the speakers in the previous meeting placing in the mouths of prohibitionists words which they never used, and making them assume positions which they never maintained.

All the speakers distinguished themselves in demolishing a man of straw of their own creation. Prof. Kent said, "The prohibitionists say we are in favor of prohibition, though the result should be that whiskey should be entirely free." In all fairness the learned professor should have stated *what* prohibitionist used such an expression and where it was used. It is not an honorable act to manufacture expressions to place in the mouths of opponents. I say to Prof. Kent that prohibitionists have made no such statement. Prohibitionists attack taxation because under taxation or license whiskey is free, and they ask for prohibition because in the light of experience they know that prohibition does and can prohibit.

The proposed amendment simply operates as an indictment to bring the liquor business into the court for the people and place it on trial for crimes against society and government. There are but two ways in our Government for trying institutions of this class—the one autocratic, by the Legislature, the other democratic, by the people. The Legislature of this State might have passed a prohibitory law outlawing the liquor business, but such a law would have been the opinion of a majority of the members, and would have been entitled to the respect accorded to the judgment and conscience of that number of men. The cry would have been at once raised that it was in advance of public sentiment, that the people were not educated up to the position, and the liquor-sellers, using these cries, would have organized to defy the statute and to continue their business in violation of law. The Legislature, in my judgment, chose the correct method when they referred the whole question to the people. Constitutional amendment is the American method of revolution. The provision for a peaceable change in the principles underlying our Government provides for a revolution by ballots, instead of a revolution by bullets, and when Mr. Duffield steps out of his way to impugn the intelligence, the honesty, the integrity, and the conscience of the Legislature by saying "Political manœuvering and tactics rather than an honest opinion on the part of two-thirds of the Legislature that this amendment is called for, is the secret of its submission," he weakens his case by introducing special pleading to justify this attack. When he says: "We recall the fact also that in 1868 an amendment was submitted to the people prohibiting license of the sale of liquor as a beverage and it was defeated by a majority of 13,000 votes," and forgets to state that the clause prohibiting the license of the sale of liquor as a beverage was in the old Constitution, which it was proposed to overturn by the new one at the same election, and that the new Constitution was defeated by 39,000 votes, he must think that the old people of this State have short memories and that the young people do not read history. And when he stated that in 1876 "the people struck out from our present Constitution the old equivocal clause forbidding the license of liquor-selling," and neglects to state that the Supreme Court of the State, by its decisions, sustaining tax laws, had made the clause utterly worthless, so that it was voted against by temperance men, he leaves the position of a lawyer and descends to the level of a pettifogger. Should the Legislature have submitted the amendment? For years the people of this State have discussed the relation of the liquor traffic to our free government and civilization. Time and again the Legislature has been petitioned to submit this question to the people; a political party casting 25,000 votes at the last election has been organized on this issue alone; and you must admit that if there was ever a question which circumstances justify submitting to the people, for their examination and final determination, it is the question of what shall be done with the alcoholic liquor traffic in the State of Michigan. But all side issues are out of place in this discussion. The fact is that the amendment has been submitted, and that on the 4th of April the question of its adoption or its rejection will be settled. The issue involved is the life or the death of the drunkard-making traffic. The business of liquor-selling and making drunkards is on trial, not the men who are in the business. The issues raised are not personal issues. If there is any liquor-seller in Detroit who labors under the delusion that he is of importance enough to have this temperance movement aimed at him, he has a very much better opinion of himself than we have. If you could catch every liquor-seller in the State of Michigan to-night, tie him hand and foot and drown him in the Detroit River, unless you could root up the accursed law which propagates liquor-sellers as a hotbed propagates vegetation, you would have another crop in three months just as mean as the old one. But if you root up the law that makes legal a business in which a man can make more money with less capital and less brains and less character than any other business on earth, the good men, if there are any such in the business, will go into other trades and professions, and the mean men will fetch up in State prisons, where they should have been long ago. The liquor business is simply on trial on account of the record it has made in society. Society never tries men or institutions for their names. It tries men for their acts, institutions for their results. The law of this State would recognize one difference between me and my friend David Preston. It would recognize me as an alien, it would recognize him as a citizen; but though I am an alien, though I pay no taxes in this State, I am as safe as my friend, that is, as long as I behave myself as well as he behaves himself; but if at the close of this meeting I should go out of the hall, and as I went out should draw a knife from my coat and bury it to the hilt in the heart of some person, then I would be arrested and locked up and he would be allowed to go home. Now you would not arrest me because my name is Finch and let him go because his name is Preston. You would not arrest me because I am a lawyer and let him go because he is a banker. You arrest me because of my own free will I had taken human life. For the act I would be arrested, for the act I would be tried, for the act I would be hung; and as society would deal with me it would deal with anybody before me. As long as man lives in society sober, temperate, honest, so long society defends and protects him; but when a man wills to commit crime, wills to injure another socially or financially, then the Government reaches out and takes that man from the ranks of other men and tries him, not for what the Government has done, but for what he has done; not because it wants to, but because it must do it. The punishment is not the result of the act of the Government, but the result of the act of the man who made the punishment necessary. As society deals with men it deals with institutions and trades.

As long as an institution or a business or a trade promotes the interests of society, so long the Government defends and protects that trade; but when a trade or a business establishes a criminal character by the production of vice, crime, pauperism, and misery, then the Government arrests the business and tries it for its results. In this way the Governments of most of the States have tried and condemned lotteries. The governments of cities try and suppress slaughter-houses, fat-rendering establishments, soap-factories, and gunpowder-factories, and the Government of the United States has tried and is punishing the practice of polygamy by the Brighamite Mormon Church. The prohibitionists ask that the alcoholic liquor traffic as represented by the saloon, the beer garden, the dance hall, the concert saloon, the dive, the brothel, and the gambling hell shall be tried exactly as the Government tries lotteries, slaughter-houses, and the Mormon Church. The charges against the liquor business are plain, positive, definite, and specific; the question raised is simply the guilt or the innocence of this business as a social institution, and if guilty the proper punishment for crime of such enormity.

I will not to-night take time to prove the guilt of the alcoholic traffic. The men in the business concede its guilt. This trial has now been going forward for weeks, and no one has stood in the pulpit or on the platform to defend the history, the record, or the results of the alcoholic liquor traffic as a social institution. If the Church had been assailed the Church would have been defended; if the dry-goods trade had been assailed the dry-goods trade would have been defended; if the school had been assailed it would have been defended, but here is a great business on trial for its life; the men engaged are worth millions of dollars; no one can doubt their ability to employ talent to present their case, if they have any case to present, and yet this trial is drawing to a close without a single defender standing before the people to urge the innocence of the charge made against it, to justify its record or to claim by its own merits that it ought to be allowed to live. If you assail the Democratic party, the man who defends it is a Democrat; if you assail the Republican party, the man who defends it is a Republican; if you assail the Methodist Church, the man who defends it is a Methodist; but if you assail the liquor traffic the man who steps up to defend it claims to be just as good a temperance man as you are. The meeting of Monday night is a sample of meetings held in defence of this system. The farmer who goes out to defend the interests of the farmers wears the weapons of a farmer; the printer wears the armor of his trade; the merchant wears the armor of his craft; but the apologist for the continuance of the liquor traffic commences his speech with the statement, "I am a temperance man," and denies that he represents the liquor interests or is friendly to its continuance. In justice to my cause, I call your attention to the fact that the saloon-keepers of this State unanimously indorse the speeches of the Monday night meeting, and that they are circulating those speeches by thousands over the State. A minister who would preach a sermon which could be indorsed and circulated by the devil to sustain and promote sin, should be expelled from the Christian pulpit. A temperance doctrine which is indorsed by the brewers, the distillers, the saloon-keepers, the dive-keepers, and circulated by them as a defence of their trade should be repudiated by all enemies of drunkenness, immorality, and vice. Mr. Duffield, Mr. Kent, and others protest again and again that they do not represent the liquor interests. Why this reiterated protestation? Why is it necessary for them to constantly affirm that they are temperance men? Is it because they feel the pressure of the old rule: "A man is known by the company he keeps," and because they know the indorsation and support of the liquor-sellers throws doubt on them and this doctrine? The speech I shall make here to-night will not be circulated by the liquor-sellers of this State, and I do not envy the speakers of Monday night—their champions and their defenders.

Ladies and gentlemen, I would go half-way around the world once and pay my own fare, to find a man with cheek hard enough, and impudence great enough, to stand on the public platform and claim that the public bar-room, judged by its history, its record, and its results in this country, was entitled to live in any decent State, in any decent nation. I have never heard such a defence, I never shall. The business is guilty, guilty, guilty, and the only question is the method of dealing with the criminal.

But two methods are proposed—the one license or tax, the other prohibition. I hardly need stand here to demonstrate that license and tax in their effects upon the liquor trade are identical. I appreciate the sneer of Mr. Duffield when he says, "Shall Tom, Dick, and Harry, hired at $10 or $20 a night, go on the stump of prohibition and claim that taxation is identical with license?" I regret as much as Mr. Duffield can that the poverty of our clients will not justify our receiving a larger fee; but our misfortune is his gain, for our clients have been made paupers by his clients. We stand here to defend the drunkards' wives, the drunkards' children, and the drunkards' homes. He stood on the platform to oppose the destruction of the liquor traffic. The millions of dollars in the liquor business of this State have been drawn from the homes, from the wives and the children of Michigan. I would rather stand before this audience to plead in behalf of the wrecked woman and the ruined child for nothing than to stand to plead in behalf of the bloated oligarchy of liquor-sellers for all the money in the blood-stained coffers in that trade in the State. His sneer was undoubtedly made to cover the weakness of his position; let us inquire what are the facts in regard to the identity of these two methods. Under license, grog-shops exist and are protected by the State; under tax, grog-shops exist and are protected by the State. Mr. Duffield says: "Were they familiar with the Michigan law they would drop their license feature and adopt the taxation and regulation style." Taxes are levied for two purposes—revenue and regulation, and Mr. Duffield admits that the tax law combines both of these features. Judge Cooley says: "The protection of Government being the consideration for which taxes are demanded, all parties who receive or are entitled to that protection may be called upon to render an equivalent." I pay taxes on my home for the protection that Government gives that home. Under license the man who has paid the license fee is entitled to the protection of Government, and Mr. Duffield will not dare claim that under taxation the man who has paid the tax is not entitled to protection! If a mob should attack a saloon would not the Government be compelled to defend it? Is there any legal process by which the saloon may be destroyed if it complies with the tax law? Is not a saloon-keeper who pays the tax entitled to protection and defence from civil government? Mr. Duffield says, "Taxes are burdens," but he is too good a lawyer not to know the burden is borne for the greater benefit of the protection afforded by the Government, to support which the tax is levied. Juggle with words as much as you please; and you will not be able to show any difference in the effects of the saloon which under regulation pays $500 license, and the saloon which under taxation pays $500 tax. Government permits everything that it does not prohibit. Under your old prohibitory law the liquor business had no existence in

Michigan, and there were no property rights in liquor. To-day under your tax law the liquor business has a legal existence in this State, and there are property rights in liquor. Now, what gives it this legal existence and what creates these property rights if it is not the tax law? To say that the Government which recognizes the existence of the saloon by receiving tax from it, and which recognizes the evil effects of the existence of the saloon by providing for its regulation, does not sanction its existence under those regulations, is to talk nonsense. And when the learned Professor Kent, from the Law Department of Ann Arbor University, confounds the taxing power of the General Government with the police power of the State, it is not to be wondered at that the country is full of poor lawyers. And when he says, "When in consequence of the war it was necessary, by Federal legislation, to tax the sale of liquor, the liquor-dealers undertook to say that in consequence of that tax their business was protected in cities where the law forbade it, they took the case to the Supreme Court of the United States, and that court decided that taxation was not license and no approval of the business," the learned professor should know and ought to have stated, that the decision was that the tax permit of the General Government was no bar to proceedings against the liquor business under the police power of the States; and with his intelligence I am sure he would not wish to be understood as holding that the payment of the $25 tax to the Federal Government is not a bar to proceedings against the liquor business by the General Government under its present law. While the United States tax will not act as a permit in the State as against the police power of the State, it does act as a permit by the General Government against its own power. But the point I wish to maintain, outside of all legal technicalities and quibbles, is that the social effects of a licensed saloon and the social effects of a taxed saloon are identical.

The quibbling and twisting over the distinction between taxation and license is a confession on the part of the advocates of tax that the liquor business is

THE DEFENCE ANSWERED.

wrong. If it is not wrong, why object to licensing it? If the liquor business is right, there is no reason why the Government should not license and permit its existence. If the liquor business is wrong, then to seek to justify its existence upon the ground that the Government has not specially said while deriving benefits from the traffic that the traffic may exist, is the trick of a sophist. But for the sake of the argument to-night, let us grant that there is a difference between license and tax, and say that the methods of punishment for the liquor crime now being discussed in this State are tax and prohibition. From this point I desire to go forward to prove that of all the humbugs, frauds, and failures ever written upon the statute-books of a free State, the liquor tax laws of this country are the worst; that they never have been enforced; that they never will be enforced; that they never can be enforced. First, because they are wrong in theory. There appear in society three classes of institutions: good—part good and part bad—and bad. Government protects and defends the good, regulates and restrains the part good and part bad, and prohibits the bad. Regulation implies something good in the thing regulated that is to be developed by regulation. You regulate to develop, not to destroy. You take your boy across your knee and regulate him, to develop the good traits and repress the bad traits in the boy; you do not regulate to kill. You take the whip in your hand to regulate the ugly horse, not to destroy, but to develop the good tendencies and destroy the bad tendencies. In one corner of your yard is an apple-tree, crooked as a horn. Shall it be pulled up? No. The apple-tree is good, the crooks are bad. You drive down a stake to regulate the crooks out of it, because in after years the tree will reward the labor. In the other corner is a thorn-bush as crooked as the apple-tree. Do you regulate that? No, because it is utterly worthless, and the time spent in regulation would be useless. There in a lot is a calf with a broken leg. What do you do? Regulate the leg so as to mend the bad fracture, and in after years the cow pays for the labor. In another lot is a mad dog with a broken leg. Do you ever regulate that leg? No. The more you fuss with the animal the worse off you are. It is utterly bad; the remedy is to prohibit existence. In your lot stands a large apple-tree with knotty limbs, with little runts of apples. Will you cut it down? No. Regulate it, trim it up, and graft it. Ten years pass away and here is a large apple, the legitimate fruit of regulation; but regulate the grog-shops of Detroit with your accursed tax law from now until Gabriel blows his trumpet, and the last fruit you will pick off the accursed things is the same you get to-day, "bummers" every time. Do you expect you can ever regulate the grog-shop so as to produce Christians; that you can ever regulate it so that its customers will be good men, their wives happy, and their children happy? Do you not know that as long as you permit the thing to exist, that just in the same proportion it will breed drunkards, broken-hearted women, and beggar children? It is bad and all bad, vile and all vile, evil and all evil, and should be destroyed. The system of taxation and regulation has been tried in England for more than 400 years, and under it the liquor business has grown to be the master of the British nation. In this country, under the system of regulation and taxation the liquor-shops have doubled in numbers within the last twenty-five years. There is not a lawyer before me who does not know that it will not take one-half the force to enforce prohibition that it does to fail to enforce license or taxation. The reason is that taxation gives the liquor business a standing in society, creates property rights, and makes a majority of all the sales legal. Under it, violation becomes the exception, and the legal sale the rule. In this way the presumption of innocence is in favor of the liquor business. To secure a conviction you must break down the presumption of the legal sale and establish the exception of the illegal or unrighteous sale. Your tax law prohibits the sale of liquor to minors and licenses the sale to adults. In this State you prohibit murder. You start down the streets of Detroit in the morning accompanied by your boy, who is seventeen years old. As you approach a saloon, he says, "Good-morning, father," and enters. You wait.

Two hours after, he comes out stupidly drunk. You have watched the door during that time, you know he has not left the place. He went in sober and came out drunk. Is that any evidence that the man in the place sold him liquor in violation of law? No. I go into another building, later; you see me come out and soon after you discover that a man has been murdered; he has been killed by a knife in his heart. You come to my home, you find blood on my coat, scratches on my hands. Is there any evidence that I killed the man? Unless I can show how the blood came on my coat and the scratches on my hands, unless I can show what I was doing in that place, how the man was killed, you will send me to State's prison for life for his murder. Yet the evidence that would send me to State's prison for murder, would not touch a taxed liquor-dealer for selling liquor to your boy and sending him to a drunkard's grave and a drunkard's hereafter. The law prohibits the sale of liquor on certain days. You enter a saloon on one of those days, see a man step to the bar, hear him call for liquor, see the liquor turned out, drank, and paid for. Can you swear that liquor was bought and drunk in that place? If you think so, go upon the witness-stand and swear that the taxed drunkard-maker broke the law and sold liquor in violation of the statute. The defendant's attorney asks you where you stood in the saloon. You answer, "Just inside the door." "How far from the bar?" "Ten feet." "Can you smell whiskey ten feet?" "No." "Did you taste that stuff that man drank?" "No." "Did you smell it?" "No." "How do you know it is whiskey?" "Well, it looked like whiskey." "Are there other things that look like whiskey?" "Yes." "Will you swear that it was whiskey?" "Well, I think it was." "You are not swearing to what you think, you are swearing to what you know; will you swear it was whiskey?" And the answer must be "No." To secure a conviction under the tax law, you must enter a saloon, induce the liquor-seller to sell liquor to you in violation of the law, thereby becoming *particeps criminis*. You must turn the liquor down your own throat so as to be able to swear you know what it was. Then enter the court room and hear the judge charge the jury that a man who deliberately induces another man to commit a crime becomes *particeps criminis*, that his evidence should be thoroughly corroborated before it should have weight with the jury. If it took the same evidence to convict a man of murder that it does of illegal liquor-selling under the tax law, the witness would have to swear that he rode astride the bullet and saw it enter the murdered man's heart. The result is that the tax law of this State is openly and impudently defied. This Mr. Duffield admits when he says, "The only objection urged against it is that it is not carried out. That may be true to some extent, but that is no fault of the law"; and again, "In some large cities there is some difficulty in enforcing the Sunday and night law, but in most of the smaller cities and in nearly all the villages it is fairly well enforced." Now, I stand here to assert, and I challenge denial, that the tax law is violated in every city, every town, and every village in the State; that convictions for violation are the exception and not the rule; that convictions under the forms of evidence required under the tax law are practically impossible; and what is true in Michigan is true in every State where a tax or high license has been tried. The grand jury of Chicago, in a recent statement to the court, said: "Having discovered that a majority of the cases of robbery sent to the grand jury by the different police justices of Chicago, originated in the low saloons in certain districts of the city, the perpetrators of which are licensed to carry on their nefarious business, and enjoy immunity from police authorities of the city of Chicago, a committee of our body was duly appointed to ascertain if such charges of irregularities and flagrant dereliction of duty on the part of the police officers were true; the committee reported that they were, and that furthermore the ordinance requiring the closing of saloons by midnight has by long custom become a dead letter in the community, and a partiality seemed to exist in favor of groggeries of the very lowest character, and they have been described on the sworn testimony of policemen before our body, as robbers' dens." Andrew Paxton, agent of the Law and Order League of Chicago, speaking of the condition of things under high license, says: "Some of the low dens are of the most infamous character and are a menace to the city. They are filled with thieves and debased women. The chances are that any man who enters them will be drugged and robbed. One of these places was raided one night, and eighteen women of the basest sort were found there. Some were drunk and nearly all partially so. Two weeks later another raid was made and about the same number was found. Our own agents went there, and were solicited by the women to go with them to their rooms. One night a young man came with a considerable sum of money. He became drunk and was followed out by the bartender and robbed. In our protest against the renewal of the man's license, we set forth these facts, and the evidence sustained them, yet the license was renewed in this infamous place frequented by the worst characters. Young girls in short dresses are kept to lure in young men. From some of these dens, women are sent out to intercept working girls on their way home, and try to induce them to accompany them. Their purpose and their deplorable results need no explanation."

The effect of high license is to fortify the immoral features of the liquor business, to destroy the semi-respectable part of the trade, and to develop its worst tendencies. In Nebraska, under low license, numbers of Germans kept grocery-stores, and sold lager-beer in connection with that business. No gamblers, no prostitutes frequented these places. The effect of high license was to close these places because they did not sell enough liquor to pay the tax; but not so with the place where bad women were kept to tempt men, or the place where gambling was carried on; not a place where men were held up and robbed, was closed by increasing the tax. "The little corner grocery-stores cannot carry these burdens and therefore they disappear," urges Mr. Duffield; but I say to him, the dive, the concert garden, the gambling hell, can carry these burdens, and therefore they remain. Mr. Duffield *prints*, speaking of the license law of Illinois: "There the tax law went into operation" (notice that he calls a high license law a tax law) "in 1883 only, and what has it done there? It closed, in one year, 1,000 saloons in Chicago alone, and blotted out 4,000 in the State." I must call your attention to the fact that he dodges the whole and the real question, viz.: "Does tax decrease the evils of intemperance?" What does it matter whether there are sixteen or fourteen saloons on a block? Cannot the people get as drunk in fourteen as in sixteen? But, as he sees fit to avoid the real question, we must follow him into his chosen field and ask what are facts. A leading lawyer of Illinois, the Hon. George C. Christian, sends me the following statement: "My grocer told me that he had just quit selling beer to families. I asked him when: he replied, 'When high license went into effect.' Why? 'Because I didn't sell $500 worth in a year, and therefore I can't afford to pay the tax and make money.' I asked, 'Is this general?' 'Yes,' said he, 'there are 3,000 family groceries in Chicago. One-half or more sold beer to families before high license. Now not over 100 take out license.' The number of saloon licenses the year before high license, was 3,820; number of saloons licensed now, 3,760—an apparent decrease of 60; total old saloons licensed, 3,820, less family grocers, say one thousand, equal 2,820. Present number of saloon licenses and only 100 family groceries selling, 3,760. Total increase in saloons 940." This shows the suppression of the class of liquor-sellers who handle liquor with other commodities, and an increase in the grog-shops proper. Mr. Duffield came within 940 of getting the correct figures, which is wonderfully accurate, considering the side of the question that he is discussing. In regard to the closing of saloons in other parts of Illinois, the State is working under local option, and the decrease in the saloons is owing to prohibition, not taxation. I challenge Mr. Duffield to show a single town in Illinois where the saloons have been driven out by tax, while it is easy to show numbers of towns where the high tax acted as a bribe, and broke down local option. Again he speaks of the working of tax in Ohio. Under tax in Ohio the Christian Sunday has been destroyed in all large cities, and it is as legal to sell liquor on Sunday as on Monday. Concert gardens and saloon dives make the day hideous, and interrupt persons on their way to and from places of worship. Desiring to get at the correct facts I telegraphed Dr. Biler, editor of the *Central Christian Advocate*, and asked him how tax was working in Cincinnati. I received the following answer:

"CINCINNATI, *March* 23.
"Dr. Biler away. I have seen Methodist preachers in the city. Unanimously for constitutional prohibition. Tax law unworkable and unsatisfactory. (Signed), H. W. WILLIAM, Asst."

How does this agree with Mr. Duffield's statement: "Everybody in Ohio is satisfied with the tax law"?

You will notice that the witnesses cited by Mr. Duffield himself, make the prohibitory feature of the law the only one which can be defended. Judge Foraker says: "Practical prohibition has been secured under the local option feature of the Dow law, in at least 150 municipal corporations in the State." His other witnesses say the local option feature pleases the prohibitionists. Nearly every day adds to the municipalities availing themselves of the local prohibition feature of the tax law. Notice this is not the result of taxation, but the result of prohibition by people who utterly repudiate the principle of taxation.

In Nebraska, the Hon. H. W. Hardy, ex-Mayor of Lincoln, the father of the high license law, says: "High license utterly fails to abolish the evil effects of the liquor traffic. As a temperance measure it is an entire and complete failure."

Rev. J. B. Maxfield, Presiding Elder of the Methodist Church, says: "Men who pay the $1,000 license resort to every possible means to secure trade. The result is that prostitution and gambling have largely increased in the State." Mr. Duffield, in his defence of the indefensible tax system, gives special prominence to the prohibitory features of the law, and admits that the taxing principle is an impure and an unsound position. He says: "Take a township or a village, for instance, where there is a pure and sound sentiment on the subject of temperance and the liquor traffic, and the trustees meet, or the board, and say we do not want any saloon in our town or village. Now let us fix the amount of the bond required from any and every man who wishes to sell at $6,000 and no less. This can be done under the law." Now, if a pure and a sound sentiment will lead men to adopt prohibition by the roundabout way of refusing the bonds offered by the liquor-sellers, then the sentiment that advocates tax and opposes prohibition is impure and unsound. Pure and sound sentiment on the subject of sentiment! I thank thee, Duffield, for the word. In speaking of the tax law he says, "That it is illegal to sell liquor where billiards and other games are played, it is illegal to sell in any hall adjacent to a variety show or theatre, it is illegal to keep open bars or places for the sale of liquor on the Sabbath day, election days, regular holidays, and all such places must be closed after 10 or 11 o'clock at night until 7 A.M.; that no child under 16 years of age shall be permitted to remain in any bar-room nor shall any saloon-keeper give an entertainment on Sunday in his place." All these features are prohibitory features, and not taxation features. If it were not for the prohibitory salt distributed through the tax law of Michigan, it would stink in the nostrils of decent people. To defend the principle of taxation he cited the opinions of eminent men in the East. When I read his speech, I regretted that a bad cause compelled him to adopt questionable methods to uphold it. To place leading men in false positions is neither fair nor honorable. To cite Dr. Theodore L. Cuyler as opposed to constitutional prohibition after Dr. Cuyler had written him a letter urging him not to make the speech, deserves a more severe reprimand than I care to give on this platform. As he had called these witnesses, and unfairly used the influence of their great names, I, knowing he had done so, telegraphed them the facts, and now want to read Duffield's witnesses against Duffield, and want you to bear in mind they are his witnesses, and he must accept what they say; that he cannot impeach them:

"New York, *March* 24.

"I am not opposed to constitutional prohibition, but sincerely hope the people of Michigan will adopt it.
"(Signed), Noah Davis,
"*Ex-Judge of Supreme Court.*"

"New York, *March* 23.

"No man has a right to quote me on the question. I simply stood for high license in the State of New York as the most prohibitory measure that could be passed at the present time.
"Wm. Lloyd;
"*Of the Central Congregational Church.*"

"New Orleans, La., *March* 23.

"I am now, and have been since the movement started, in favor of constitutional prohibition. Theodore L. Cuyler."

Under the present law of Michigan there were, in 1885, 4,180 liquor manufacturers and dealers. Will any man claim that there is any difficulty in obtaining liquor or that drunkenness, and crime, and vice are not the result of these taxed saloons? The case summed up against taxation is this: 1. Taxation creates property rights in liquor, gives a liquor-dealer a legal standing in the community, and renders the enforcement of the law practically impossible. If Mr. Duffield doubts this, let me suggest that he commence to-morrow to try and enforce the tax law in this city. When the liquor-dealers sell liquor to minors let him enter a complaint. When they sell liquor on Sunday, enter a complaint. When they sell liquor on holidays, enter a complaint. If, at the end of six months, he is not a prohibitionist, I will buy him the best suit of clothes he ever wore in his life. Is it not a fact that under the tax system of this State the business men are terrorized and intimidated so that they do not dare to make complaints, but ask the Woman's Christian Temperance Union, the temperance organizations, or some irresponsible parties who have no property to be injured by the liquor-sellers, to undertake the enforcement of this law?

2. It reduces the number of groceries that sell liquor incidentally; it increases saloons that sell nothing else.

3. It permits a business in cities and towns that makes drunkards, paupers, and criminals.

4. The tax paid by the business goes into the city and town treasuries. The taxes to support the crimi-

nals and the paupers made by the business comes from the entire State, thereby laying on the shoulders of those who receive no part of the revenue of the liquor traffic the burdens of the liquor traffic itself.

5. It leads to the desecration of the Christian Sabbath, to the debauchery of workingmen, and the degradation of workingmen's homes.

6. It is everywhere violated, and little or no attempt is made to enforce it.

7. The prohibition obtained under it can only be procured by false methods and in circuitous ways, which makes it valueless when obtained.

8. It creates a class of drunkard-makers who live by working to increase the sale, and consequently the consumption, of liquor.

9. It is a failure as a temperance measure.

Mr. Duffield is the father of the tax law. The tax law is openly and impudently violated in Detroit. Mr. Duffield is a lawyer and a man of wealth and standing in the community. Why does he not make his law work? It will not do for him to ask prohibitionists to enforce a law in which they do not believe, and yet his sneer that "no prohibitionist ever attempted to enforce the law," is utterly unfounded. In fact, it seems to me that a man of his experience and knowledge of the affairs of this State, must have known it to be untrue. It is the prohibitionists who have tried to enforce the tax law and thereby demonstrated its utter worthlessness as a regulative measure. The members of the law and order leagues of this State are largely prohibitionists. Prohibitionists have furnished the money and done the work to attempt the enforcement of this law, while Mr. Duffield, and men who like him advocate the tax law everywhere, do nothing to make the law operative, and justify their indifference and idleness by sneering at prohibitionists, and insisting that they shall enforce the tax law. I challenge Mr. Duffield to show that the tax law of Michigan has decreased the crime, pauperism, and vice resulting from the use of intoxicating liquors, or made it more difficult for the drunkard to obtain liquor. I challenge Mr. Duffield to prove the tax system is workable by trying to enforce it. I say the law is so bad that it cannot be worked by the constitutional machinery of Government, and challenge Mr. Duffield to prove my statement false, by enforcement in Detroit.

The question is now, Will the prohibitory law work better? I repeat my statement that it will not take one-half the force to enforce prohibition, that it does to fail to enforce license.

The trial of prohibition in this State was made during the terrible period of our civil war. The whole attention of the nation was absorbed in the issues of that great struggle. Churches languished, schools grew weak, but the liquor business flourished. With the close of the war there came a reaction, and with the reaction an attempt to enforce the law. The last year that the law was on the statute-book of this State, the grog-shops decreased 2,862. Yet Mr. Duffield presumed upon the ignorance of his audience, and asked: "Did you ever hear, Mr. Sheley, of a prohibition law that wiped out ten saloons?"

Mr. Sheley—"No, never."

And then in the next breath he claims that the tax law has largely reduced the number of saloons, quoting figures one year from the United States internal revenue reports and the next year from the State reports, but neglecting to state whether there were any saloons in that year that continued selling without paying the tax, and also neglecting to explain that a red-ribbon movement which swept through the country, and the consequent temperance sentiment created by that movement, was the real cause of the reduction, or the seeming reduction of the saloons in Michigan, instead of the tax law. When this pressure was brought to bear upon the liquor-dealers, a brewers' congress, held in Detroit, August 12, 1874, demanded the repeal of the law. If the law had injured them sooner, a demand would have sooner been made for its repeal. It was not until the law was becoming effective that the liquor-sellers demanded at the hands of the politicians of this State that the law be strangled. The conditions to-day are entirely different. The temperance forces are thoroughly organized. Total abstinence is taught in the schools. The churches are thoroughly awake on the question. The politicians are aware that they can no longer slight it, and prohibition, if adopted in this State, will be enforced. I am surprised and astonished to see the statements made by Mr. Duffield against prohibition in other States. When I read the speech I knew that the statements, or rather the inferences from the statements, were not true. So I telegraphed gentlemen of undoubted integrity that he had seen fit to drag into the controversy, in the States referred to, and asked for the facts in the case. The witnesses I shall call are honored in the States where they live. I regret that in discussing this question I am compelled to meet Mr. Duffield in two ways—first, Mr. Duffield as printed; second, Mr. Duffield as spoken—and that he deemed it necessary to make one speech for the people of Detroit, and one for the farmers of the country. In his attack upon prohibition he bases his whole charge upon the statement of the Internal Revenue Commissioner of the United States. Mr. Duffield is a lawyer and knows that the tax permit issued by the General Government to the saloon is identical with the tax permit issued to the drug-store, or any place that retails alcoholic spirits. He also knows that in a State under tax the man who obtains the permit holds the permit for an entire year. That is, a man under prohibition who wants to violate the State law pays the United States tax to prevent an interference of that Government, so that he shall only have one power to fight. That if a man is arrested and imprisoned, the permit appears in the records of the United States; so that in one town in Kansas where twenty-one permits were granted, nineteen of the liquor-sellers were in the jail, and the other skipped the country, and the town did not have an open grog-shop during the year. Mr. Duffield is either very ignorant or else he knows that the tax permit of the United States is absolutely no evidence, that it does not show that a single liquor-shop is open, or that the State law is violated; that it simply shows the intent of the party in paying twenty-five dollars to violate the State law if he can. In exposing the fallacy of his position I desire, in all cases where possible, to criticise the printed speech, and only refer to the speech that he really made, in order to get an explanation of his views.

Mr. Duffield printed: "Let us, for instance, take the State of Rhode Island. There the prohibition law has been in operation now for six months, and carries with it very stringent provisions for its enforcement. What record has it already made for itself? The records in Providence County show that of the whole number of cases tried for the last six months there were but three convictions. In the September term there were 106 liquor cases on the appeal docket, and in the December docket 116, and of the whole number there were but four verdicts of 'guilty' rendered; the rest of the cases were variously disposed of by discontinuances on payment of cost, discontinuances on conditions and disagreements of juries. The same state of things is being enacted here that prevailed under our prohibition laws of twenty years ago. The result is that already the best men in the State are deluging the General Assembly with petitions for the law's repeal, many signers being those who voted for the prohibition law. One petition represented men of property to the amount of $3,000,000, another of $12,000,000, and the Legislature is now pondering on what is its duty in the premises. At a recent meeting of the Law and Order Society in Providence, President Robinson, of Brown University, admitted that 'the frequency of intoxication upon the streets, notwithstanding the prohibition law, was a scandal and outrage upon decency.'" Mr. Duffield gives no authority for his statements, nor does he tell where he got his figures.

To find out whether this statement, in regard to a resubmission of the question, was true or false, I telegraphed Hon. E. A. Wilson, Speaker of the House, and received this answer:

"PROVIDENCE, R. I., *March* 23.

"Proposition to submit repeal of prohibitory amendment indefinitely postponed without debate, unanimously. The liquor nuisance will be served with equal unanimity. Prohibition will prohibit in this State. E. A. WILSON."

To meet another statement, I telegraphed Professor Robinson, who answered:

"PROVIDENCE, R. I., *March* 23, 1887.
"Constitutional prohibition is good. Political intrigue attempts to thwart reform in Providence. W. H. ROBINSON."

Desiring to give the people of Michigan the real facts in the case, I telegraphed the Rev. H. W. Conant and C. R. Brayton, Chief of State Police. They replied as follows:

"PROVIDENCE, R. I., *March* 23.
"Increase of arrests for drunkenness and revelry in Providence last six months license, over eighteen per cent. Decrease in first six months prohibition, over forty-two per cent. Common drunkenness in same time decreased in Newport 100 per cent.; Pawtucket fifty per cent.; last two months seventy-five per cent. Official figures.
"H. W. CONANT."

"PROVIDENCE, R. I., *March* 24.
'The statistics from the city of Providence, the largest city in the State, show an increase of drunkenness during the last months of the license law of 183 per cent. While during the first six months of prohibition, as compared with the corresponding period under license, drunkenness decreased more than forty-two per cent. The commitments to the State Workhouse, whose inmates are largely victims of the intemperate use of intoxicating liquors, for the first six months under prohibition, as compared with the corresponding period under license, show a falling off of more than one-half, and resulting in the large saving to the State of more than $1,800,000 per annum in the item of board alone. The 'growler,' or tin-kettle trade, has almost entirely disappeared from the streets, and children are not now seen frequenting liquor-saloons for supplies of liquor, as before prohibition went into effect. Many families that never saw a penny of the weekly earnings of its head, now receive the full benefit of his labor. The Legislature, now in session, has just indefinitely postponed, by an almost unanimous vote, a proposition to submit the repeal of the prohibition amendment to the people, and will at this session make the prohibition law more effective. C. R. BRAYTON."

Mr. Duffield says in regard to Kansas: "Take the State of Kansas. Under free traffic" (you see that he admits that traffic under license or tax is free traffic), "before the prohibition law of last year was enacted, there were 2,339 liquor-dealers. In 1886 under prohibition there were 1,850." You will notice he fails to say how he knows there are any liquor-dealers in Kansas. Against his empty assertion I want to put Gov. John A. Martin, who recently said: "The liquor sold in the city of Topeka amounted under license to two-thirds as much as is sold for all purposes in the whole State under prohibition." He estimates that under license the

State sold $60,000,000 per year, and under prohibition less than $5,000,000.

Mr. Duffield prints: "In Vermont, with thirty years of prohibition, the United States revenue shows 446 open saloons." I know it showed no such thing. Mr. Duffield presumed upon the ignorance of his audience when he insinuated that any men could determine from the United States revenue whether the tax permit was issued to an open saloon, "a hole in the wall, or a drug-store." Yet Mr. Duffield said, but did not print, "while there is a number of saloons, and that does not reckon in hotels, club-houses, or private drinking places." I submit this is either reckless assertion or impudent pettifoggery. Dare Mr. Duffield claim that the United States Government allows hotels and club-houses and private drinking-places to be carried on in Vermont without the necessary permit?

To prove the falsity of his statement I telegraphed the Hon. Frank Plumley, one of the most brilliant Republican leaders of the State of Vermont. He was chairman of the last Republican State convention, and has been in the Republican campaigns of this State several times. He answered:

"NORTHFIELD, Vt., *March* 23.

"Your denial of open saloons in Vermont to my knowledge is absolutely correct. FRANK PLUMLEY."

Mr. Duffield prints: "In the State of Iowa, before the prohibition law, there were 3,834 dealers; under prohibition in 1886 there were 4,033, and the manufacture of 5,894,544 gallons." Mr. Duffield seems to be ignorant of the fact that in the State of Iowa they have had prohibition of the sale of distilled liquors since 1853; that a recent prohibitory statute simply added to the prohibitory law the prohibition of vinous and fermented liquors.

To show the absolute working of prohibition in Iowa I telegraphed Hon. E. R. Hutchins, Commissioner of Labor Statistics. Mr. Hutchins answered:

"DES MOINES, Ia., *March* 23.

"Governor and Attorney-General both say prohibition has constantly improved the moral, financial, and social condition of Iowa, and is successfully enforced in eighty-five of the ninety-nine counties, also growing rapidly in favor in the remainder.   E. R. HUTCHINS."

I will not quote his statement in regard to Maine. It is the old one, and has been so often answered, that there is no need of replying to it in detail. But I would call the attention of the audience to the fact that in quoting the *Maine Farmer* Mr. Duffield fails to tell where the paper is printed or to give the date or number of the issue containing the statement. But if he make another speech he should be honest enough to say that the *Maine Farmer* is and always has been a consistent advocate of prohibition. His own showing of figures in regard to Maine prove that the prohibitory law more nearly suppresses liquor-selling and drunkenness in that State, than the tax law in Michigan. However, to corroborate the statement of James G. Blaine, William P. Frye, Eugene Hale, and all other public men of Maine, I telegraphed Joseph R. Bidwell, the Governor. He answered:

"AUGUSTA, Me., *March* 23."

"The finances of the State never more prosperous. Drink habit is fatal to prosperity in any community. Prohibition promotes morality everywhere. Nearly all crimes can be traced to rum, either directly or indirectly. The law is well enforced in the country towns. In some of the cities it is not quite so effective. The new law will aid the enforcement there.   JOSEPH R. BIDWELL."

Hon. Nelson Dingley, Congressman, and editor of the Lewiston *Daily Journal*, writes me:

"LEWISTON, Me., *March* 23, 1887."
"The prohibitory law is well enforced, and is a blessing to the State.
"NELSON DINGLEY."

Mr. Duffield makes a great point by citing Rev. A. L. Ladd, of Bangor, Me., as opposed to prohibition. Mr. Ladd telegraphs me:

"BANGOR, Me., *March* 24, 1887.
"Prohibition is a success throughout the State. The amendments since passed to the law will make it still more effective in cities.
"A. L. LADD."

In 1844, after the prohibition law of Maine had been on trial for thirty years, the people, by a majority of

47,000, placed it in the State Constitution. Few men in this country will presume to claim that the people of Maine are either fools or idiots, and yet to charge that they made prohibition a part of their organic law when it increased pauperism and crime and vice, is to challenge their judgment and intelligence, because prohibition with them was not an experiment. They had lived under it and seen its workings for thirty years.

Mr. Duffield prints, in speaking of the State of Georgia: " Take the State of Georgia, where it is claimed that prohibition and local option have been at work, and we find that, according to the Internal Revenue Office of the United States, there are to-day more distilleries in the State than ever before, and they are rapidly increasing. The increase is not alone in the number of stills, but in their capacity—old ones having increased from five bushels to fifty." As a public man Mr. Duffield must know that immediately following the war Northern Georgia, Eastern Tennessee, Western North Carolina, and South Carolina were filled with moonshine distilleries. All attempts to enforce the necessary internal revenue laws resulted in unblushing crime. But as time has passed on, the enforcement of the law has become more uniform, and the so-called report of increase in distilleries is simply a statement that the law is better enforced, and that the distilleries of the South are becoming more law-abiding. Desiring to call reliable witnesses, I telegraphed the business men of Atlanta. The answers were as follows:

"Atlanta, Ga., *March* 23.—Georgia, 115 of 137 counties absolute prohibition. With imperfect system of assessment taxable valuation constantly increasing. State in a very prosperous condition."—(W. E. Wright, Controller of State.)

"General merchants from all parts of the State report business good."—(J. T. Henderson, Commissioner of Agriculture.)

"Atlanta, compared with same dates last year, increased population 5,000; most moral city in the world. Prohibition does prohibit."—(Howard Van Epps, Judge City Court.)

"Business increased $50,000 last two months."—(Kizer & Co., wholesale dry-goods.)

"Business never so good."—(E. P. Chamberlain, dry-goods.)

"Never saw anything like it."—(G. T. Dood & Co., wholesale grocers.)

"Will transfer $200,000 of real estate this week, on eve of biggest kind of boom; workingmen buying homes."—(S. W. Goode, real estate.)

"Sales of school-books increased 100 per cent."—(J. M. Miller, book-store.)

"It is doubtful if Atlanta has ever been the scene of such a religious movement as at present."—(*Daily Constitution* this morning.)

Indorsed by Rev. J. B. Hawthorne and every minister of the city.

"Every business but undertakers' doing well. Not a drop of liquor for better than in ten years."—(J. B. Thromer, contractor.)

I might close my case in favor of prohibition by this statement: Under prohibition in 1882, Maine paid taxes upon spirituous liquors amounting to $25,247.05. On fermented liquors, $2,993.34. Michigan, under tax, the same year, paid on spirituous liquors, $129,405.02. On fermented liquors, $323,137.02; total, $452,542.04. The effects of prohibition in restraining immorality, vice, and crime, are such that the prohibitory law of Maine is indorsed by every public man, by every teacher in their colleges, by every minister in their pulpits, while the effect of the tax law in Michigan is such that it is antagonized by the churches, the ministers, the teachers, the women, and most of the farmers of this State. The contrast between prohibition and license is ably drawn by Dr. C. L. Randall, of your own State, whose statements I have not seen contradicted: "That during the last two years the prohibitory law was on our statute-books there was a reduction of 2,862 places where liquor was sold, and $39,142.25 in United States revenue and 11,393 barrels of beer, and we had but one State prison at Jackson with 703 inmates. How was it ten years from that day? After ten years of taxation or legalized rum, we find more than one prison as follows: State prison at Jackson with 670 inmates; State Reformatory, Iona, 611 inmates; Detroit House of Correction, 314 inmates; total, 1,595. Draw the contrast. Prohibition twenty years with a terrible war, 723 criminals. Taxation one year with peace and plenty, 1,595; although our population has increased but twenty-two per cent., our criminal population increased about 120 per cent."

Then I urge in favor of prohibition:

1. That it destroys property rights in liquor obtained after the law is passed, and makes possession *prima facie* evidence. It destroys all legal sales for beverage purposes, and so removes all legal protection from the drunkard-maker. Proof is simplified and prosecution aided.

2. That it makes liquor-selling a crime.

3. That it forces the liquor-dealer into business and trades which develop the prosperity and general morality of the public.

4. That it turns the earnings of the laboring man from the grog-shop to the store, and from the bar-room to the school.

5. That wherever tried it has reduced liquor-selling and the effects resulting from liquor-selling.

6. It destroys the open, popular saloon and the social habits of treating which drag young men to lives of debauchery and crime.

If prohibition be adopted on the 4th of April, and it will be, if an honest ballot and fair count is guaranteed, the question raised by Prof. Kent when he stated, "In my judgment, this amendment, if passed by a majority, will be utterly ineffectual," and gave as a reason that it interfered with the property rights of the liquor-dealers, is entitled to consideration. The question is simply, Will the State be compelled to compensate the manufacturers and dealers in liquor for the injury which may result to breweries, distilleries, saloons, and stock on hand, from the prohibition of the beverage sale of alcoholic liquors? Prof. Kent, with the greatest solemnity and with due judicial deliberation, says: "In my judgment, if the amendment is adopted, it will be held void so far as it undertakes to forfeit the rights of individuals in the liquor which they now have." Prof. Kent should know that the prohibitory law does not contemplate the forfeiture of the rights of individuals in the liquor which they now have. It simply says to those individuals that you shall not sell those liquors to injure public morals, public intelligence, and public prosperity. The attack upon the liquor business is the result of the wrongs of that business. But for its own wrongs there would never have been a prohibitory amendment. The prohibitory law is a police regulation made necessary by the wrongs of the liquor business itself. The law on this question simply is: *"The trade in alcoholic drinks being lawful as capital employed not being duly perfected by law, the Legislature then steps in and by an enactment based on general reasons of public utility, annihilates the traffic, destroys altogether the employment, and reduces to a nominal value the property on hand. Even the keeping of it for the purpose of sale becomes a criminal offence, and without any change whatever in his own conduct and employment, the merchant of yesterday becomes the criminal of to-day, and the very building in which he lives and conducts the business which before the amendment was lawful, becomes a subject of legal proceedings and liable to be proceeded against for forfeiture. A statute which can do this must be justified upon the highest reasons of public benefit, but whether satisfactory or not, the reasons address themselves exclusively to legislative wisdom."*

Government compensates for private property taken for public use. Government never compensates for prohibiting the wrongful or injurious use of private property. If the liquor business had produced the same results as the dry-goods business, there would have been no attempt to prohibit it. The prohibition is the result of the effects of the business. It has made its own suppression necessary and cannot plead its own wrongs in any court of equity. The Professor concedes the weakness of his position when he says in the first part of his speech: "I do not advocate the right of any man to keep a saloon." The tax assessed against a saloon-keeper is for one year, the bond is for one year, and when the saloon-keeper enters a business, pays his tax, and gives his bond, he knows that at the expiration of the year, all privileges and all rights under that tax and that bond expire and no mandamus will lie, to compel the officers of the village or city to renew the privilege. I rent a farm for a year; the man who rents, stocks the farm. At the end of a year I refuse to renew the lease. It would be a very poor lawyer who would claim that the man could recover from me the value of the stock upon the farm because I had refused to renew the lease. The liquor-seller knows that his privilege is annual; with the expiration of the privilege he takes the risk of renewal. Prof. Kent would certainly not claim that if the tax law drove out of the business in a certain town twenty saloon-keepers and left ten in the business, that the twenty who were driven out could recover compensation for their liquors, business, and fixtures. One argument made by both Mr. Duffield and Prof. Kent in favor of taxation is that it reduces the number of saloons. No man will claim that if taxation drove half of the liquor-sellers out of the business they could recover against the city for damage done. Now if the one-half driven out could not recover compensation, where is the argument that would give the other half compensation when they were driven out of the business for doing exactly the same thing that the others had done? The fact is, that the liquor-sellers of this country, sitting in their idleness, have grown rich off the ruin of the homes of the country, and if they are in favor of equitable compensation, the people will have no reason to fear the settlement. If they will return to the tax-payers of the State the money that the tax-payers have been compelled to pay to take care of the products of their business; if they will return to the families of the State the money that has been squandered by husband, by father, and by son, the State can afford to pay for every distillery, every brewery, every saloon, and all the fixtures and liquors in those establishments.

But, really, the worst feature of his whole canvass is, that this business, realizing that it has no legitimate defence, is stooping to methods which threaten the social, the industrial, and the commercial prosperity of this country. The temperance men have simply asked an intelligent examination and discussion of the question. They have been met by boycotting, bulldozing, and outrage. The safety of our institutions depends upon the right of the people to assemble and discuss all matters of public policy, and anything that prevents such assemblage and such discussion is an enemy of our liberties and our free institutions. The proposition to boycott business men for their honest opinion, the attempts to burn churches, the threats to take human life, should prejudice everybody against a business that has no other defence. In Holly the other night the people were assembled in the Methodist church to listen to a prohibition speech. The liquor-sellers, to break up the meeting, fired the building, and to say that I was astonished hardly expresses my feelings as I read the statement made by Prof. Kent when he said, speaking of this outrage: "Again, gentlemen, when men feel that way, if you consider them altogether, how are you going to enforce the law? I know of no way. And what are the means they are likely to use in withstanding any attempt to enforce them? I will tell you what means they will use. They will begin with legal means probably. They will prevent juries from convicting, they will undertake to overthrow the law and probably they will succeed. If they do not succeed in that, then they will use what means God and nature has placed in their hands to defend what they regard as their most sacred rights."

I ask now, ladies and gentlemen, if a more outrageous and more dangerous sentiment ever fell from the lips of a public man. . He says: "I am the last one to excuse or defend the attempt to burn the Methodist churches." But does he repudiate it? Read: "And can we, whose fathers secured their liberty in ways not unlike these, can we say that if our rights, which we thought were sacred, were assailed in that way, we should do otherwise? I fear not." Such language says to every liquor-seller outlaw in the country. "If I were in your place and my business were attacked, I would burn churches, destroy property, or use any means that God and nature had given me to defend myself." There is no excuse for the use of these words. This discussion is the discussion of a matter of governmental policy. The people are intelligent. This is a government of the people, by the people, and for the people, and to attempt in any way to extenuate the burning of buildings, the boycotting of business men, the taking of human life, is to open the doors for murder and anarchy in this country. Some enemy of Ireland certainly must have been whispering in the ears of Prof. Kent, or he would have made no attempt to compare the ragged, homeless outcast of Glenbeigh with the bloated liquor-sellers of this State. Look: a woman is driven from the home of her fathers in rags and misery to starve beside the street. Look again: a man is sitting in the doors of a saloon in entire idleness, growing rich off the homes, the misery, the suffering and agony of the women and children. Then compare the Irish mother, shivering in the storm, trembling in the blast, with the drunkard-maker of Detroit. To insinuate that our forefathers secured their liberty by boycotting, by attempting to fire churches filled with women and children, is to insult the noblest dead of the nation. Later, in his endeavor to extenuate the use of this language, Prof. Kent says in *The Free Press*: " The meeting to which my remarks were addressed was composed almost wholly of our most conservative and law-abiding citizens. There was no danger of exciting them to mob law." But Prof. Kent is a public man, the speech was made in a public place, it was printed in the public press, and he had no right to make a speech before that audience that he could not have made before any audience in this country. " There was no danger of exciting them to mob law," but suppose that building had been full of the liquor-sellers and their tools in this city, would it have excited them to mob law? Does not every inference of the statement justify the use of force, of bloodshed, and of murder to defend the nefarious traffic?

I want to say, calmly and deliberately, that this is a free country; our forefathers fought and died at Bunker Hill, at Brandywine, at Yorktown, and starved at Valley Forge to build on this continent a republic. For a hundred years this country has prospered.

The broadest discussion of all questions has been allowed. The will of the majority has been the controlling power, and now at the close of the first century of our history, it sounds strange to hear men born in other countries, who have fled to this country to escape despotisms, say to American business men: "You shall not think, you shall not act, you shall not follow your own conscientious convictions upon matters of public policy; if you lay your finger upon a public evil we will boycott your business; if you endeavor to destroy a public nuisance, we will burn your property; if you endeavor to enforce the law against law-breakers, we will murder you." Ladies and gentlemen, if there is any man in this country who is dissatisfied with American institutions, with American ideas, with the American methods of procedure in public matters, it will not cost him any more to buy a ticket from New York to go to the country from which he came, than it did to buy a ticket from that country to this. America is a free country. The freedom of action, the freedom of speech must be upheld, and all attempts at mob violence, all attempts at anarchy, all attempts at outlawry, must be suppressed by the hand of law, and that law upheld and sustained by the people. The idea of a teacher of young men in a public institution like An'n Arbor justifying, even by implication, the burning of a Methodist church, where men and women were assembled to listen to the discussion of a public question, shows the dangerous and alarming tendencies of our times. The saloon is the hotbed of anarchy, the hotbed of lawlessness, the hotbed of mob rule, the hotbed of murder, and those in favor of good order, those in favor of the enforcement of law, must strike down this enemy of the civilization and liberties of this country.

It has been urged by the opponents of the amendment that if the amendment be adopted, there is no guarantee that the Legislature will enact laws to enforce it. The amendment, if adopted, will be adopted by a majority of the voters. If a majority of the voters are in favor, four-fifths of the women are certainly in favor, and that would give a preponderance of sentiment in favor of the enactment. In the State of Iowa the amendment, after being adopted, was declared unconstitutionally adopted by the Supreme Court of the State, but despite this fact the Legislature of the State enacted a stringent prohibitory law, and at each session since, the stringency of the law has increased.

In Kansas and Rhode Island the same results followed the adoption of the law, and in Michigan if a majority of the voters of the State declare in favor of the amendment, it will not be safe for any political party or any politician to defy the will of the people in this matter. This is a government of the people and a majority of the people must rule. Let politicians defy the will of the people and the political undertaker will not complain for want of business.

In conclusion, let me urge that the grog-shop is the primary school of crime, pauperism, and vice. This is admitted. License and tax have been tried in this country and in Europe for hundreds of years, and have failed to diminish the evils resulting from the public bar-room. The only features of license and tax regulation, which are urged in their defence, are the prohibitory features, and if the prohibitory features are the only part of the license laws which can be defended, then why not reject the license features and make the laws wholly prohibitory? The tax features of the law have failed. Mr. Duffield again and again concedes this in his speech. Urging its good features he says: "If we should run out into the country where they claim this temperance sentiment is so strong—although I don't believe there are many of them who know anything about it—they would find how it works." Thereby conceding that it does not work in cities and that the people in the cities realize no benefits from the law.

Again, he says: "It contains three elements—local option, license, or prohibition. Where the community wants prohibition, and in the cities here this traffic cannot be suppressed or abolished, and when you look at the law and analyze it in that respect you will be astonished how much worth, how much merit, how much strength there is in our present tax law against the liquor traffic."

But is it not strange that with the law working for years in Detroit, the people of Detroit do not realize the beneficial features it is claimed to possess?

Again, he says: "I doubt very much whether any of our people here, except those who have given special attention to it, know how great the benefit of these provisions in the tax law are, to say nothing about what has been done." But the people here do not know that out of over 300 complaints against liquor-dealers in Detroit last year, but twenty-two of them have been tried, and that the rest are pigeon-holed or linger in the courts of the city. The trouble with Mr. Duffield's argument is that the tax does not work and that the ordinary machinery of government cannot work it. His constant iteration and reiteration that the people ought to ascertain the beneficial features and make it work, reminds me of the Irish porter who, at the Adams House, in Boston, was one night sent by the night clerk to accompany a gentleman to his room. After Pat had deposited the baggage, the gentleman said: "I want to be called at six o'clock in the morning." The Irishman replied, "Faith, I go on at twelve and off at twelve. Do you think I will be sitting up all night to call you?" "I don't care whether you call me or not, I want to be called." "Oh, you want I should lave word at the office?" "Leave it where you please, only say that I am to be called." "All right, sir," and the Irishman left. A few minutes later he went back and rapped on the door. The gentleman opened the door and said: "What do you want?" "Faith, sir, for fear there might be some mistake about calling you I thought I would come back and tell you there is no need of calling a gentleman in this hotel. Do you see that little bunch up there with a knob in the middle (pointing to the electrical bell call), when you want to be called in the morning just turn over, put your thumb on that bunch and push, and the boy will come up and call you, sure."

The tax law of this State, in the hands of the proper officers of the State, has been demonstrated to be unworkable, and the people are left to call themselves, and to perform the duties that other men are elected to perform and paid for doing. After ten years of failure the people propose to repudiate the fraud, and Mr. Duffield hastens forward, to say in substance, that it is the duty of the people to create a Government inside the Government and work the fraud themselves.

In closing his speech, Mr. Duffield has seen fit to say that two banners have been erected in this campaign—the one, the banner of prohibition, the other the banner of taxation and license—and by this he seeks to draw an invidious comparison between the followers of one banner, and the followers of the other. I am glad he has done this, for when he says, "All bad men are in favor of the amendment," it justifies me in showing what kind of people indorse him and his speech and how utterly reckless he is in his statements. I want to challenge his statement by saying: When, on the 4th of April, the vote on the amendment has been counted, one of two camps in this State will rejoice; and, while I do not wish to insinuate that every man who votes against the amendment is a bad man, I do want to say that the bad men and the bad women in this State are not in favor of the amendment.

Desiring to meet his empty statement with evidence which he could not break down, I sent a trusted detective to take a census of the gambling hells, the saloons, and the houses of ill-fame in Grand Rapids. He telegraphs me as follows:

"GRAND RAPIDS, *March* 26.
"Visited professional gamblers, sixty-four against the amendment. Saloon-keepers, twenty-six against the amendment. Houses of ill-fame, six against the amendment. None for the amendment."

Another equally trusty officer working the city of Detroit visited the houses of ill-fame in this city to take a canvass of the inmates; to show you their feeling, let me read the interviews, omitting the name of the keeper and the name of the street. If anybody doubts the correctness of these statements and will come on the platform at the close of the meeting, I will give them the name of the keeper and the number and name of the street:

In the first house visited, the proprietor said: "Oh,

stuff! The amendment can never be carried. See what *The Free Press* said the other day; it had about one-half of its paper filled with speeches against it, and with good big men here. Why, the Opera-House was packed with men who thought as they did. If carried, good-bye Detroit! I am off to some other place; no drinks, no money here, and that is what I want. I tell you, lots of it is drunk in these houses, and if it was not for that, girls would be in hard luck, but the boys will beat it sure."

The keeper of another house said: "No prohibition here. That Duffield meeting was the thing! You can't do without it. Men will drink. Why, look, how many there are in the business, and they ain't going to shut up, and don't you forget it."

In another house the proprietress said: "You can come here any time in the next ten years and get what you want, if you pay for it. Prohibition won't be carried and I know it. All the men say so. Why, you can't do it. When they want to drink they will do it, and those who don't want it will let it alone. Say, did you read the papers the other day? You ought to see the speeches made by all the big men here. They say it can't be done—that license is right, and so it is."

In another house: "I will bet you the drinks all around that the amendment won't carry. Too many want their drinks. See what a large amount is drunk in the sporting houses. That is how a good many of the men spend their money, having the girls to while away a few hours with. They take enough to make them feel good and generally behave themselves. Better for them to take it in a comfortable house than in saloons with a lot of dead-beats waiting to be treated. We pay our license and will have it."

In another house: "I don't believe it can be carried. Too many want the stuff, and the best men in town patronize our house and like to treat the girls. It does no one any harm, and gives the men lots of pleasure to spend a social hour. Mark my words, you will never see prohibition in this State. The whiskey men have a good deal of money that is to be used to defeat it, and you bet they will do it. These politicians know their business, and know where they get help on election day. The speeches of Duffield and Kent were just to the point."

The proprietress of another house said: "It never can be carried. Look at what the big men say here. If it should be carried it will make our houses dull here. I have been here only a few months, but I have seen enough to convince me that a great many men come into houses, and are drunk or pretty well set up when they come, and when they wake up in the morning in our room, curse and swear to find where they are. Of course it will be dull, but if the business is prohibited I guess it will be no good."

A canvass of eighty saloons showed a unanimous vote against the amendment and a unanimous indorsation of Duffield's and Kent's speeches. Mr. Duffield should not have invited this comparison, for the world knows that the professedly good and avowedly bad are working together, to defeat the amendment in Michigan.

On the night of the 4th of April, if the amendment be defeated, where will the rejoicing be? Down in the slums where bad men chink glasses with bad women! In drinking houses and drinking hells, where mothers' boys are ruined! In the saloons, where husbands are made brutes! In bar-rooms, where fathers are wrecked! But if the amendment be carried, there will not be a drunkard's wife or a drunkard's child who will not see the stars of hope breaking through the clouds of despair! The church bells will ring, the moral people of the State will rejoice, and the angels in Heaven will sing an anthem over a State redeemed from the licensed promoters of vice, crime, and immorality!

IX.

WHAT, WHY, AND HOW.

An Address delivered in Tremont Temple, Boston, Mass., Sunday, December 16, 1883.

Ladies and Gentlemen: The temperance reform has for its object the development of manhood and womanhood along the lines of intelligence and conscience. A sound mind in a diseased and rotten body is the exception, not the rule. The use of alcoholic drinks by persons in health, causes muscular and nervous degeneration and disease. Hence the temperance reform aims to prevent the use of alcoholic drinks, and by such prevention, avoid the effects of such use.

Alcoholic drunkenness is caused by the use of alcoholic liquors. The results which temperance workers wish to prevent are caused by alcohol affecting nerve and brain tissue. Bring a barrel of whiskey into this Temple and place it on this platform, call up Dr. Ellis, and have him read and pray over it; then let this large audience, with their different temperaments, drink it, and there would be a fight before they left the hall. It is not the place where it is sold, it is not the man who sells it, it is alcohol affecting brain and nerve tissue that produces the results which temperance reform seeks to prevent.

To prevent the use of alcholic drinks, the person must be treated in his dual nature, as individual and citizen. It is of the person as a citizen I wish to speak to-day in order to develop the reasons for the interference by Government with the alcoholic liquor trade.

That intemperance is a withering, blighting curse, is axiomatic. That the alcoholic liquor trade is an ulcer on social, civil, and business life, no sane man dares deny. The person who thinks it necessary to stand upon the public platform to prove that the use of alcoholic liquors causes more misery, pauperism, and crime than any other or all other social customs, insults the intelligence of his audience.

A contagious disease breaks out in your city, your people have suffered from its ravages in former years, yet the cry goes up to your board of health: "What can we do?" The board of health hires Tremont Temple, and places on this platform an eminent physician to answer your question. He stands here for an hour to describe the workings of the disease on the human system, and after he has described all its loathsome characteristics, tells you, "You had better be careful and not catch it." Would not the disgusted and impatient audience cry: "Doctor, we do not need to be convinced of the terrible nature of the disease! We know that, because the disease has visited our city before. What we want is a *remedy* for the disease. The question is not: Is it a contagious disease? — of that we are thoroughly conversant,— but, What shall we do to prevent the spread of a contagious disease? Simply a question of remedy, doctor." So in dealing with the national disease of intemperance, the people need no additional proof of the horrid results and nature of the plague. It has crowded too many poorhouses, asylums, and penitentiaries, filled the streets of too many cities with its debauched and ruined victims; blighted the flowers of hope and trust and love in too many homes; turned too many days into pandemoniums and nights into hells, for an intelligent people to remain ignorant of its nature and effects. The people are satisfied that intemperance is a terrible disease, threatening the nation's life. From Cape Cod to Cape Mendocino, from Hudson Bay to the Gulf, they recognize the fact.

"Intemperance is threatening our civilization and liberties," is an axiom. The question remaining to be settled is, what are the remedies for the disease? Certain well-settled propositions will enable us to start right. Experience and science have these statements:

1. Alcoholic beverages are a product of man's work,

consequently the desire for, and disease resulting from the use of, must follow their manufacture.

2. Alcoholic drinks being a manufactured curse, the supply must precede and create the demand for them.

3. The use of alcoholic liquors in all ages and nations has been proportionate to the public popular facilities for obtaining the supply.

4. The effect of alcoholic drinks on the habitual user are, primarily, muscular and nervous degeneration and disease; secondarily, weakened intellect, sensibility, and will.

5. The treatment of the alcoholic patient must be such as to arouse the weakened will to force the patient to wholly abstain from all alcoholic liquors. This accomplished, the sick body must be treated with physical remedies, and the sick soul with spiritual remedies.

6. The old rule, " an ounce of prevention is worth a pound of cure," is truer in this case than in any other.

Intemperance (alcoholism) injures primarily the individual, but the individual is a social unit, and anything that injures him injures society, of which he is a part, and while the Christian and philanthropist would work to save the victim because he is one for whom Christ died, society must work to save him because he is a social unit.

Man is a social animal. Society is necessary for his development. To isolate him is to destroy him as an intellectual being, and to degrade him to the level of the brute. The effects of solitary confinement in the prisons of France and the United States, the history of persons lost on uninhabited islands, all prove that man was created as a social being; that, removed from his fellows, he ceases to be human. Therefore, any system of ethics is weak and defective which fails to recognize the dual nature of man as an individual responsible to God, and as a social unit responsible to society made necessary by his very nature. Man is dependent, and his individuality must bend to that fact. Perfect natural liberty means liberty in accord with nature. The liberty or freedom of will that has a tendency to destroy society, and thereby deprive man of social intercourse, which nature has made imperative for his development, is opposed to the laws of nature and of nature's God—and wrong.

The ability of society to fulfil its high function depends almost wholly upon the character of the social units. This Temple is a brick building. The unit of the structure is the individual brick in the wall. The strength of the building depends somewhat upon its form, and the work done upon it; but all architectural calculation is based upon the strength and durability of the material which is used. Suppose that the architect had drawn the plan, the master-workman and masons been ready to do good work when the material came, and an examination of the material had shown it to be poor, weak, soft, would the men have gone forward with the building? No! The strength of the building depends upon the strength of the material, and it would be worse than useless to erect a building of weak, poor material. If it would be useless to erect a building of poor material, would it not be criminal to allow persons to weaken and destroy the material of a structure already erected, when its destruction means the destruction of the building and the thwarting of the purpose for which it was erected?

Society is a structure—its material composed of reasonable, ethical human beings. Any business or custom which develops or strengthens the God-nature of man, develops and strengthens society, of which he is a part, and the converse of the proposition is equally true. Any business or custom which develops the animal nature of man at the expense of the intellectual God-nature, weakens and degrades society. To fulfil its mission, society must establish and maintain institutions and customs, necessary for man's development, comfort, and happiness. Trade is a social institution, born of society, developed by society, and subjected to society, to assist in promoting the interests that necessitate society.

This statement of fundamental truths is expressed by the axiom: "The use of alcoholic liquors in all ages and nations has been proportionate to the public popular facilities for obtaining the same," or, in other words, it depends on the open alcoholic liquor trade. The alcoholic liquor trade is a social institution, subject to the social law governing all trade, viz., to assist in promoting the interest that necessitates society. True, millions of dollars are invested in it, and thousands of men depend upon it for a livelihood; but its magnitude only gives it greater power to do evil, if its results are bad. It is entitled to the same protection from society as other trades, if its work produces the same social results. Only gravest charges, fully sustained, can justify its destruction; but if charges sufficient are sustained, its very magnitude must bar the dealers from pleading the "baby act" as an excuse for their crimes. They can only be held responsible for the results of their trade, but they must come into the people's court and answer for them. The open bar-room, exposing the supply of liquors, with tempting signs and alluring accompaniments, constantly creates a demand where no demand existed before. Two men passing along the street, with no thought of drinking, see the tempting sign, and step into the public popular place and drink; not that they care to drink, but to be social. Several young men enter a saloon to play billiards. They do not care for liquor, but "when they are with Romans they must do as Romans do," and they drink to be social. The business, outlawed and driven into holes, would be followed by the victims it had already ruined and chained, but not by the boys of the land who care nothing for drink. Drinking, in its incipiency, is the result of social customs; in its advanced stages, of diseased, nervous, and muscular conditions, which create an unnatural craving, falsely called an appetite. The treatment of the victim as an individual is one part of the work of the reform, but the fact of his relation to society, and society's relation to him, must not be lost sight of. If alcoholic drinks injure the user, then they injure society, of which the user is a part, and it is a matter of self-defence for society to discourage their use. Granted the effects of alcoholic drinks on the habitual user, are:—primarily, muscular and nervous degeneration and disease—secondarily, weakened intellect, sensibility, and will, and it follows that the individual thus injured, being a social unit, society must suffer from the use of alcoholic liquors; and that the public bar-room, by stimulating the use, becomes an enemy to society, and, therefore, subject to trial, conviction, and destruction. Society tries men for their acts,—institutions for their results. If the liquor traffic builds up its customer socially, morally, intellectually, and financially, no argument can justify its overthrow; but if it tears down its customer socially, morally, intellectually, and financially, no sophistry can justify society in continuing it. I hope I have liquor-dealers before me to-day, and if so, they will please correct me if I misstate the results of their traffic.

Four workmen were paid off last night. Each received twenty-five dollars. On the way home, one spent a large part of his money in a dry-goods store, one in a boot and shoe store, one in a hardware store, and the other commenced last night, and is continuing to-day to spend it in a saloon. Each of these men has a family to provide for and educate. Next Wednesday let us visit the homes of these men. We enter the home of the man who spent his money with the dry-goods merchant, and ask what his family received in exchange for his hard-earned dollars. His wife would show us the new dresses, and say: "We needed the clothes, the merchant needed the money, so we traded," —an exchange of values benefiting both parties. The same answer, simply varied by the articles purchased, would be given by the wives of the men who traded at the boot and hardware stores; but when we enter the home of the saloon customer to ask, the misery, wretchedness, and poverty would answer before the lips could utter the question. The saloon takes material values from the customer, and returns what is worse than nothing. Far better for the man if the drunkard-maker had simply robbed him, for then he would have had a clear head and sound muscles to go on and provide for his family,—while by purchasing and drinking liquor he is temporarily unfitted for work, and sent home a maddened brute to abuse and insult those he should love and protect. To illustrate more fully let me ask a liquor-dealer a hypothetical question: "Mr. Dealer, suppose a young man, standing high in social and business circles, commenced to patronize you to-day, and does so for the next ten years, all the while increasing the time spent in your saloon, and the money spent at your bar. At the end of the ten years, what will you have done for that man in return for all the money and time he has given you?" Must not the dealer answer: "He would have been better socially, morally, intellectually, and financially if he had never entered a saloon." Another, please: "Suppose a man with a family patronizes you the same way, for the same time, what will you do for his family in return for the father's money and time?" The answer must be: "The family would be better off, and the children would have a better chance for happiness, if the father had never entered a saloon." No liquor-dealer dares deny that the whole tendency of the saloon is to degrade its customers. The bar-room, under whatever name, is a nursery where criminals and paupers are bred — a cradle where vice is fondled and rocked. Its path through the ages is stained with blood and tears, and made horrible by the countless skeletons of its victims, who, decoyed by its influence from the up-hill path of denial and duty, into the by-way of sensual pleasure and drunkenness, have then been dragged, by the cravings of diseased bodies, in disgrace and madness, to dishonored death. Judged by its own record, the traffic is a curse to all the higher elements of manhood and womanhood, a disgrace to our Christian civilization, and an ulcer on the nation's life.

That the liquor traffic, and the men employed in it, constantly outrage that part of society not engaged in the traffic, follows from what has been stated, and the punishment and destruction of the traffic must come from the society founded on the relations of right — the State. It is the duty of the State to destroy this traffic, and thereby prevent its results.

If I should ask a school-boy, "What is Massachusetts?" he would probably get an atlas and say, "Here is a picture of it." Of course the child would be wrong, for the map would be a picture of the house where Massachusetts lives. Land and water do not constitute the State. They were here before Massachusetts came. Birds do not organize States. Beasts do not organize States. A State is a society, and a society, as before stated, is composed of ethical, reasonable human beings. The science of its life and powers is called politics. The power which it exercises is inherent in the individuals that compose it. It is the duty of every person to understand the science of the right use of the powers delegated to the State, or, politics. The old cry, "Keep moral questions out of politics," is the most damnable political heresy ever taught by empty-headed demagogues. In this country every man is a political factor, bound by his honor and patriotism to do his duty, on all occasions, for the upbuilding and development of humanity. Every influence that makes the man better makes the Government better, and to keep a reform out of politics, it must be buried so it shall not influence the individual who is a unit of the State. What the country needs in its politics is more school-houses, prayer-meetings, and pulpits, and less saloons, gambling hells, and houses of prostitution. Politics, made respectable, is the great need of the times. The effects of the use of alcoholic liquors on the individual as a social being, would justify the State in destroying any trade that encouraged its use, but the political effects of the use make such destruction imperative.

A pure ballot-box, made pure by intelligent electors, is necessary if the Republic is to live. A man who will corrupt the ballot-box is a traitor to the Government. A man who will buy a vote will sell his vote if he gets elected. A man who will corrupt a voter, will accept a bribe if he succeed in winning official position. But notwithstanding these admitted truths, voting in our large centres of population is a farce, and an honest count a thing of the past. For years the question asked of Presidential candidates has been, "Can he carry New York State?" This means, "Can he carry New York City?" or, in other words, "Will the liquor traffic of New York support him?" The infected political centres of the cities are the slums. A slum is licensed grog-shops gone to seed.

It is election morning. Here stands an American workman in front of his cottage home. Inside are wife and baby boy. The workman owns his home, has a good job, is sober, intelligent, happy. Offer him ten dollars for his vote and he would knock you down. He is a *man*, with a man's honor and conscience. In the hands of such men the ballot-box is safe. To-morrow let the same man enter a saloon and commence to drink, and for ten years take the same course of political training the saloon gives its customers, and at the end of that time graduate a sot. Election morning comes and finds him in front of the tenement where poverty has driven his wife, who takes in washing and does the most menial work to support herself and children. He is a drunkard, ragged, dirty, hungry, and worse still, the diseased craving for liquor almost drives him wild. He has no money, no employment, and he could not do work if it was offered him; conscience is stupefied, will-power gone. A villain offers him five dollars for his vote and he sells it. Such are the political results of the alcoholic liquor traffic. A corrupt ballot-box means corrupt voters. To pass laws to guard against corruption of the ballot-box, and license institutions to corrupt voters, is working at the wrong end. You cannot expect a fountain to rise higher than its source. The effect of alcoholic drinks on the user makes him, to a certain extent, the slave of the liquor-dealer who will supply the stimulant his diseased system craves.

Dishonest politicians have long recognized this fact, and leave money with the dealer, with instructions to "set up the drinks and fix things with the boys." To such an extent has this corruption of the voter in centres of population been carried, that intelligent thinkers, like Kasson of Iowa, and Winchell of Michigan, do not hesitate to pronounce our form of government a failure when applied to great cities. The user of alcoholic stimulants is not only unfitted as a voter, but for such other public duties, as witness, juror, or officer. Four thousand bar-rooms in the city of Boston, open six days in the week and eighteen hours each day, are constantly turning out men thus unfitted for their duties as citizens and electors. That the State should destroy the liquor traffic, has ceased to be a debatable question; that the question must be determined by political action, the liquor-dealers themselves have made certain. They are not content to carry on their business as other tradesmen do, but have banded themselves together as political autocrats, and decreed the death of any party that refuses to be their pliant tool. They have drawn the sword and thrown away the scabbard.

In the year 1875, Louis Schade, attorney of the Beer Brewers' Association, and editor of the Washington *Sentinel*, said :

"If we find that one or the other political party is against us, we must support the opposition party that is not against us. The principle of self-protection must, in such instances, be our only guide—first beer, and then politicians.

. . . .

"Support that party that supports you, and go against that which wants to destroy you."

In August, 1874, the representatives of the liquor interests of Michigan met in convention, and recorded themselves in these words :

"*Resolved*, That we believe that national legislation can be secured by co-operation and concert of action, and we hereby pledge ourselves to make this issue one of paramount importance to all others."

The following declaration and instruction is from the *Liquor Dealers' Advocate :*

"*Resolved*, That we will support all political papers advancing the true principles of liberty.
"*Resolved*, That we find it necessary, in a business point of view, to patronize only such business men as will work hand in hand with us."

In August, 1867, the beer advocates of Chicago met in mass convention, and, after the passage of resolutions denouncing Sunday and temperance laws, passed the following :

"*Resolved*, That we firmly stand as one man by these declarations, and that no party consideration shall lead us to indorse a platform, or vote for a man, whose course will be in the least doubtful on these conditional points."

The ninth National Beer Congress, held in Newark, N.J., June 2, 1869, adopted this:

"*Resolved*, That we hereby reiterate and reaffirm as our standing creed and unchangeable purpose, to use all honorable means to deprive puritanical and temperance men of the power which they have so long held in councils of the political parties of this country. And that, for this purpose, we will support no man for any office who is identified with this illiberal and narrow-minded element."

At the 13th National Beer Brewers' Association, held in Cleveland, Ohio, June 4, 1878, the president, in the last words of the opening address, said: "The last Presidential campaign has shown us what unity among us can do. Let our votes and our work in the future be heard from in every direction."

Thus an examination of the causes, nature, and results of the disease, shows the necessity of State action.

An examination of the purposes and powers of the State, shows its power and right to act.

An examination of the utterances of the conventions representing the traffic, shows that the State is given the alternative of destroying the traffic, or becoming the vassal of the liquor organizations, which are yearly growing more powerful by destruction of the citizens.

Remember, the use of alcoholic drinks, in all ages and nations, has been proportionate to the public popular facilities for obtaining the supply.

If the State wishes to diminish the use, it must destroy the public places where the citizen is tempted to use alcoholic liquors.

In the Ohio campaign a leading political speaker said, in a public speech: "There is no harm in a glass of beer *per se*." The next night a gentleman asked me if there was; and I, using the answer of my friend, Geo. W. Bain, said, "*Per se* means by itself. Certainly there is no harm in a glass of beer by itself. Place a glass of beer on a shelf, and let it remain there, and it is *per se*, and will harm no one; but if you take it from the shelf, and turn it inside a man, then it is no longer *per se.*" The prohibitionists agree with the Ohio judge. He says: "There is no harm in a glass of beer *per se.*" We believe the same thing; and are trying to keep the accursed thing *per se* for all time, and out of the stomachs of men.

To do this work the State is asked to use no new power; simply to extend its police power over poisoned drinks as it now does over poisoned foods. This power is the ability which the State has to protect its own political health. In our Republic all power, not properly delegated to the General Government, is reserved to the States, and this police power is one of the reservations. In its exercise, the State should be governed by its own nature and functions. The State is a political body. The power to exercise it is inherent in the people who compose it, and is by them delegated to be used for the public good. The power of the State to accomplish the object that necessitates its existence, depends upon its own health. The State must be healthy as a whole; and this can only be when its members—counties, towns, villages, and cities—are themselves healthy. The tendency of vice and crime is to congregate. "Birds of a feather flock together." The tendency of society, then, is for bad centres to become worse, and good centres better. But the State is a whole, and disease in one part means bad health in other parts of the political organism. A man cannot be healthy who has a fever-sore on the skin, an ulcer on the arm, and a cancer on the face; neither can a State be healthy with the political ulcers caused by the liquor traffic located on its joints—the great cities. The political health of the State can only be maintained by bringing its whole vital power to bear on the diseased centres.

This leads us to an objection to one method of State dealing with the liquor traffic, viz., the delegation to towns, cities, and counties of the State, power to prohibit the traffic, known as "local option." Counties, towns, and cities are not independent political organisms, but simply members or parts of the political body—the State. They assist it in performing its functions, as the legs and arms of a man assist him. The moral and social conditions of the cities affect the whole State. The elector of a city votes as an elector of the State. The corruption in a voter in a city, means the corruption of the State. The legislator elected as the tool of the slums in the cities, assists in making laws for the whole State.

The political health of New York City has injured the political health of New York State for years. With the tendency of vice to congregate, apply the local option principle to the other forms of political and moral disease. If Brighamite Mormons establish a town and have a majority of the voters, let them license polygamy. If prostitutes and their followers are in majority in the city, let them license the social evil. If gamblers and their cappers are in majority in the city, let them license gambling. The objection to this would be, that since the State is a society of justice, the granting to vile men and women power to control in centres where they congregate, would weaken the power of society to do its work; besides, the effect of these vices is in no sense local, and how can the State in justice give the vicious in cities the power to injure the moral people of the country? The liquor traffic, like all other vile institutions, tends to centralize. It is leaving the country towns and getting in cities where, by its debauched following, it makes and unmakes the officers who have in charge the enforcement of law. The saloon, by its following, elects the city government, the city government appoints the city police, the police arrest the saloon-keeper for violating the law, a saloon-keeper demands protection from the government that he elected, and the government removes the policeman from the force. The people object, but how can you expect a creature (the government) to be greater than the creator (the saloon-keeper)? The slums of the city are simply great ulcers on the body of the State. There is not vitality enough in the cities to remedy the low condition to which they have been brought by the slums. The only hope is to bring the vitality of the whole body to bear on the diseased centres. The objections to local option, are:

1st. The law does not make liquor-selling a crime, but teaches that a majority vote of the people can make it either right or wrong. The effect of such a law is to constantly demoralize public sentiment, because law is always an educator. If it is based on right principles, it educates right; if on wrong principles, it educates wrong.

2d. It applies to the municipality, which, if it adopt prohibition, may be surrounded by others granting license. The outlawed liquor-seller knows if he can bring the law into contempt the people will vote for license next year, and everything is favorable for such violation as will bring it into contempt. Under such conditions, prohibition can never have a fair trial.

3d. Citizens of a town will say, "Drinking men never come to a prohibition town to trade, if there is a license town equally near, and we cannot afford to kill our town even for principle."

4th. Local option delegates power to a municipality to prohibit the traffic, but does not give the municipality the power to fix an adequate penalty for violations. A local option law is a license law, with license law penalties for violation, which are wholly inadequate to enforce it. Penalties sufficient to destroy the traffic will never be made until the State recognizes the business as an outlaw and enemy. License recognizes it as a good thing, regulated to destroy bad incidentals.

5th. Local option degrades the struggle into a personal fight. It is the citizen of the town against the saloon-keeper of the town. Many business men who would vote for State action, will not vote for local prohibition, because it brings the fight into their local affairs.

6th. It is an unsafe principle to introduce into municipal matters, because it subordinates all business interests to the one issue of saloon or no saloon. If a first-class business man was nominated for the council, or mayoralty, who favored license, and a man poorly qualified be nominated for the same position who opposed license, prohibitionists, as a matter of principle, would be compelled to vote for the man poorly qualified, claiming that a less evil than licensed grog-shops. Each year this issue would be forced. Neighbors who should be friends become enemies, all because an issue of national character has by cowardly politicians been forced into municipal elections, to be fought over every year, with the knowledge that the municipality can never settle it, and the certainty that, though prohibition be adopted, the Legislature can change it at any time, without consulting the municipality.

7th. Prohibition can never be fairly tested by local option. Local option is determined by annual elections. No law changing the social customs of the people, and destroying a social institution, can be honestly tested in a single year.

8th. The people in the cities where the evil element controls, are entitled to protection by the State. Is it a truly brave man and leader who would say to the drunkard's wife and child in Cincinnati, "I regret that you live in the city, but as you do, I see no help for you, for the saloon-keepers control the city, and I am in favor of local option"? It is treason to God and humanity, to advocate the policy of the State turning the helpless in the great cities over into the hands of the drunkard-makers, by local option. Ohio is a State. Every home in it is entitled to State protection.

To advocate local option is to make the State a nonentity. We said this when, in obedience to the demands of the liquor ring, the Legislature turned the Christian Sunday over into the hands of the saloon-keepers to be destroyed, and we say it now, when it is proposed to desert the workers in our great cities, and turn their homes over to the vile elements.

When a State has passed a local option law, workers should work for local prohibition under it, not as an end, but as a means to accomplish an end, and this is best done by making the fight for State and National prohibition. The drunkard-makers always follow and take possession of the camp abandoned by prohibitionists as they advance. Where temperance men fought for license, drunkard-makers fought for free beer and whiskey; where temperance men fought for high license, drunkard-makers fought for low license; and when temperance men declared for State and

National prohibition, the drunkard-makers and their allies shouted for high license. In this reform the greater takes with the less. In a State where a hot and bitter war is waged for State prohibition, more towns are carried for local prohibition than in States where the fight is allowed to degenerate into a selfish local contest. Where a State has not local option, the worker is foolish indeed who will petition or work for it. The idea that a traffic can be made right in one part of the State, and wrong in another, is absurd.

The system of restriction by license for the evils of the traffic, has been thoroughly tried in nearly every State in the Union, and has everywhere proved itself utterly impracticable and defective. The only redeeming qualities of the system are the prohibitory features it contains, and these are rendered useless by the State license or permission, granted to the few, in consideration of the few sharing their profits with it. The State, by an attempt to regulate and restrict, admits that the traffic is one dangerous to the true interests of society. Of this fact society is thoroughly convinced, and the only sensible rule of State action is: If an institution is wholly evil, the State should outlaw and destroy it; if an institution is productive of both good and evil results, it is the duty of the State to license it and regulate it, so as to destroy the evil and promote the good. Possession is nine points of the law. License gives the traffic possession and creates a presumption that its rules are legal, and places upon the people the burden of disproving the presumption of innocence, and establishing the exception over the rule. The system is based on incorrect principles, is utterly impracticable, and never was and never will be enforced. There are more saloons selling liquor in Chicago without license under the license system than in any prohibitory city in the world, and this in addition to the licensed saloons. In this cultured city of Boston, I am informed by good authority, that there are more than one thousand places which sell liquor without license, in addition to over two thousand licensed places. In Nebraska, under high license, drug-stores almost equalling the saloons in number, sell liquors as a beverage without license to do so. The system, wherever tried, has been a failure, and it is utterly useless to waste any more time or money trying to make it work.

I am aware that some of my friends would say: "Men must organize to enforce law." Certainly, but who organize? Burke said: "When bad men conspire, good men must combine." The State, through its machinery, the Government, gives the only safe method of enforcing law, and only when a conspiracy exists of such formidable character as to prevent the operation of the Government, is a private organization of citizens justifiable. The Government is the State machinery to enforce law, and every tax-payer is taxed to pay for such enforcement. Public officers take oaths to enforce laws; if they do not do it, the statute which creates the office provides for the removal of the incumbent, and the remedy is not the organization to do the officer's work, but proceedings to remove and punish the officer for his neglect of duty. This people does not need or want two Governments to enforce the law. Demonstrate that two Governments, one public, one private, one supported by public tax, one by private contribution, are necessary to enforce law in this country, and you have proved our republican Government to be fatally weak and defective. You say to me: "It is your duty to give money to help enforce law." I answer: "I pay taxes to support a Government to enforce law, and if that is a failure, and cannot do so, the remedy is not to create a Government within itself, but to find what are its defects and remedy them."

If a law is defied, it is proof either that the law is not public opinion crystallized into public will; that bad men have conspired to thwart the will of the people; that bad men are in office; or that the law is defective and cannot be enforced by the ordinary machinery of Government. The remedy for the first condition is to repeal the law; for the second, is for good men to combine; for the third, is to arouse the vitality of the political system, so that bad men will be driven from office; for the fourth, to substitute a good law for the bad one. No man will claim that a license law is in advance of public opinion, so the first reason does not apply to this case. There is absolutely no proof that any conspiracy exists among the liquor men to defy the license laws except in a few places like Chicago. On the contrary, all of their great organizations have again and again declared in favor of license. That liquor-dealers all violate the license laws is certain; but they do it as individuals, not as parties to a conspiracy: consequently the second reason does not apply to license laws, although it does to prohibitory laws, for all the liquor organizations were brought into existence to destroy prohibition.

The real cause of the failure of license laws is, that the laws are defective and cannot be enforced, and that bad men are in office. The remedy, then, is plain: substitute a good for the bad law, and kick bad men out of office. When an officer neglects his duties, the remedy is not to do his work for him, but to punish him for his neglect of duty.

In Kansas, when corrupt officials refused to prosecute liquor outlaws, the Kansas State Temperance Union, led by the Hon. A. B. Campbell, did not undertake to perform the officers' work, but it commenced proceedings against the rebellious city government and corrupt officers. The result was, the corrupt officers were driven from power, public conscience was quickened, public faith in the power of the State to enforce its laws was strengthened, and the law will be enforced in that State. Every officer knows if he neglects his duty he will be proceeded against, and, if found guilty, removed from his position. The law is better enforced in the city of Quincy than in any other city in Massachusetts, and it is done by the Hon. Henry Foxton as an officer, not as a private citizen. In his own words, "The remedy is to elect good men to office," and he might have added, "to prosecute any officer who fails to do his duty."

Anything else is a quack remedy, which will injure and not help. No evidence of a conspiracy to defy the license law exists, and if the State cannot enforce the law against single individuals, it is positive the law is a fraud, and that all time spent trying to make it operate is wasted. Certainly no evidence of a conspiracy exists such as would justify private individuals organizing a government within the existing one to perform the works of the State, and try by extra constitutional means to make a law effective which the State, by a hundred years' trial, through the ordinary and legitimate channels of enforcement, has proved absolutely inoperative and bad. These statements made by those organizations, that the people are to blame for not enforcing the license law, are false. The trouble is with the law, not with the people. License laws have had a fair trial for more than a hundred years in this country, and have utterly failed to accomplish the object for which they were passed. The temperance men upheld these laws and gave money and time to make them operative, and only abandoned them after years of trial had proved them wholly useless. If the license system had proved practical, there would never have been a thought of prohibition; and these people who come around, and, with an air of "I'll tell you how to do it," inform temperance workers that they must enforce the license laws, simply air their ignorance of temperance history and their superficial knowledge of the reform. The license laws are fatally defective both in principle and construction, and the statement frequently made, "There is no need of further legislation until the present law is enforced," is idlest nonsense. Let me say again, the fault is with the law, not with the people. The blame laid on the people for not making a bad law operate well, shows a shallow thinker or a tricky demagogue who wants to lay the blame where it does not belong, and thereby have an excuse for not perfecting legislation. "If the law is in fault, then the law must be amended, and that will make the liquor-sellers mad; but if we can take the blame from off the law and place it on its enforcement, then we are safe," say the politicians; and many a law and order league has received support from these men for the purpose of creating a false public opinion as to the real cause of a failure, and thereby give a plausible reason for inaction. I object to a law and order league organized to enforce a license law as a license law, because no evidence exists that would justify its organization, and because it creates the false impression that the fault is with the people and not with the law. They constantly say: "Enforce the present law before you ask for more." As well have said in years gone by to the farmer: "You should make this old mower do good work before you get a new one." Would he not have answered: "Fool, if it did good work I should not want a new one. I have tried it for years, it does not half cut the grass, and I am not going to waste any more time or spoil any more work fussing with it." His answer is good sense. As well say: "We have tried for a century to cut down this tree with a beetle; it will not work, but we must make it work before we get an axe; we have tried for a century to dip up water with a sieve; it will not work, but we must make it work before we get a bucket," as to say: "License has failed to work well for a hundred years, but we must make it work well before we ask for prohibition." Away with such twaddle! If license works well, prohibition is unnecessary; and it is only because license has proved a failure that prohibition is sought. To hope to destroy the liquor traffic with license laws reminds me of the man who was nightly disturbed by the barking of his neighbor's dog. Night after night he endured until at last with patience exhausted, he jumped out of bed in his night-clothes and rushed out into the snow. He was gone for a long time, and his wife, alarmed, left her bed to look for him. Opening the door she saw him standing in the snow holding the dog. "What are you doing?" she cried. Through chattering teeth he answered, "I intend to hold this dog in the snow until I freeze him."

Every dollar given to make license work is virtually given to prove that prohibition is unnecessary. As a temperance man I formerly believed in license, and gave both time and money to make the system operate so as to destroy the evils of intemperance. The time and money were wasted. You ask me, "Will you help enforce a license law now?" Certainly, as a citizen I will do a citizen's duty in helping to enforce all laws on the statute-book, but as a temperance man I will not give one cent of money, or one minute of time in trying to make the license fraud operate as a temperance measure. As a temperance measure it has utterly failed, and the liquor men, recognizing that fact, have adopted the system as theirs, and work for and defend it. All efforts of temperance workers to make it a success simply deceive the people, and lead them to expect and hope that something good may come of the license system. Temperance workers should attack the false system, and demonstrate to the people how utterly worthless it is, for when the people are convinced of the fact they will demand effective legislation, and not until then. You ask, "Will not leagues organized to enforce license laws do good?" Yes, they will demonstrate to the people the fact that the license laws are so vicious, that the State cannot enforce them, even when assisted by a private organization of citizens.

The law and order league may be necessary to enforce a prohibitory law, because of the great organizations whose only purpose is to defy it; but I fear the effect of organizations, whose avowed purpose is to assume the duties which belong to the Government. Three of these private organizations frequently appear within the State, viz., the mob, the vigilance committee, the law and order league. The mob usurps all the power of the State, the vigilance committee take the power of the prosecuting attorney, court, and officers, and the law and order league assumes the duties of the prosecuting officers. That each in its time may do some good, many will claim; that the law and order league does accomplish good, no one will doubt; but it is doubtful if the good it does is commensurate with the evil it will do if it is to be more than a temporary organization, for, by assuming to do what the State should do, it impeaches the integrity of the State, and, by teaching the people to distrust the Government, weakens public faith and individual patriotism. If the law is defied by conspirators who are too strong for the State, the organization of good men should be to meet the specific danger, and should be limited to the existence of the necessity that called it into being, which will be the recovery by the State of the power to perform its own functions. If the failure of the law is caused, by what a celebrated writer calls "atony" of the State, viz., political indifference, inattention, and carelessness on the part of the citizens, by which active bad men are enabled to control matters, and place their tools in executive office, the only remedy is to arouse the political conscience and patriotism of the citizens, and thereby increase the vitality of the State; and in this case the law and order league is a positive injury, because it acts as a sedative, and individual conscience leads to a postponement of irksome political duties and increases the danger.

These organizations must have this effect, for the elector will say: "If we, to advance the interests of our party, elect a weak man, or a man pledged to the vile elements, the law and order league will stand behind the laws, and the country will not suffer. Another business man will say: "I have not time to attend to the political caucus, to work for men who will enforce the law; I will give the law and order league fifty dollars, and it will look after things." Another injury these organizations must do is to teach the public that the special law they are organized to enforce cannot be made operative by the State, which, if true, proves the law defective. They give the prosecuting attorney a chance to shirk his duty and to say: "You have an organization to enforce this law, and why don't you do it?" The laws dealing with the liquor traffic should stand with all other laws, and their enforcement be made a political, and, if necessary, a party issue. Tools of the liquor interest should be kicked out of power. The country has no use for men who work for party first and country afterwards; who say: "If the law is enforced it will hurt our party, we will lose the German vote." Such men are traitors to humanity, civilization, and liberty. I fear the results of any organization which will act as an excuse for lazy electors, and quiet their political consciences. What this country needs are not anæsthetics and narcotics to soothe the conscience of electors, but the burning iron of intelligent action, and the knife of righteous law freely used upon the loathsome ulcers on the body politic, by officers whose official tenure depends upon the honest enforcement of law, they having been elected by a party based on that principle. It is my opinion that if half the money and time and effort had been used to induce the people to apply the common-sense methods of political treatment for political disease, that have been spent in devising false remedies, and studying "how not to do it," there would not be an open bar-room in this country to-day. The fault is not with the masses, but with the leaders, or so-called moral guides of society. When the leaders of Kansas and Iowa and Ohio mustered up grit enough to lead the way, they found the masses true as steel. Our leaders have become stumbling-blocks whose inaction smacks strongly of cowardice, inability, or treason. The old worn-out cry: "The people are not educated up to the point," is an insult to the intelligence of the American nation. The State having failed to destroy the evils of the traffic by license, or by giving communities the power to deal with it, should now outlaw it, brand it as infamous, and the people should put in administrative offices men whose honor, conscience, and party fealty all say: "You must enforce the law." Cowards may cry: "You are going too fast," but every interest of home, humanity, civilization, and country demands immediate action. The last time I was at home, my little boy stood by me to say with a laugh, " Papa, I's almost a man." For a moment I was as happy as he, in the thought, and then this cloud came: " Every inch he grows taller, every day he grows older, brings nearer the time when he will go out on the streets of a city, that opens more schools to make him a devil, than it does to make him a man." I bowed my head and asked God to give me courage and muscle and nerve to stand in the front of the fight with my fellow-workers, and assist in freeing Nebraska from this curse before my boy should be in danger. "In a hurry?" How many more hearts must be broken? How many more babies be starved? How many more women must have the light of love and hope taken out of their lives? How many more fathers, and husbands, and sons must be offered up on the altar of this devilish license system, and other compromises, before this Christian people will stand shoulder to shoulder, and for wife and babies, and friends and home and country, cry: "Out of the way, cowards! This is a battle to the death, and may God defend the right!"

•

X.

COMPENSATION.

An Address delivered in Berkeley Street Methodist Church, Toronto Canada, Sunday, May 24, 1885.*

> PORTIA—" Then take thy bond, take thou thy pound of flesh;
> But in the cutting it, if thou dost shed
> One drop of Christian blood, thy lands and goods
> Are by the laws of Venice confiscate
> Unto the State of Venice."
> GRATIANO—" O, upright judge! Mark, Jew—O, learned judge!"
> SHYLOCK—" Is that the law?"
> PORTIA—" Thyself shall see the act;
> For as thou urgest justice, be assured
> Thou shalt have justice more than thou desirest."
> —*Shakespeare.*

IN discussing the rights, duties, and obligations of man, the primary laws of his being must be taken into consideration. Man is a social animal. Society is necessary for his development. When associated with his fellows he becomes the God-man; isolated, he becomes the brute-man. It is impossible to think of man out of society. It is wasting time to talk of man's entering society, because he was born in society, a part of society, and it is impossible for him to remain a man and exist outside of social influences. Government is made necessary by the fundamental laws of man's being. In society there must be an institution of justice, which shall determine the individual rights of the various members, in order that the weak may be protected against the strong, avarice restrained, vice and crime prevented, and man elevated. If we could think of man as existing by himself, we could think of him as a comparatively free and independent being—that is, free from all social restraint and law. Man in a country by himself can violate but

---

* The Canadian Parliament had been considering the question of indemnity to brewers and distillers. The R. W. G. Lodge met at Toronto this week, and Mr. Finch, who had just completed his first term as R. W. G. Templar, was invited to speak on "Compensation." —ED.

one class of laws: God's laws—God's laws which control his own being—God's laws written in nature—God's laws written in the revealed Word. When we think of man following the dictates of his own nature, and, as a social being, accepting the protection of society, profiting by the advantages which make him truly free, we must always consider him as an individual whose rights are limited by those of other individuals who have the same rights, duties, and obligations that he has himself. The privileges of free schools, churches, colleges, and the right to acquire property, to have life and property protected, all take with them corresponding obligations and duties, and give Government the right to say that in consideration of these social benefits, the individual shall so conduct himself and his business, as not to interfere with the rights of others. Government is an institution of justice, which determines obligations and duties, and punishes crime. It is a necessity growing out of man's nature and coexistent with him. Robbers defy all social law, but have among themselves an iron code. Pirates laugh at the authority of Government, but their own leader is a despot. Sailors mutiny and kill their captain, but they must at once form a government or they cannot navigate the ship. In Western towns of the United States, beyond the limits of organized government, men have again and again organized a court, and called "Judge Lynch" to the bench, to take the place of government.

Government, being necessary for man's development, and his protection, must have powers commensurate with its duties. If it is to administer justice, it must have power to protect the innocent and punish the guilty. It must be the supreme power, for any greater force will dominate it. If it is to protect others, it must have the power to protect itself. Self-preservation is the first law of life. Self-defence is a good defence, in the legal sense. Every individual has a right to defend himself from assault and injury. This defence must be conducted in accordance with the necessities of the case. If it is necessary, the one assaulted is justified in taking the life of the assailant, to protect his own life. This absolute right to life, inherent in every individual until he forfeits it to society, is inherent in the Government until the latter is repudiated by the people.*

In times of civil war, the Government may draft soldiers from the ranks of its citizens. Whether they want to go to battle or not, does not affect the right to send them. The Government is the judge of the necessities of the case, and if it deems their assistance necessary to save itself, it may take them from home, from wife and children, from business, dress them in uniform, strap the knapsack to their backs, put the guns in their hands, and march them to the battle-field, to be shot to death to preserve its own life. The right to life is absolute, yet the Government may arrest the individual who has killed, and, after trial, take the life of the offender. I am aware that some may urge—and I am of their opinion—that the right of the Government to take human life is governed by the same rule that governs the right of an individual to defend himself, viz.: the necessities of the case. No one can doubt that there was a time in the civilization of the world, when government, without prisons and reformatories to confine the vicious and criminal, was justified in killing men; but that right is limited by the necessities of the case, and I question whether any government with its present civilization and facilities for imprisonment, has a right to do what is in point of fact unnecessary. The right of the Government to protect its life, and the lives of the people, by taking individual life, is the same right by which society, acting through the Government, destroys trade to protect its life, and remove obstacles which prevent it from fulfilling its mission. Great Britain, on the first day of January, 1808, entirely abolished the slave trade. In most civilized countries the trade of the gambler has been prohibited by Government, and in the United States, after years of existence, the lottery trade was prohibited by most of the States for the same reason. When the trade is not wholly bad, Government regulates, restrains, and legislates so as to destroy its bad tendencies and develop good results. It prevents the employment of children under a certain age in factories. It compels manufacturers to provide fire escapes for their employés. It compels the removal of slaughter-houses and soap-factories in cities, and prevents the keeping of gunpowder in more than certain quantities in populous centres. The power of the United States Government in such matters is clearly stated by Chief Justice Shaw, of Massachusetts, in the leading case of Fisher against McGirr: "*We have no doubt that it is competent for the Legislature to declare the possession of certain articles of property, either absolutely or when held in particular places or under particular circumstances, to be unlawful because they would be injurious, dangerous, or obnoxious, and by due process of law, by proceedings in rem to provide both for the abatement of the offence by the seizure and confiscation of the property, by the removal, sale, or destruction of obnoxious articles.*" In the case of the State, Sanford, Relator, *vs.* the Court of Common Pleas, New Jersey, Van Syckles, Justice, said: "*While alcoholic stimulants are recognized as property and entitled to the protection of the law, ownership in them is subject to such restrictions as are demanded by the highest considerations of public expediency. Such enactments are regarded as police regulations, established for the prevention of crime and pauperism, for the abatement of nuisances, and the protection of public health and safety. They are a just restraint of the injurious use of property.*"

In England, the Court of the King's Bench has decided: "*There are many cases in which individuals sustain an injury for which the law gives no action: for instance, pulling down houses or raising bulwarks for the preservation and defence of the kingdom against the king's enemies. The civil law writers say that the individuals who suffer have the right to report to the public for satisfaction, but no one ever thought that the common law gave an action against the individual who pulled down the house. This is one of the cases to which the maxim applies,* 'Salus populi suprema est lex.'"

In the United States, upon the adoption of the Fourteenth Amendment to the National Constitution, it was claimed the rule was changed. The amendment is as follows:

"All persons born or naturalized in the United States, and subject to the jurisdiction thereof, are citizens of the United States and of the State wherein they reside. No State shall make or enforce any law which shall abridge the privileges or immunities of citizens of the United States ; *nor shall any State deprive any person of life, liberty, or property, without due process of law,* nor deny to any person within its jurisdiction the equal protection of the laws."

The United States Supreme Court construed this amendment in December, 1872, in the Louisiana Slaughter-house cases.

By act of the Legislature a corporation was created and given the exclusive privilege for twenty-five years, to have and maintain slaughter-houses, landings for cattle, and yards for inclosing cattle intended for slaughter, within a territorial area of 1,154 square miles around and about and including the city of New Orleans, and *prohibited* all other persons from building, keeping, or having slaughter-houses, landings for cattle and yards for cattle intended for sale or slaughter, within those limits.

The effect of this act was thus stated by an able attorney:

"The only question, then, is this : 'When a State passes a law depriving a thousand people, who have acquired valuable property, and who, through its instrumentality, are engaged in an honest and necessary business, which they understand, of their right to use such, their own property, and to labor in such, their honest and necessary business, and gives a monopoly, embracing the whole subject, including the right to labor in such business, to seventeen other persons—whether the State has abridged any of the privileges or immunities of these one thousand persons?' "

The Supreme Court held "that this grant of exclusive right or privilege .... was a police regulation for the health and comfort of the people, within the power of the State Legislatures, unaffected by the Constitution of the United States previous to the adoption of the Thirteenth and Fourteenth Articles of Amendment. Such power is not forbidden by the Thirteenth Article and by the first section of the Fourteenth Article."

The power of the Government to prohibit without compensation was not removed by the amendments, but remains in the Government to be used as circumstances require.

In Canada, to-day, the power of Government is being exerted to destroy a great trade. The men engaged in it make no defence of the trade as a social institution, but demand, in consideration of its destruction, that the Government shall compensate them for the property, which will be injured by prohibiting its criminal use. By prohibition of the alcoholic traffic the Government does not destroy property, or take private property for public use. It simply prevents private parties from using their property to the injury of the public. In discussing the equity of this claim of the liquor-dealers, it will be better for us to examine when and how Government grants compensation, and whether this demand of the liquor-dealers is sustained by precedent or equity.

It is certain: 1st. Such compensation can only be secured by special enactment concurrent with the prohibitory law. In Canada, as well as in Great Britain, Parliament is supreme. The right of the subject to compensation is entirely statutory.

"*We have no law or general principle by which compensation is to be given; in such cases it is entirely statutory.*" (Sir Montague E. Smith, in Drummond *vs.* City of Montreal, House of Lords' case in 1876.) From this it follows that if the Parliament of Canada should at any time elect to suppress any business, or expropriate private property for public use or public good, without providing for compensation to the owners of such business or property, the latter would seek in vain to obtain damages from the courts, and the books would fail to produce a single case where a precedent for such an action exists. The Governor and Company of the British Cast Plate Manu. *vs.* Meredith *et al.*, 14 Term Reports, 794, decided in the Court of the King's Bench in 1792, and Dungey *vs.* The Mayor and Cor. of London, 3 Law Journal (C. P.), 298, are both in support of this principle. In the first-named the defendants, who were Commissioners under a Paving Act, in the exercise of the powers given to them by the Act, raised a pavement two feet and a half in front of the plaintiff company's premises, causing them substantial injury. In deciding this case, Lord Kenyon,

Chief Justice, said: *"If this action could be maintained, every Turnpike Act, Paving Act, and Navigation Act, would give rise to an infinity of actions. If the legislature think it necessary, as they do in many cases, they enable the commissioners to award satisfaction to the individuals who happen to suffer; but if there be no such power, the parties are without remedy, provided the commissioners do not exceed their jurisdiction. . . . . Some individuals suffer an inconvenience under all these Acts of Parliament, but the interests of individuals must give way to the accommodation of the public."*

The second case cited is a much later one, in which the principles, as laid down in the older case, are reviewed and confirmed.

From these decisions it may also be stated: 2d. Parliament has a right to refuse such compensation. In this respect there is a wide difference between English and American legislation. The Constitution of the United States expressly provides that private property shall not be taken for public use without just compensation. Most of the States have a similar provision. (Amd. Com. U.S., Art. V., March, 1789.) A point is sought to be made in Canada by quoting Chancellor Kent, who says: *"The settled and fundamental doctrine is that Government has no right to take private property for public purposes without giving a just compensation; and it seems to be necessarily implied that the indemnity should, in cases which will admit of it, be previously and equitably ascertained and be ready concurrently in point of time with the actual exercise of the right of eminent domain."* (Kent's Com., Vol. II., p. 409, note f.)

It will be observed that Judge Kent speaks of taking property for public use. He does not speak of preventing the injurious use of property. The American law given by the Supreme Court of the United States, is: *" The trade in alcoholic drinks being lawful, and the capital employed in it being duly protected by law, the legislature then steps in, and, by an enactment based on general reasons of public utility, annihilates the traffic, destroys altogether the employment, and reduces to a nominal value the property on hand; even the keeping of that for the purpose of sale becomes a criminal offence, and without any change whatever in his own conduct or employment, the merchant of yesterday becomes the criminal of to-day, and the very building in which he lives and conducts the business which to that moment was lawful, becomes the subject of legal proceedings if the statute so declare, and liable to be proceeded against for forfeiture. A statute which can do this must be justified upon the highest reasons of public benefit; but whether satisfactory or not, the reasons address themselves exclusively to the legislative wisdom."*

British governments have never recognized the principle stated by Judge Kent in its entirety, but have invariably exercised their discretion in the matter of granting compensation, and in the few cases where the courts have been asked to interfere, the judges have unhesitatingly refused to dictate to Parliament, but have confined themselves to interpreting the law as it stood.

3d. Should Parliament neglect to provide for compensation, no injustice will be done, and the precedents in similar cases will be followed. There being no common law or constitutional right for the liquor-dealers to grasp, they must come and present their claims for compensation before the Prohibitory Act is passed, as by standing by and failing to claim, they will waive any right they may now possess. While the power of Parliament is supreme, it has always been a leading principle of its enactments, that they should be to a large extent guided and controlled by ancient precedent, and many sensible and excellent principles which from their great value in directing the exercise of legislative power have acquired almost the force of law. The principle laid down by Kent is among these, and English Parliaments have always been careful to do full justice to the owners of property whenever they have been entitled to such. English and Canadian statutes abound in provisions for compensation, based upon this very principle. It is not proposed, however, to appropriate these breweries, distilleries, warehouses, etc., for public purposes, but to entirely destroy their right to exist for the purpose of furnishing alcoholic drinks as beverages. The penalty for violation, in all probability, will be forfeiture and imprisonment. Parliament has frequently seen fit to enact that certain trades cease to be prosecuted in the country (for the public good), and in no case have the courts held that Parliament was bound to provide for compensation for those who suffered pecuniary loss. In a few instances provision was made at the time the law was passed, and the reports of English cases do not cite a single instance where a private individual sought to recover against the Crown. There are numerous cases where courts have interpreted the statute and have decided what Parliament intended. In Rex *vs.* Watts, 2 Carrington and Payne, 466, the Court of the King's Bench decided with reference to a business, previously declared a nuisance in a certain locality by statute. It was held that a person violating the Act, was not entitled to damages or compensation at that time, even if the Act itself provided for compensation.

Abbott, Chief Justice, said: "*If the defendant's slaughtering-house was so conducted as to be a public nuisance at common law, the parish might at any time have caused it to be removed, and I am clearly of opinion that in this case it was so conducted as to be a nuisance at common law, and that the defendant would not have been, and is not, entitled to any compensation.*" It will be observed that this case, like all the others reported respecting nuisances, turned entirely upon the statute and the ordinary common law definition of a nuisance. In dealing with this question, therefore, no advantage can be obtained from consulting the decisions of courts. First principles, and an examination of what Parliaments have formerly done, must be the sole factors in presenting the claims of the liquor business. In the latter connection, reference is made to the abolition of slavery by the English Parliament in 1833, and the advocates of compensation for liquor-dealers seek to strengthen their position by showing what was then done. Let us go back, however, a few years and a parallel will be found to the question of prohibition as it stands to-day. In 1806 an Act was passed prohibiting all British subjects from engaging in the slave trade, either for the supply of conquered colonies or of foreign possessions. A large amount of capital was at that time invested in this very profitable trade, but the question of compensation was never mooted, and when, on the first of January, 1808, the trade was entirely abolished, not a shilling was paid the traders for their loss, but Parliament in 1811 followed the former laws with an Act making participation in the slave trade a felony, punishable with fourteen years' transportation, and in 1824 it was declared to be piracy, punishable with death. Thus was the business of dealing in slaves dealt with, and the above was the kind of compensation the dealers received. If the liquor-dealers insist on the Canadian Parliament dealing with them as the British Government did with the slave-traders, prohibitionists ought not to object. When, however, in 1833, it was decided to emancipate the slaves in the West Indies, a new element had to be considered, namely, the effect of such an action on the business of the Colonies and Britain.

"*If by his manufacture a man creates an appreciable nuisance to those around him, his act becomes wrongful.*" (Mayne on Damages, page 8.) If Parliament then decides that the manufacture of liquor must be suppressed because it is an injury to the public, every principle of common law, and every precedent to be found in the reports of parliamentary proceedings, support the contention that the liquor-dealers have no just rights to compensation. For it is settled: 1st. Government never grants compensation for diminution of the value of property by the prohibition of its injurious or wrongful use. 2d. Where Government grants compensation for property taken or destroyed, it never takes into consideration indirect damages. Though the British Government granted financial aid to the owners of liberated slaves, it wholly ignored all indirect damage done by emancipation. But it may be advantageous for us to examine fully into the equity of this particular case. It must be borne in mind that the retail trade exists by license granted annually, and the wholesale trade by sufferance. Under the Canada license system, the common law right to sell liquor is destroyed by police regulation. In other words, no individual can compel the granting of a license. A man in Toronto may build a fine hotel, comply with every requirement of the law, and still the commissioners have the right to refuse him license, and no action will lie to compel them to issue a license. If they deem it wise, they may issue a license, but it is for them to say who shall have a license and how many licenses shall be granted. The license granted is for one year. At the end of the year there is no guarantee, either expressed or implied, that it will be renewed. A man leases a farm for a year, and during the year buys farm machinery and stock. At the end of the year the owner of the farm refuses to renew the lease. The property purchased by the lessor being useless to him, will depreciate in the forced sale, but the owner of the farm would not be responsible for the depreciation in value, because the man who leased the farm, knew his lease was for but a single year. The lease or license given retail liquor-dealers to set up their drunkard-factories in a city, is an annual lease, and, when their lease has expired, for them to claim compensation for the tools with which they have been injuring the public, simply because they have been prohibited from continuing to use the tools for that specific purpose, is, to express it mildly, a preposterous claim. In examining the claim of the drunkard-makers, the rule of the courts must be the rule of the people, viz.: "A man who comes into court demanding equity must come with clean hands and a pure heart before God." The liquor business does not and cannot come with clean hands. The suppression of the liquor trade is caused by its own crimes. When the liquor trade was introduced into this country, it was admitted on the same social, civil, and religious basis as all trades. There was a time in the history of Canada when it was as religious to sell rum as it was to sell molasses, and I presume a majority of the people, if they could only have had one of the two, would have taken the rum. I think the fact is that they usually took them together. As late as 1813, a majority of all the distillers of America were members of the Christian Church. As late as 1820, a majority of all the liquor-sellers were members of the churches. As late as 1835, the Rev. George B. Cheever was arrested in the city of Salem, Mass., for libel, and sent to jail for daring to maintain, in that celebrated cartoon, "Deacon Giles' Distillery," that the business of selling rum and peddling Bibles, was not consistent with the professed Christian life of a deacon of the Church. As four boys, born in the same family, are given the same opportunities to become honorable men, loved and respected by their fellows, so the dry-goods trade, grocery trade, liquor trade, and the Church were, at the organization of society on this continent, given the same chances to make honorable records, and endear themselves to the people. The road before the liquor trade was broad, and the sky over its head bright. It was given every chance to endear itself to this people and make an honest record. Everybody was its friend, nobody was its enemy. Liquor was used at the raising, at the log-rolling, at the corn-husking, at the wedding, in social life — everywhere and under all circumstances. With this start, what has the liquor trade done for itself and for the society that nursed and protected it? One day while I was sitting in front of the Commercial Hotel in the city of Lincoln, Nebraska, talking with a prominent liquor-dealer, a couple of little girls ran laughing by us. Touching me on the shoulder, he said: "Those are my girls." I said, "Pretty girls." He said, "I think they are." After a moment's silence, he said: "I am going to go out of this liquor business pretty soon," and when I told him I was glad to hear it, and asked him for his reasons, he answered: "Not because I think it all bad, as you do, but because my girls will soon be women, and when my girls grow up, I want them to go in good society, and a whiskey-seller's girls cannot go in good society in this city." He simply told the truth. The social rule which makes liquor-sellers and their families social outcasts, is the rule generally observed throughout the United States. Why is it? It was not always so. Do you believe that if the liquor business had made good men and happy women and children it would meet with any greater opposition to-day than the dry-goods trade or the grocer's trade? Do you believe that if the liquor-seller had made his customer a better man, a kinder husband, a more loving father, society would treat him any differently than it treats the clergyman or merchant? The Christian Church has been tried on this continent by its social, its civil, and its business record. After all these years of trial, it never had a stronger hold on the hearts of intelligent people than it has to-day. The dry-goods trade has been tried, and after a record of a hundred years, it is as respectable to sell dry-goods now as then. The grocers' trade has been tried, and has lost neither its character nor standing. The liquor trade has been tried, and is it as respectable to sell liquor now as it was a hundred years ago? Is it as respectable to drink it as it was a hundred years ago? Is it as respectable to make liquor? If not, why not? What is the matter with this villainous traffic? You know that from the day society welcomed it to the marts of commerce, it has deliberately and maliciously buried its arms to the elbows in the blood of the best interests of a free people. These crimes have not been committed in moments of passion, in moments of excitement, but after coolly and deliberately figuring the profits to come from such ruin, and paying for the privilege of carrying forward the work. Its record in Canada is a record of crime, vice, sorrow, misery, wretchedness, agony. On this record it has been tried, and the prohibitory law is simply a sentence for crime committed.

Crimes forfeit rights. The right to life and liberty is the primary and greatest right; but let a man murder another and he is arrested and brought into court for trial. Suppose his solicitor would object: "This man is a free-born British subject, entitled to life and liberty, and I demand his release." His Lordship would probably answer: "This man is now charged with crime and has two rights: the right to a fair trial in accordance with the forms of law; if convicted, the right to be executed in accordance with the method prescribed by law." So to-day the liquor business is indicted for social crimes, and is entitled to a fair trial, and punishment commensurate with its crimes.

I come to your city, buy a lot, and this summer erect a slaughter-house. During the cold weather of next winter I use it as a slaughter-house; but, when the warm air comes, breathing up from the southland, and the place becomes a nuisance, the city officers would call on me and demand that the building be disinfected, and that I cease using it for such purposes. If I should protest, "I own this building," they would answer, "We are aware of the fact. That is the reason we come to you. If another man had owned the property we would have called on him." I answer: "I have the deed of this property. My fortune is invested here. I make my living by slaughtering cattle. If you drive me out of here you will ruin me. I pay my taxes and behave myself. Why are you here disturbing me?" The answer would be: "We should not have thought of disturbing you if the smell of your building had not disturbed people and injured the public health of this city. You, by your own act, by your own business, have made your place a public nuisance; now disinfect this building and stop your work." Who would be to blame for that result? Not society who acted, but I who compelled society to act. Bear in mind that it is the thief who compels society to arrest him, that it is the murderer who compels society to punish him; that it is the liquor trade that has compelled society to proceed against it. Society assails the liquor trade to protect itself, and in dealing with the liquor trade has ever been governed by the law of self-defence, viz., that the means used must be in proportion to the danger to be overcome. It has tried mild measures in dealing with these criminals, before proceeding to extreme measures. Low license, high license, and civil damages have all been tried; but despite these warnings, the traffic has continued the same malicious, hardened criminal. All other remedies have failed. No man doubts that if low license had removed the vicious character of this trade, high license would never have been adopted. If high license and local option had accomplished the results desired by society, the death sentence, in the form of prohibition, would never have been passed. Notwithstanding this self-evident fact, it now seeks to use the forbearance of Government, as the basis for its present demand for compensation. Its friends urge that the Government, by license, gave it a right to exist. There is not a lawyer in Canada who does not know that the liquor license law is a police regulation, passed to regulate and restrain the traffic, not for the purpose of raising revenue from it. The liquor traffic, before the days of license, existed by common law right. Repeal the license law, and the right to sell liquor everywhere would be universal. License does not create rights; it simply aims to curtail and limit pre-existing rights to prevent public injury. The license fee is a police fine assessed in advance for the purpose of regulation, not for revenue. License is partial prohibition. By it Government has simply kept in view the law of self-defence: "The force and means used must be proportionate to the danger." This attempted regulation never created a right, nor indicated approval of a system, any more than for a man to seize an assailant and try to hold him, would indicate approval of the assault, because he did not kill the assailant. The Government has shown its desire to do justice, by trying all other methods before killing the traffic, and, by chaining and fining the criminal, has not become its partner or responsible for its crimes. The common law right of the traffic to exist was disturbed because of its criminal use. The traffic refused to heed the warning, and has compelled Government to destroy the right. Had it contained an element of decency it might have lived. But it has defied every law, and gone on with its work of debauching and degrading public morals. It stands in the court of the people, surrounded by the evidence of its infamous crimes, and asks for justice, and justice it shall have. Its demand is that the people who have been compelled to prohibit it shall pay its representatives for the tools with which they are carrying on the infamous work, to stop which the Government prohibits the traffic. My wife has a property interest in my brain, nerve, and muscle. If I should be killed on the railroad she could collect from the company damages for injury done her rights; but if I should commit murder, and society should hang me, she could not collect damage from the Government, because the hanging was caused by my wrongful act. If the Government had taken the property of the liquor trade for public purposes, or prevented its use in a certain way because it desired to promote the public good; if this had been done when the liquor interest was benefiting society, then compensation would have been just; but the Government does not prohibit liquor because it prefers that method of dealing with it; it prohibits the liquor traffic, because it is compelled to do so to promote public good. Prohibition is the result of the wrongful act of the liquor trade, and the liquor interest cannot demand compensation for something compelled by its own wrongful act. This principle has been recognized in all the restrictive measures adopted with a view to reform this criminal traffic. When your Government limited the number of liquor-dealers by license, those driven out of the traffic had no thought of demanding compensation for damages done to their property. If it was right for the Government to destroy one-half of the liquor-shops of the country without compensating the dealers, and the brewers and distillers who were injured by the reduction of the trade, who will dare urge that it shall compensate when the remainder of the trade are treated in the same way, for continuing the very crimes for which the others were suppressed? No man questions the right of the Government to regulate the number of liquor places in each city and town in the province, and no one would dare claim compensation, if the Government should deem such regulation necessary. The restrictive statute would injure the entire liquor trade; but the liquor men never remonstrate until the last one is suppressed, and when the last one is suppressed for exactly the same reasons that led to the suppression of the others, where is the justice of the claim for compensation? I know it is urged that Great Britain compensated slave-owners when she emancipated slaves, but the distinction should be borne in mind, that in one case she destroyed property, in the other case Canada simply proposes to prohibit wrongful uses of property. The slave-owner had a property interest which he might sell. No liquor-dealer can sell his license. License is not property. If the slave-owners had used their slaves for the purpose of robbing and plundering, and the

Government had prohibited such uses of property, does any one suppose that compensation would have been granted? Suppose the only way in which the slaves could have been made profitable to the owners had been by using them as pirates and robbers, and the Government had absolutely prohibited such use, would the demand for compensation have been sustained because the slave would have been diminished in value? To claim that the Government should compensate criminals because it had suffered them to commit crime, would be to claim that Great Britain would pay for the ships and property of every negro-stealer, who was for long years suffered to carry on his terrible trade, under the protection of a free flag. The same logic would compel France to pay for the furniture in every house of prostitution, when, restrictive measures having failed, prostitution is prohibited. When a Government is compelled by the social results of lotteries to prohibit lotteries, the same logic would compel the Government to purchase the wheels, dice, and boxes. To examine more fully into the merits of this case, let us see what it is these men have been prohibited from doing, to what uses the property for which they demand compensation has been put. I was standing at the corner of Reade Street and Broadway, in the city of New York, last October, chatting with a friend. On my way from the elevated railway station I had purchased an apple, which I was eating. Something attracted my attention, and looking down at my side I saw a boy, a genuine street arab. His coat had evidently been made for a full-grown man, and unless his feet had grown rapidly, his boots were never made for him. As I looked down at him he looked up to me and said, "Say, Mister, would you mind giving me the core of that apple when you get it eat?" At first I was tempted to laugh, but as I looked at the pinched face and ragged clothes the temptation disappeared, and I asked my friend and the boy to come with me to the apple-stand, where I told the proprietor to give the boy all the apples he could carry off in his pockets. The boy, half doubtingly, looked up to me and said: "You are not a-fooling, are you, Mister?" When I assured him I was not fooling, it would have done you good to have seen how many pockets that boy had. He seemed to be a sort of universal pocket. The holes in the knees of his pants certainly served him one good turn, for I saw him put several apples through the holes, between the lining and the outside, using the bottom of the trouser leg as the bottom of the pocket. As he went away with an apple in each hand my friend said to me: "I am going to pay for those apples, because I have enjoyed them more than any I have eaten in five years." An after-investigation showed that the father of the boy was a drunkard.

One night last February, returning from Cambridge, Mass., to the city of Boston, accompanied by my friend Mr. Mitchell, we left the street-car at the corner of Temple Place and Washington Street. A little boy ran up to us, holding in his baby hands a paper, saying, "Please buy the last paper." He was not as tall as the five-year-old in my own home. Mr. Mitchell said, with a tremble in his voice, "He is not as big as my baby," meaning his youngest boy. In the bitter cold of a winter's night the little fellow stood pleading for us to "buy the last paper." It was the same story—drunken parents.

If I have any one affection greater than others it is love for babies. Not the big babies who whine, "The liquor traffic ought to be stopped, but we can't stop it." I have neither respect nor love for them. Little babies are the ones I love. There is something in the honest eyes and dimpled form of a baby, that has always had a strong fascination for me. A year ago, in Boston, I saw a baby in a wretched tenement-house on North Street. It was not such a baby as I should see in some of your homes—with laughing eyes, cheeks sinking into dimples as he laughed, while with little hands he held his big toe and tried to get it into his mouth. It was a baby with hands like bird's claws, face pinched and purple, that lay moaning and restless in its sleep. I asked the gentleman accompanying me what was the matter with the baby. He answered, "Starving. If you doubt it, look at the mother." It was true. Baby was dying because mother was dying. He assisted her. He was a city missionary. As we left the place, I said: "Madam, where is your husband?" She replied, "In the city prison, serving out a sentence for being drunk and disorderly." I am aware that the liquor-dealers will claim that the drunkard is as responsible as the seller, but I stand here to maintain, that it is the duty of Government to protect the wife and baby, from the crimes both of the liquor-sellers and the drunkard. If there is anything which should make the hot blood rush in surging torrents through the veins of any man, it is the sight of a woman with a baby in her arms, injured, maltreated, and starved by the accursed liquor traffic.

If the argument that the drinker is alone responsible for the results of the liquor traffic is good, it would justify every gambler, courtesan, and lottery-dealer, for the customers of each of these death-traps patronize them of their own free will.

No one will doubt that it is the duty of a State to protect its women and children. If any one will injure a baby, it is the duty of the Government to protect it, even if it is necessary to put bayonets around its cradle-bed for that purpose. Canada is at last moving forward to give this protection.

The men who have grown rich by what accomplishes the ruin of women and the degradation of children, demand, if they are no longer to be allowed to carry forward this crime against humanity and civilization, that they shall be compensated for the tools with which the crime has been committed, because they cannot make as much money by using them in an honorable business as they have made by using them in ruining the homes of this Dominion.

Justice! Yes, give them justice. Surely every man must be anxious to give the liquor trade justice. The men in the business are men of intelligence and good judgment. They knew the results of the trade before they entered it. No one compelled them to enter. Of their own free will they took up the fearful work, simply to make money out of the wretchedness and misery of others. They are responsible as social units for their social acts. They would not be in the business if it was not for the fact that it is the most profitable of trades. When one knows the actuating motives of the drunkard-makers, and then looks at the destitute homes and ruined families of their victims, the only conclusion can be is that, to do justice, would be to repeat the Shylock verdict, "Confiscation of property and death." But the wronged ones in this case are more merciful even than in that case, for they only ask that the guilty shall be stopped from continuing their crimes, and are willing to leave with them all their ill-gotten gains. The liquor men ought to be happy to be let off so easily. The people only ask a verdict on the record that this accursed trade has made for itself. The ruined homes, the degraded men, the broken-hearted wives and beggared children, made by the liquor-dealers in their attempt to amass wealth, are witnesses in the case. The results of the traffic as shown by the police court, the almshouse, the penitentiary, and the scaffold, must all be considered in making up a verdict. Try it as you try a man, as you try a woman, as you try a boy, as you try a girl. If you find that the men representing the traffic stand in the court of the people with clean hands and pure hearts before God, and that their property has been taken for no wrong of their own, pay them every cent of the amount to which it has been damaged; but if you find that the traffic was admitted to the country as a friend, given every opportunity to be decent, and that now, like an adder warmed to life in the bosom of its benefactor, would sting to death the life that warmed it into existence; if you find it has ruined public morals, degraded public virtue, lowered public intelligence; if you find that its representatives have sold liquor to minors, to drunkards, and to Indians; if you find that in their efforts they have not heeded the prayers of the wife, of the mother, of the children; if you find that they have defied all restriction, and when warned by gentle measures, continued their accursed work, until it has become necessary for the Government to suppress their business for the public good, then the demand of the liquor-sellers should be treated with the loathing and contempt which such a crime and villainy excites in the breasts of honest men!

XI.

THE PRACTICABILITY OF THE MOVEMENT PROVED BY ITS SUCCESS.

An Address delivered at Decatur, Illinois, March 30, 1882.

LADIES AND GENTLEMEN: The liquor traffic in this country is based upon ignorance and superstition. The acme of liquor-drinking civilization is debauchery, vice, and crime. The hope of the temperance workers must be the moral, social, and intellectual elevation of the race. The two armies now arrayed in this country, are,—on the one hand, all that is debauched and vile; and on the other, the highest hopes of the world. A battle-field such as this must be interesting to every lover of his race, to every friend of humanity, and to every one who believes in a future life, and in a personal God. Ay, and it must be interesting to those who only aspire to see, here in this life, the intellectual and physical development of the race, the curbing of animal passions, and the restraining of vicious ignorance.

Members of temperance organizations and societies recently formed, into whose minds the light has come in these latter days, in the fresh enthusiasm of souls just brought from semi-darkness into the light, exclaim: "The principles underlying the reform are self-evident. The criminal results of the traffic are not denied. It stands a criminal without a defender. Why is it not overthrown?" To some, this impatience, and the loss of faith in humanity which always results from it, may seem reasonable; but to me, looking from the stand-point of one of the oldest temperance organizations in this country—the Independent Order of Good Templars—which dates its labors from the year

1852, the reasons why the reform moves so slowly are self-evident.

It is a slow work to lift humanity from a lower to a higher plane of civilization; it is a difficult work to disabuse the public mind of delusions long cherished, and of ideas which are strengthened by their avarice, by their intemperance, and by their strong party affiliations.

The impressions made upon the brain in childhood are never effaced. In the language of one of the greatest of living scientists, "Scars on the brain can be removed only by the destruction of the brain." Teach a child a lie as a truth, and such instruction will influence him, even after manhood's years have convinced him of its absurdity. Ask the old men in this audience at what period in their lives they received lasting impressions most readily; they will answer, "The mind retains most clearly the details of events which transpired when we were between the ages of five and thirty years."

I visited an old lady in my native State, New York, some years ago, who was ninety-two years of age. I was sitting and chatting with her, when, interrupting me, she said: "I want to tell you something," and then she told me of a wedding that had occurred fifty-seven years before. She described how the groom was dressed, told who were there, gave their names readily, and related the details of the affair as minutely and accurately as though she had been reading from a book. When she had finished her story, I said to her, "Mother Stewart, will you tell me what you had for dinner yesterday?" Putting her hand up to her head, she said: "Law, ain't it strange how we forget!" She could remember accurately, distinctly, things which had occurred fifty-seven years before, but what had occurred only twenty-four hours previously had left no impression on the brain. The brain of childhood receives impressions and retains them.

Once, while visiting an insane asylum in the East, I asked the superintendent if he would allow me to see a certain Methodist minister. I had known the minister in my home as one of the best and truest of men, who, by overwork, physical and mental, had wrecked himself and become a raving maniac. The superintendent of the asylum said: "You will not want to see him"; but I said, "Yes," and he took me to the ward of the asylum known as "Bedlam ward." Unlocking the door of one of the cells, we entered. The inmate was locked up in the "strait-jacket," to prevent him from injuring himself. As we entered the room, the most terrible, the most vile, the most vulgar oaths which I ever heard in my life, came from his lips. I touched the superintendent, and told him I did not wish to stay longer. Going down the corridor, I turned to the superintendent and said to him: "What can this mean? When I knew that man he was one of the grandest Christians—true, noble, and good in every respect; and now, to hear such vile language coming from him surprises me." Said the superintendent: "He learned to swear when a boy. The impressions made on his mind during that period of his life when the brain most readily received impressions, now that reason is dethroned, become the governing power and control the thoughts and speech. In this asylum we can almost uniformly tell what have been the habits, the customs, and abuses of insane people when they were children. The brain at such times receives impressions readily; the impressions are permanent; if they have indulged in vile practices, or used terrible language, the dethronement of reason and intelligent consciousness will give the early impressions and habits control of the mind. If people could only realize, as we have learned here, that it is the education of the children which moulds the character for life, the race would be better off."

Not only are these impressions permanent, but, as we grow older—although we may in a measure disabuse our minds of belief in them—they are ever present to bless or curse us to a very great extent.

My grandmother believed in ghosts, sincerely, honestly—she believed in them just as sincerely as she trusted in the Bible—and I think she was one of the grandest Christians I have ever known. She would frequently entertain us children—we were seven in number—by gathering us around her and telling us ghost stories. She would tell these stories in a way which made every one of us believe them. My grandmother never lied; knowing her veracity, knowing her integrity, knowing her regard for the strict letter of the truth, we believed all she said. She knew there were ghosts; she had seen them, heard them, and we believed her. I grew to boyhood. I never passed a cemetery at night but I gave more attention to that side of the road than to the other, and when I had passed by the graveyard preferred running to walking. When young manhood came, and I went to college, I never entered the dissecting-room and turned down the cover from a cadaver to commence work, without a feeling of horror and fear—that feeling of terrible awe which I had felt in my boyhood days while listening to my grandmother's stories. It intimidated me, and made the hand nervous. I tell you to-night I do not believe in ghosts; and yet, honestly, I scarcely know whether I do or not. The teaching of my boyhood says, "There are ghosts"; the teaching of my after-years says, "The belief is nonsense"; reason and intelligence say, "It is absurd and foolish"; but childish impressions say, "It is true."

I was crossing a divide on horseback in my own State some months ago, late at night. Tired and worn I allowed my pony to have his own way. I presume I was half asleep. The pony was picking his way along the bank of a draw (in this country it would be called a ravine), when he stumbled and nearly fell. I do not know how long I had been riding in that semi-conscious condition when aroused by the jolt. A rapid glance showed me that I was in an Indian burying-ground. The shape of the mounds told what tribe had buried their dead there, and I knew they were hundreds of miles away in the Indian Territory. I was well mounted and armed—certainly not afraid—yet, as I rode through the graveyard and down the slope on the other side, something cold started at the region of the heart, and went down toward my toes, then up toward my head, and my hair became wonderfully strong, and my hat wonderfully light. The first look was a look back over my shoulder. I stopped the horse and asked myself the question, "Why look back?" and I had to admit I had looked back for ghosts.

So I say to you, I do not believe in ghosts, and I do believe in ghosts. The teaching of my boyhood days will go with me to my grave; although I may study, although I may work, although I may do everything I can to overcome it, I am sure that in moments of weakness, of suspense, perhaps of fear, the early teachings will always come up and govern, to a certain extent, the inclinations and the impulses of the heart.

You older men know this is true of your own experience. If, when young, you were taught to plant your corn at a certain time of the moon's changes, you will still plant it at that time. If you were taught that a dog standing with his head toward a house and barking at midnight, meant death in the family within a year, you will never feel comfortable when hearing the dog bark, and seeing him in such a position. If, when a boy, you were taught to put an angleworm on the hook, and then to spit on the worm to make the fish bite more readily, you will spit on the worm yet, though for your life you cannot tell whether fish like tobacco-juice or pure saliva.

From these natural laws and tendencies of the brain we must draw our conclusions. If we would understand the conditions of this reform, and what we have to overcome in order to win, we must stop and ask, "What theories, what ideas, and what opinions, were entertained by the fathers, mothers, and teachers of the present generation of men and women in this country, regarding the sale and use of alcoholic liquors?" The question to settle, when we come to investigate this movement, and desire to judge how rapidly we may succeed, is : "What teaching, what instruction, and what superstitions implanted in the brain of this generation have we to overcome?"

The liquor business in this country is founded on superstition. There is not a thing modern, not a thing intellectual, not a thing elevating about it. The drinking customs of this land were born back in the misty past, and every one of them is hoary-headed with

THE PRACTICABILITY OF THE MOVEMENT. 243

superstition and moss-backed with age. They are but remnants of legends of the past that have come to us, not through the educated minds of the race, but perpetuated in other countries, as they have been perpetuated in this country, in the baseness of the lusts and passions of humanity.

For a moment let us see in part, if we may, what some of these impressions have been. You know that every one of the drinking customs of this land comes down to us from the pagan worship of devil-gods. A woman takes a glass of wine in her fingers, raises it to her lips—she is imitating the example of the drunken courtesans of Greece, as, amid the revels of Bacchus, they gave up their honor for place and power.

A man takes a glass of the nasty, dirty, bitter swill, known as beer, gulps it down, and, as he rolls into the gutter, debauched, and with his manhood soiled and tainted by contact with this heathen relic, he cries out, "Great is Gambrinus, the god of beer!" In this city you erect temples to the traditions and institutions of Bacchus and Gambrinus, two of the most beastly heathen gods, and pay more money to continue their worship than you pay for the support of your churches and your common schools.

Enter a saloon with a young man; watch him a moment or two, and study the delusion under which he is acting. You know him to be good, kind, and affectionate. What has he in his hand? It is a glass of liquor. It is a bitter cold day, and, as he raises the glass to his lips, you step up to him and say, "Hold on, Tom; why are you drinking that liquor?" With a face as long as grandmother's was when she told the ghost stories, he tells you he is drinking the liquor "to warm him up." You say to him, "Tom, does drinking liquor warm you up? Do you not know the physiologists of this country say that is a false idea?" He says, "I don't know anything about physiologists, and I don't want to."

Six months pass, and August with its severe heat, is here; you see the same man enter the saloon, and as you follow him again you see him take up a glass of the same kind of liquor. "Tom," you say, "what are you drinking that liquor for?" and he tells you with the same long face that it is a fearfully warm day, and he is drinking it "to cool him off."

Suppose I were to bring a stove on the platform, fill it with fuel, start a fire, let the stove become hot, and then say to one of the little boys who are present to-night, "Come up here, Willie." As he comes at my suggestion, he puts his fingers to the stove and is burned; he snaps his fingers at me and says, "Oh, you thought you were smart, didn't you?" Again, it is summer-time. Now put in the fuel, start the fire; the stove gets hot, and I say, "Willie, come up here and sit down on this stove; it will cool you off." What would be the answer of the child? "If fire burns in the winter, it will burn in the summer." Any child will readily recognize the foolishness of the drinker's position. And yet full-grown men, men with gray hairs, men with wrinkles on their brows, drink whiskey as fire in the winter to warm them, and whiskey as fire in the summer to cool them off!

Will you laugh at grandmother, who taught me to believe in ghosts, if you talk like that, my friends?

Again, see a man in a saloon drinking liquor "to warm him up." If it warms him it must be fuel and food. The heat of the body is generated like the heat of the stove, by combustion of fuel taken in at the mouth. The drinker, if his theory is correct, is simply taking in firewood. With this he loads his physical system all day, and at night starts for his home out on the prairies of this country. The next morning he is found by the roadside, dead. What killed him? All the preceding day he was taking alcoholic firewood to warm him up, and if his theory that alcohol generates heat is true, he must have burned to death. The coroner's jury say, "He froze." Nine out of every ten men who have perished with cold in this northern land, labored under the foolish, idiotic superstition, that alcoholic liquor adds heat to the physical system, and drank that which reduced their power of endurance, and hastened their death.

Again, a broad-shouldered man enters a saloon. You ask:

'Charlie, why are you drinking?"

He replies: "I am drinking alcoholic liquor because I have a difficult job on hand, and I want to add a little to my strength."

"How does alcoholic liquor give you strength?"

"I do not know, but it does."

"Do you not know that alcoholic liquors act as the whip to the tired, exhausted system, simply using up the reserve force, enabling you to use up a fund of strength you ought not to draw upon?"

"But I feel stronger."

"Yes, and if you sit down on a pin rightly fixed, you would feel stronger. It would stimulate, not strengthen."

He persists, and during the day takes liquor to make him strong. Late at night you start for your home. You hear a grunt in the gutter, and looking down you see a man holding on to the earth to keep from falling off. He cannot stir hand or foot. You roll him over to see who he is, and lo! he is the man who was drinking liquor to make him strong. "What ails him?" Why, if his logic is right, he is too strong.

Again, I asked a gentleman recently, why he drank beer. He replied, "I drink beer because it is good as food." Now this is a common delusion, yet I wish to assure you, my friends, that the German drinks his beer, the Frenchman drinks his wine, the Irishman drinks his ale and gin, and the Yankee all kinds of drinks, for the "drunk" there is in them. They all drink for the intoxicating principle there is in the drinks.

To this proposition you may demur for an instant. Let me prove it. You drink beer for the food or nourishment it is supposed to contain. Very well. Send to the saloon, buy a gallon of beer, take it home, and put it in the cellar, place ice around it to keep it cool, let it remain there until the next morning, then bring it up-stairs to drink. No, you will not use it. Why? "It is dead." Yes, the devil has got out of it, the drunkard-making alcohol has run away. It has only the food (?) left, while the alcohol and carbonic acid gas, neither of them food, neither of them nourishment, have partially escaped.

An old German in the city in which I reside, once said to me, when I made that assertion: "Vell, I tole you vat I tinks. I tinks you vas mistaken yourself." He said: "I drinks beer for food." "Very well," I said to him, "you get some beer and let us see whether you do or not." He brought me some beer. I took a retort, improvised a still and then distilled the alcohol from the beer. When I had thus removed the alcohol, I took the remainder, cooled it on ice, turned it into a tumbler, and gave it to him to drink. He drank about half a glass of it, when all he had swallowed and his breakfast came back together. From that day to this the old man will tell you, "Feench put somedings in dot beer vot makes me sick right avay quick," while the fact was, I simply took from the beer what would have made him drunk.

One of the greatest chemists the world has ever known,* (and, by the way, this chemist was a German,) said, after eight years of thorough experiment: "I have proved, with mathematical accuracy, that the amount of nourishment you may take upon the point of a table-knife, inserted into a sack of flour, contains absolutely more nourishment for the physical organism than the nourishment contained in eight quarts of the best Bavarian beer, and if a person is able to drink two gallons of beer each day in the year, he would get about the same amount of nutrition from the beer in twelve months that he would by consuming a five-pound loaf of bread, or three pounds of lean meat."

Another person may say: "I do not drink beer for the food there is in it, nor for the alcohol which it contains, but I drink it for the hops. Hops, you know, are healthy." My friend, if you will go to a drug-store, buy ten cents' worth of hops, and steep them in two gallons of water, you will get more hop tea than you can get in five gallons of beer. Can you convince any sensible man that you buy five gallons of beer,

---

*Baron Justus Von Liebig, born in Darmstadt, 1803, died in Munich, 1873. He is best known to English readers by his "Familiar Letters on Chemistry." Baron Liebig was an enthusiast in regard to America, and at one time thought of making his residence in the United States.—ED.

and pay the price for it you do, to obtain ten cents' worth of hop tea?

These are some of the delusions which find a lodging place in the minds of the people, but they are losing their hold gradually, as science and intelligence break down the fortifications of ignorance and superstition. You older men can tell these boys in the audience to-night, that when you were boys, liquor was the first thing ever drank by children, and it was the last thing used when people died. It was present on all occasions. The theory was that it was universally beneficial and universally necessary.

Some may object, and some do object, on the ground that humanity is not advancing, that temperance work acts and reacts, and that these superstitions are not fading away. To set at rest forever these croaking moralists (who, having chronic dyspepsia, think it is religion, and seeing the whole world from the observatory of their diseased stomachs, proclaim it is going to the bad), it may be best for us to contrast the past with the present.

The idea that universal benefit was derived from the sale and the use of alcoholic liquor was held in common fifty or sixty years ago by nearly the whole people of this country. It was supposed to be necessary when persons were sick and when they were well; when people were sad and when they were happy. It was supposed to be necessary when persons were cold and when they were hot; when they were wet and when they were dry. It was universally considered a panacea and cure-all for every ailment to which human flesh was heir. To doubt its being "a good thing of God" was to be called a fanatic, a zealot, and a fool.

The men who controlled the business of this country, who employed laborers on contracts and in manufactories, thought it absolutely necessary that workmen should use alcoholic stimulants to enable them to stand the physical strain and do a good day's work. Farmers held the same belief. There could not be a logging, a raising, or a threshing-bee without the jug.

Said an old lady to me, " Nobody ever tells about the quiltings, but when we had our quiltings in the afternoon, we always set the milk punch up for our husbands when they came in the evening."

Take, for example, the digging of the Erie Canal across the State of New York. When that canal was dug, a boy, known by the cognomen or title of "Grog-boy," was employed on every sub-section. On the Pennsylvania and Ohio Canal he was known as "Jigger-boy." What was his business? To take liquor, bought by the contractors, and carry it out to the laborers. The idea was held that all men required liquor, and that no man could do a good day's work without stimulants. This idea was so thoroughly impressed upon all, that they not only hired men who drank, but they bought the liquor and hired a boy to carry it to them.

Fifty years have passed, and what do we see now? The other day I was writing to Samuel D. Hastings, of Madison, Wis.—one of the grandest, best, and truest of men I have ever known. He is intimately acquainted with the affairs of his State, and I asked him to inform me what rules were made by the railroads of Wisconsin in regard to the use of liquor by their employés. March 18th I received the letter I now hold in my hand, from which I read the following:

"Among the questions proposed to the railroad companies by our railroad commissioner are the following, viz.:

"'Has your company any rule governing your conductors, engineers, and trainmen concerning the use of intoxicating liquors? If so, what is it, and is it enforced?'

"[Answers from the report of 1877.]

"Answers are given as follows, to wit.:

"Chicago, Milwaukee, and St. Paul Road—'It is a rule of this road not to employ or retain in service men who make an immoderate use of intoxicating liquors, and this rule is enforced.'

"Chicago and Northwestern Road—'The rules of this Company absolutely prohibit the use of intoxicating liquors by conductors, engineers, and trainmen, and they are strictly enforced.'

"Chippewa Falls and Western Road—'Perfect sobriety is required, and no liquors on the property.'

"Green Bay and Minnesota Road—'Employés not allowed to use intoxicating liquors.'

"Milwaukee, Lake Shore and Western Road—'The use of intoxicating drinks on or about the premises of the company is strictly prohibited, and any employé appearing on duty in a state of intoxication is forthwith dismissed: those who totally abstain will receive the preference in promotion and employment. These rules are strictly enforced.'

"Wisconsin Valley Road—'Total abstinence? Yes.'

"Answers from the report of 1881:

"Chicago, St. Paul, Minneapolis, and Omaha Road—'The use of intoxicating liquors involves instant dismissal.'

"Wisconsin Central Road—'Rule No. 2 of our book of instruction reads: "The use of intoxicating liquors of any kind by any employé is detrimental to himself and the interests of the company, and only those who abstain from its use will be employed." This rule is rigidly enforced.'

"Wisconsin and Minnesota and Chippewa Falls and Western Road —'Have the same rule as the Wisconsin Central; substantially the same owners.'

"Fond du Lac, Amboy, and Peoria Road—'Drunkenness on duty will be considered sufficient cause for instant dismissal. This is enforced.'

"And in Illinois.

"Wabash, St. Louis, and Pacific Road—Rule 88: 'Intoxication, or habitual or frequent use of intoxicating liquors will be sufficient reason for dismissal. Persons employed in running trains in any capacity who are known to drink intoxicating liquors will be forthwith discharged.'"

These rules are fair samples of the rules of all the railroads and manufactories of this country from the Atlantic to the Pacific.

Fifty years ago, a man who employed laborers thought it necessary they should drink.

To-day the great contractors and business men of this country give the preference to abstainers, and are frowning upon men who use intoxicating liquors.

I recently saw in a newspaper published in this State, an advertisement for a bar-keeper. It was a request by a saloon-keeper for help; the last words of the advertisement said: "The applicant must be a total abstainer."

Suppose two young men of equal physical strength, mental force, and education, should contemplate going to Chicago, to seek situations in business houses. A leading banker in that city wishes the services of a clerk. These young men learn of the vacant clerkship, and each wishes to secure the position. They know they must obtain it on the record of their past lives and business qualifications. What are the records of those lives?

At the commencement of his business career one of these young men made up his mind to win; he counted the cost of success; looked out over the future before him, and realized that to be successful he must have knowledge, health, and good habits. Carrying out this idea he took the money he earned in the store, bought books, and spent his leisure hours, few though they may have been, in study; if he wanted pleasure he sought it in the society of respectable young men and ladies of his acquaintance; when the Sabbath came he went to the Sunday-school, and, although considered old-fogyish, he was known to be an attendant at church.

The other young man thought he would have a good time in the beginning of his business career, and then catch up. He took his money and went to the saloon to play billiards, drink beer, and have a good time.

These young men, with such records, take steps to get the clerkship. The former goes to his minister and says: "Will you give me a certificate of character to the gentleman in Chicago?" and the minister writes: "I know this young gentleman to be moral, honest, and truly worthy. He attends Sunday-school regularly, and is a member of my church; he is sober, temperate, and industrious." To this letter the minister signs his name. The young man then goes to his employer and says: "Will you give me a recommendation?" and his employer gives him a certificate to the same general effect as that received from his pastor.

The other young man goes to the saloon-keeper with whom he has associated, and says: "I want a certain position in Chicago; will you give me a certificate to the banker?" The dram-seller writes: "He is a good fellow, and can play the best game of billiards of any man in the city. He can play seven-up and win five times out of six; he can drink more beer in the same length of time than any other man of my acquaintance. He is a bright, jolly man." The young man then goes to his employer and asks him for a recommendation, and he receives a certificate relating the same general facts.

Both young men go to Chicago, ask for the banker, and lay their recommendations before him. Does it matter whether the president of the bank drinks beer or not? Whether he is an infidel or Christian? Whether he is a prohibitionist or license man? No matter what his personal views or habits may be, he will hire the man who comes with credentials certifying to a record of total abstinence and morality.

An acquaintance of mine wanted a clerk. The man was an infidel and an habitual drinker. A boy said to me, "Will you give me a credential to Mr. ——?" I simply certified to the fact that I knew the youth; that he was a good Christian boy, a total abstainer, a member of the Good Templar lodge, and that he was thoroughly industrious, studious, and honest. The boy applied for the position. I afterward learned that some five or six other boys applied for the same position. Some of the boys were reckless and fast. The boy to whom I gave the recommendation got the position. A few days afterward, passing down the street, I put my arm through that of the gentleman who had employed the boy I recommended, and said: "Mr. ——, tell me why you hired that boy; he was a total abstainer and a Christian, and the other boys who applied for the position could drink beer, play cards, and disregard the Sabbath, which you approve. Why did you hire the total abstainer?"

"Oh," said he, "such principles as he follows are good to have around a counting-room."

Go where you will, up and down this nation to-day, the temperance work is rolling humanity steadily upward. The business man recognizes this truth, that the man who drinks liquor is injured intellectually, physically, and morally by such use.

This is one line of advance. Look at another.

The Rev. J. B. Dunn, the celebrated author of the "History of Temperance," gives a bill presented to and paid by one of the oldest churches of Hartford, Connecticut. It was during the year 1784—less than a hundred years ago. There had been an assembly of ministers to ordain a young aspirant for ministerial honors. The church had sent the visiting clergy to an inn at Hartford to be entertained, telling the innkeeper to present the bill to the church for payment. The bill was a copy of the original presented by the innkeeper to the church for the expenses of the ministers, and is given in the record as follows:

The South Society in Hartford, Conn., paid the following bill for the entertainment of the ministers at the ordination of a pastor:

	£	s.	d.
May 4, 1784—To keeping ministers—			
2 mugs tody	0	2	4
5 segars	0	5	10
1 pint wine	0	3	0
May 5—			
To 3 bitters	0	0	9
To 3 breakfasts	0	3	6
To 15 boles punch	1	10	0
To 24 dinners	1	16	0
To 11 bottles wine	3	6	1
To five mugs flip	0	5	10
To 3 boles punch	0	6	0
To 3 boles tody	0	3	6
	£7	11	9

The ministers' toddy and wine cost the church a little over twenty dollars for two days, and there were only thirteen ministers entertained, and liquors were far cheaper in those days than now. What would be thought of such a bill presented to a church in Illinois to-day, and paid by them without complaint?

Four years since, speaking in Lodi, Wisconsin, for the Order of Good Templars, at the conclusion of the meeting an old gentleman came up to me and said, " I want to tell you something. I am a superannuated Baptist minister." (I learned afterward that he was one of the most loved and honored men of that denomination in the State.) " I commenced preaching in Ilion, New York. While preaching there a young brother was to be ordained in Ogdensburg, in the northern part of the State. There were no railroads then. I was to go up the Mohawk River to Rome, then up the Black River; another was to come from Oswego, another from Canada, and another from Plattsburg. We met on a certain day, held a meeting in the afternoon, and another in the evening. At night I was to sleep with the brother from Oswego. After we went to our room I opened my satchel to get my Bible, but found that I had left it at the church. My companion said, ' Have my Bible,' and opened his satchel to get it. Under it were four or five bottles of whiskey. You ask me what he had it for; if he had it to drink, and whether he offered it to me? No, he did not ask me to drink with him, nor offer to drink any of it himself. I will tell you how he came to have it in his possession. His son ran a distillery, and as the father was to preach on this long trip through Canada and Northern New York, he had taken the whiskey along as samples, and acted as a commercial agent for the distillery on the trip, preaching and selling whiskey."

A few weeks later I stood before an immense audience in Northern New York, near where the incident was said to have occurred, and related the story. After the meeting was over a man came to me and said, "Why did you assail me?" I said to him, "I do not know you." Said he, "I am the man who peddled the whiskey." Then he introduced himself. I called on him the next morning, and for more than an hour I was entertained by reminiscences, as he told me of the customs and practices of his early ministry. He said, "In that day ministers, deacons, class-leaders, and church members drank—in short, the drinking customs were almost universal."

In 1835 a large distillery was run at Salem, Mass., by an old deacon. The Rev. George B. Cheever, D.D., passed along the road and saw the sign, "Distillery—Corn wanted—Bibles to sell." This suggested his celebrated cartoon, in which he pictured devils as running the distillery, and called it "Deacon Giles' Distillery." The coat fitted, and Dr. Cheever was arrested, tried by a Christian jury, convicted of malicious libel, and sent to jail. A close examination of the case convinces me that the verdict was based upon Dr. Cheever's statements against the Christian character of the deacon distiller. In that day ministers, church officials, and Christians not only used, but manufactured and sold, intoxicating drinks. The public did not look upon these acts as degrading Christian character, or inconsistent with a Christian life. To-day the ministers of the Lord Jesus Christ are the veteran corps of our whole reform work. Other brigades, other corps, and other armies are in the fight, but the principal weight of the movement rests on the Christian centre. I have never yet, in the bitterest strife, called upon a minister in Nebraska for assistance and been refused. As I go up and down through the State of Nebraska, I do not ask the question, "Is such a minister a temperance man?" I know he is. I know he could not preach in our State if he was not. Even the denominations which in the East are apathetic toward the movement, are quite positive and aggressive in the West. A clergyman who spoke in this State only a few weeks ago in favor of saloons was told by his church, the Episcopal, that his resignation would be accepted, and an opportunity was given him to step down and out, and he embraced it.

Look at another line of advance. Fifty or sixty years ago the sale of liquor was open, and as common as the sale of tea, coffee, dry-goods, and groceries. It was piled up in every grocery-store, and men who sold dry-goods said they must have liquor to treat their customers. It was not regarded as a disreputable business. It was not deemed necessary to screen the door of the grocery, where it was to be found, from the observation of the general public, and the business of selling was not regarded as of so injurious and deadly a nature that men must petition the city authorities, to be permitted to engage in its sale.

Look at it now. In Maine, New Hampshire, Vermont, and Kansas, the whole business is outlawed. In license States like Nebraska everybody knows it is looked upon as disreputable to patronize a drunkard-factory, and he who engages in the sale is regarded as a bad man. To-day, in my State, the very fact that a man wants to sell liquor is in the eyes of the law *prima facie* evidence that he is a scoundrel.

A man may come to Nebraska to-morrow and desire to take out a license to sell liquor. If he go to a city council and ask for a license, the very fact that he applies for such a license is deemed *prima facie* evidence that he is disreputable, dishonest, and, before the council can grant it, he must get thirty freeholders, residents of the ward wherein the saloon is to be located, to certify he is decent and moral. He must get a character made to order as you get a coat, and then, when he gets it to fit (I suppose our Greenback friends would call it a fiat character), the law believes every man who signed the petition lied, and says, despite the fact that the would-be drunkard-maker has their certificates, he must give a bond of five thousand dollars, signed by three good sureties, to indemnify the people for the evil his business will create. No man is now bold enough to stand up and defend the business upon its merits. The drunkard-makers themselves favor "judicious license laws." No man dares advocate taking the chains off this old curse and letting it go free.

Look at another line of advance. There was a time in the history of this reform when everywhere, in almost every house in the land, people expected to find wine or some kind of liquor, on the table or on the sideboard. It was deemed useful and hospitable, and necessary on all occasions.

Now, the custom of turning the parlor into a bar-room, and using a beautiful daughter as a bar-tender to manufacture drunkards, who will afterward curse the fair hands that tempted them to take the first glass, is rapidly becoming obsolete everywhere.

These, ladies and gentlemen, are a few of the changes made by persistent work to educate the masses, to lift the fog of ignorance, and let in the sunlight of knowledge and scientific truth. The struggle has been severe, but no cause has ever had grander heroes.

Years ago, when Dr. Hunt, who led the reform in the East, went on the platform, the common answer of the drunkard-makers was rotten eggs. At one time when eggs were thrown at him he stopped in his speech and said: "Gentlemen, let them come; your arguments are just like your business."

I look back over the band of workers and wish I could mention them all—grand men and women who have stood shoulder to shoulder in the contest. What cause was ever supported by clearer heads and warmer hearts!

What has this work accomplished? Fifty years ago the business world furnished liquor to its employés; to-day it makes abstinence from the use of liquor a rule for workmen. Fifty years ago the Church, by its example and influence, sustained the drink customs and trade; to-day its leaders are fighting the traffic to the death. Fifty years ago the liquor traffic was respectable; to-day it is either outlawed or a criminal bound with the chains of law. Fifty years ago society held it fashionable to furnish wine to guests; to-day it is regarded vulgar and low.

Yes, the line of the reform has advanced; but, while proud of the progress of public sentiment, we would not have you forget that all along the line of march of these years there are other evidences of successful, victorious work, made sacred by the memories of men whose redeemed spirits, now in heaven, look back to rejoice that this movement came to save!

Let me give you an instance: I addressed an audience in a Western city some years ago. At the close of the talk, an old man—muddy, dirty, drunk—came and reached out his hand. His face was bloated and congested from the use of alcoholic liquors; his eyes were bleared and watery, his tongue was thick from indulgence; he was a wretched, terrible specimen of what liquor does for its victims. He said: "S-a-a-y, Mister, am—hic—go—go—in to er—hic—sign that are p-pledge, an—I am—hic—an' I'll keep it, or I'll—hic—*bust*."

As I looked at him—poor, besotted wretch, with just the faintest trace of his once glorious manhood lingering in his determination to sign the pledge, and make one more effort for the restoration of his lost character and honor—I pitied him. One could not help seeing his physical and intellectual condition—native pride gone, stomach almost destroyed by drink, feebleness in every part of his physical organism. I took his hand and told him I hoped he would keep the pledge; that I believed God would give him strength to stand. He signed and went away. The attention of some of the Good Templar friends was called to him. I went from that place, and it was more than a year before I returned. The first night after my return, I was speaking again, After the meeting, an old lady came to me and said:

"I want to shake hands, and ask you if you will come and take tea with us to-morrow?"

"I think I can come," I replied.

She went away. I did not recognize her. Turning to a minister who stood by, I asked:

"Who was the lady?"

"Why," said he, "you remember that old bummer who signed the pledge when you were here last year?"

"Yes," I answered, "did he keep it?"

"Yes, he did," was the reply; "that lady is his wife; he is now a member of my church."

The next day I went to their home. The man and his wife were both there, and greeted me most cordially. After a time the husband went to the business part of the city. When he had gone the wife said to me: "I wanted you to come so I could tell you how much my husband's reformation has done for me and my home, and to bid you God-speed in your work"; then she told the old, old story that every person who has ever worked to reform men has heard so often. A happy courtship and marriage, the sunlight of wifehood and joys of motherhood; a happy wife, busied with household cares, the pathway of life strewn with the flowers of hope and love. How the gentle voice of love, the happiness and thanksgiving had day after day thanked God for her husband, the best and bravest and noblest of men. How he had endeavored in the battle of life to shield and protect her from every discomfort and hardship. Then of the time when the husband had been enticed into a saloon and persuaded to drink his first glass; how he fell into the horrible habit of drunkenness, and how she, thinking she might reclaim him, and hardly realizing the terrible character of the loathsome serpent which had stolen into her paradise and robbed it of its purity and happiness, had followed, pleading, praying, hoping, and working. "But," said she, "hope failed, my pleadings availed not, and my prayers seemed offered to a god of brass. Oh, human heart can hardly imagine what sorrow, what grief, what bitterness of soul was mine! For fifteen years, fifteen years of a hell on earth, he drank almost incessantly; every nickel he earned went to the saloon for drink, and he did not provide anything for our home. I did washing to support myself, till rheumatism attacked me, and my hands became so I could not use them. At last I could not work more, and then the poorhouse door stood open to me. Perhaps you will think I was wicked, but, Mr. Finch, I have often gone to bed at night praying God I might never wake in the morning. During my whole life I had tried to do my duty, at least to be respectable, and the thought of *dying a pauper in a poorhouse* was enough to drive me mad. Kind women, God bless them, watched with and looked after me while I was sick. It was at that time John signed the pledge. He came home from the meeting and went directly to bed. The next morning he rose early; it was his usual custom to rise early and go down-town to get his drink, but that morning I heard him building a fire. I couldn't think what it meant. He went out of doors and soon came back, and I heard him filling the tea-kettle; then he said to me:

"'Mary, where is the hammer?'

"I asked him why he wanted the hammer.

"'I want to fix the door-steps out here.'

"The door-steps had been broken a long time. He had tumbled over them drunk many a time, and never thought of fixing them. As soon as he wanted to fix the steps it flashed into my mind what he had done, and I asked, 'John, have you signed the pledge?' and he said, 'Yes, Mary, and with God helping me, as they say down at the meeting, I am going to keep it.' Perhaps I am getting into my dotage, but the tears of joy came, and calling him to me I put my arms around his neck and kissed away the dark memories of the past. Since then the shadow of the pauperhouse has not darkened my home, and with my old-time love I feel a girl again. The Good Templars have given me back my old lover, to stand up in his redeemed manhood by my shoulder, to love me, sustain me, to go down to the grave and up into heaven with me, and I will ever thank and bless them."

This is but one of thousands of cases. There is hardly a temperance organization in America, but has in it saved men snatched from the downward road.

Thus history proves the practicability of the movement. The reform found the business world opposed to it, and by facts and arguments the business world has been convinced that total abstinence is right. The reform found tippling regarded as moral; by facts and arguments the moral world has been convinced that tippling is the A-B-C school of drunkenness. The reform found the State blind to the nature of this cut-throat traffic; by facts and arguments the eyes of the State have been opened, and it has everywhere chained the traffic and in some instances killed it. The reform found thousands of men on the road to ruin, and saved many of them.

Yes; it is a grand, a glorious success! No other movement can show a more glorious record of victory against fearful odds, and in so short a time. As we go forward encouraged, let us remember that the reform is greater than any man or organization of men. The men who stand on the platform are simply aids. Every worker has a task to do, and all our labors are essential to accomplish the work before us. Let us stand shoulder to shoulder in the places that are ready and open for us, pressing forward side by side on the battle-fields of this reform, firm and unwavering in the faith that God will give victory to the right, and that truth and purity shall triumph over vice and error. But let not this faith make us blind. The enemy will die hard. Every defence that avarice, lust, and crime can suggest, may be expected. Every means to trick the workers will be used. Local option, high license, civil damage are all subterfuges of the enemy, to postpone the inevitable hour when a prohibitory law will pronounce its death sentence.

Be not deceived! PROHIBITION in the National and State Constitutions *made effective by a live, vital political party, pledged to carry out its provisions as a matter of principle, not as a matter of policy*, is the *only* remedy for this most terrible of social and political evils—the liquor traffic! Stand by this position, though apostates and cowards cry compromise, and victory will come to bless our homes and our nation!

National Temperance Society.

T. L. CUYLER, D.D., *President.*   WM. D. PORTER, *Treasurer.*   J. N. STEARNS, *Cor. Sec. and Pub. Agent.*

THE NATIONAL TEMPERANCE SOCIETY, organized in 1865 for the purpose of supplying a sound and able temperance literature, have already stereotyped and published over one thousand publications of all sorts and sizes, from the one-page tract up to the bound volume of 1,000 pages. This list comprises books, tracts, and pamphlets, containing essays, stories, sermons, argument, statistics, history, etc., upon every phase of the question. Special attention has been given to the department

FOR SUNDAY-SCHOOL LIBRARIES.

One hundred and fifty-two volumes have already been issued, written by some of the best authors in the land. These have been carefully examined and approved by the Publication Committee of the Society, representing the various religious denominations and temperance organizations of the country, which consists of the following members:

PETER CARTER,   REV. A. G. LAWSON,   A. D. VAIL, D.D.,
REV. W. T. SABINE,   T. A. BROUWER,   R. R. SINCLAIR,
A. A. ROBBINS,   D. C. EDDY, D.D.,   JAMES BLACK,
REV. HALSEY MOORE,   J. S. CHADWICK, D.D.,   J. N. STEARNS,
    REV. ALFRED TAYLOR.

The volumes have been cordially recommended by leading clergymen of all denominations and by numerous Ecclesiastical bodies and Temperance Organizations all over the land. They should be in every Sunday-school Library. The following is a list of some of the latest and the best issued:

Susan's Sheaves. By Mrs. C. M. Livingston. 12mo, 364 pages.... $1.25
Mama's Stories. By Laura J. Rittenhouse. 12mo, 96 pages....... .50
Brooklet Series. By Miss L. Penney. 6 vols., each 25 cents; set... 1.50
Story of Rasmus; or, the Making of a Man. By Julia McNair Wright. 12mo, 338 pages........................ 1.25
Bird Angel (The). By Miss M. A. Paull. 12mo, 147 pages........ .75
Dave Marquand. By Annette L. Noble. 12mo, 357 pages........ 1.25
Let It Alone. By Edward Carswell. 12mo, 294 pages............ 1.00
Under Ban. By Miss M. E. Winslow. 12mo, 325 pages........... 1.25
The Old Tavern and Other Stories. By Mary Dwinell Chellis. 12mo, 386 pages................................. 1.25
Miss Belinda's Friends. By Mary Dwinell Chellis. 12mo, 360 pages... 1.25
One More Chance. By Mrs. S. M. I. Henry. 12mo, 598 pages.... 1.50
The Hercules Brand. By A. M. Cummings. 12mo, 445 pages.. 1.50
The Dragon and the Tea-Kettle. By Mrs. J. McNair Wright. 12mo, 288 pages................................. 1.00
Miss Janet's Old House. By Annette L. Noble. 12mo, 428 pp. 1.25
Spinning-Wheel of Tamworth (The). By Rev. W. A. Smith. 12mo, 206 pages.. .90
Haunted Islands. By M. E. Wilmer. 12mo, 383 pages.......... 1.25
Millerton People. By Faye Huntington. 12mo, 313 pages........ 1.00
Profit and Loss. By Mary D. Chellis. 12mo, 387 pages.......... 1.25
Congressman Stanley's Fate. By Harriet A. Harp. 12mo, 403 pages... 1.25
How Billy Went Up in the World. By Annette L. Noble. 12mo, 396 pages... 1.25
Competitive Workmen. By Faye Huntington. 12mo, 272 pp... 1.00
Hannah: One of the Strong Women. By Mrs. J. McNair Wright. 12mo, 290 pages............................... 1.00

Address   **J. N. STEARNS,** Publishing Agent,
58 Reade Street, New York City.

LATEST PUBLICATIONS.

THE NATIONAL TEMPERANCE SOCIETY has recently added the following to its list of cheap publications, in pamphlet form. At the prices at which these are issued, they should have the widest possible circulation.

Origin of the Maine Law, and of Prohibitory Legislation. 12mo, large size, 52 pages.................................. .10

This is a pamphlet compiled by D. F. Appleton, Esq., giving an able and exhaustive report of General James Appleton, a member of the Legislature of Maine and chairman of the Committee on License Laws in 1837. It is a remarkable document, clear, logical, convincing, and complete. All histories of the Maine law leaving this out are incomplete. Mr. Appleton was born in Ipswich, Mass., in 1786, and in 1832 wrote several articles for the Salem *Gazette* of wonderful vigor and ability, which are gathered together for the first time and printed in this little pamphlet. They dissect the license system, expose its weakness and wickedness, and present unanswerable arguments for prohibition.

High License Weighed in the Balances and ——. By Herrick Johnson, D.D. 12mo, 12 pages, thick paper, with cover... .05

Cheap campaign edition, 3 cents; per hundred, $2.50.

A keen and logical argument on the High License Question, by Rev. Dr. Herrick Johnson. Put in convenient and cheap form it should be used as a campaign document everywhere, to refute the claims of the advocates of High License.

Prohibition. By Petroleum V. Nasby (D. R. Locke). 12mo, 24 pages... .10

This is putting in pamphlet form the masterly article of Mr. Locke's (P. V. Nasby), which appeared in the October number of the *North American Review* on Prohibition. Exhaustive and able, it is one of the best and most convincing arguments for the Prohibition of the Liquor-Traffic yet presented.

The Temperance Alphabet. 8vo 16 pages. By Edward Carswell.. .10

A new and cheap edition of the popular "Temperance Alphabet," designed by the children's friend, Edward Carswell. The work is printed on fine paper in best black ink and style, with illustrated cover, and is just the thing for the little folks. The sketches are very attractive, the alphabet letters large and plain, and the mottoes teach the lessons of temperance.

Alcohol and Science. By Wm. Hargreaves, M.D. 12mo, 366 pages. Cloth, $1.50; cheap paper edition........... .50

A cheap edition, pamphlet form, of the excellent $500 prize volume of Dr. Wm. Hargreaves, entitled "Alcohol and Science," giving the large work, 366 12mo pages, for 50 cents. This places the book within the reach of all, and it should be in every home. Divided into ten parts, as follows: Part 1. What is Alcohol? Part 2. What becomes of Alcohol when Ingested? Part 3. Physiological Action of Alcohol. Part 4. Is Alcohol a Poison? Part 5. Is Alcohol Food? Part 6. Does Alcohol Sustain Vitality? Part 7. Disease caused by Alcohol. Part 8. Nervous Diseases from Alcohol. Part 9. Alcohol: its effect on Progeny. Part 10. Is Alcohol a Medicine? It touches all phases of the scientific physiological effects of alcohol.

Talmage on Rum. By Rev. T. De Witt Talmage. 12mo, 114 pages. Cloth, 50 cents; paper.......................... .25

Eight sermons and addresses by Rev. T. De Witt Talmage on rum and tobacco, giving startling statistics, arguments, and appeals in his most vigorous style. They show "The Evil Beast," "Red Dragon," "Arch-fiend of the Nations" to be the "Worst Enemy of the Working-Classes," and "High License the Monopoly of Abomination," etc., etc.

National Temperance Almanac, 1887. By J. N. Stearns. 12mo, 72 pages.............................. .10

This admirable handbook is now ready for 1887. Full of interesting facts, figures, statistics, illustrations, etc. Printed on fine tinted paper.

All the above sent post-paid on receipt of price. Address

J. N. STEARNS, Publishing Agent,
58 Reade Street, New York

THE PEOPLE

VERSUS

THE LIQUOR TRAFFIC.

SPEECHES OF
JOHN B. FINCH,

DELIVERED IN THE

PROHIBITION CAMPAIGNS OF THE UNITED STATES AND CANADA.

TWENTY-FOURTH (REVISED) EDITION.

WITH AN INTRODUCTION BY J. N. STEARNS.

EDITED BY CHARLES ARNOLD McCULLY.

NEW YORK:
Published by the R. W. G. Lodge,
B. F. Parker, R. W. G. Secretary.
1887.

VOTERS OF,

Texas, Tennessee, Oregon, and West Virginia.

The Legislatures of your States have submitted to you for adoption or rejection, amendments to your State Constitutions, prohibiting the manufacture and sale of alcoholic beverages.

The amendments simply act as indictments to bring the liquor traffic into the court of the people for trial.

The hope of the maintenance of a democratic Republic must be founded on the intelligence of the people. Any institution which breaks down the intelligence or degrades the morality of the citizen is an enemy of our free institutions.

The alcoholic liquor traffic is charged with crimes against the citizen, with crimes against business, with crimes against the School, with crimes against the Church, with crimes against the Home with crimes against the Ballot-box, and with crimes against the Government.

To aid you in the investigation of the questions which will arise in the amendment campaigns, we send you this book. It will to some extent explain why the Good Templars and Sons of Temperance ask the destruction of the liquor traffic. The Good Templars and the Sons stand together in this struggle. They are the strongest temperance organizations on earth. Years of practical work, to overcome the evils of intemperance, have convinced them that all moral work is largely nullified by the presence and influence of the licensed bar-room. In behalf of a higher, better, and truer civilization, we ask you to investigate the issues involved, and then to vote against the legalized drunkard-factory.

Respectfully yours,

JOHN B. FINCH,
Right Worthy Grand Templar of the Good Templars.

EUGENE H. CLAPP,
Most Worthy Patriarch of the Sons of Temperance.

THE YOUTH'S TEMPERANCE BANNER.

The National Temperance Society and Publication House publish a beautifully-illustrated four-page Monthly Paper for Children and Youth, Sabbath-schools, and Juvenile Temperance Organizations. Each number contains several choice engravings, a piece of music, and a great variety of articles from the pens of the best writers for children in America.

Its object is to make the temperance work and education a part of the religious culture and training of the Sabbath-school and family-circle, that the children may be early taught to shun the intoxicating cup, and walk in the path of truth, soberness, and righteousness.

The following are some of the writers for THE BANNER: Mrs. J. P. Ballard (Kruna), Mary D. Chellis, Mrs. Nellie H. Bradley, Mrs. S. M. I. Henry, Ernest Gilmore, Edward Carswell, Geo. W. Bungay, Miss A. L. Noble, Faye Huntington, Hope Ledyard, Miss Julia Colman, Mrs. Helen E. Brown, Mrs. E. J. Richmond, Rev. Alfred Taylor, Mrs. J. McNair Wright, Rev. E. A. Rand, Mrs. M. A. Kidder, etc.

MONTHLY AND SEMI-MONTHLY.

The regular Monthly Edition will continue to be published as before, unchanged in character except for the better, and specially designed for Sunday-school distribution. A Semi-Monthly Edition will also be published for those who desire it.

TERMS, IN ADVANCE, INCLUDING POSTAGE.

MONTHLY EDITION.

Single copy, one year......................................**$0.25**
One hundred copies to one address.....................**12.00**
For any number of copies less than one hundred and over four, to one address, at the rate of

12 cents per Year.

SEMI-MONTHLY EDITION.

Single copy, twice a month, one year..................**$0.40**
One hundred copies, twice a month, to one address......**24.00**
For any number of copies less than one hundred and over four, to one address, at the rate of **24** cents per year.

The National Temperance Advocate.

The National Temperance Society and Publication House publish a monthly paper devoted to the interests of the Temperance Reform, which contains articles upon every phase of the movement from the pens of some of the ablest writers in America, among whom are: T. L. Cuyler, D.D., A. M. Powell, Prof. J. C. Price, M. L. Holbrook, M.D., Mrs. E. J. Richmond, Ernest Gilmore, Mrs. J. McNair Wright, Geo. W. Bungay, Rev. J. M. Van Buren, Rev. A. Willey, Mrs. F. M. Bradley, Mary Dwinell Chellis, Miss Julia Colman, Mrs. J. P. Ballard, etc., etc.

It also contains a history of the progress of the movement from month to month in all the States, which is of great value to every worker in the cause and to those who are in any way interested in the work, and no pains will be spared to make this full of the most valuable information to all classes in the community.

Terms (cash in advance), including postage: One dollar per year for single copies; ten copies to one address, $9.00; all over ten copies at 90 cents per copy.

All orders should be addressed to

J. N. STEARNS, Publishing Agent,
58 Reade Street, New York.

Constitutional Amendment Campaign.

CHEAP PROHIBITION LITERATURE. Paper Edition.

The National Temperance Society has published the following valuable and important publications upon the Prohibition of the liquor traffic, which should have a wide distribution in view of the vote by the people for or against the drink traffic.

Constitutional Amendment Manual. By J. Ellen Foster. 12mo, 100 pp. Containing Argument, Appeal, Directions, Explanations, Form of Petition, Constitutions, Formula of Amendment, Modes of operation in different States, together with Constitutional Amendment Catechism, prepared by Mrs. Foster, the talented Iowa lawyer, and covering the entire question. Important for every temperance worker in the land................................. $0.25

The Prohibitionist's Text-Book. 12mo, 312 pp. This volume contains the most valuable arguments, statistics, testimonies, and appeals, showing the iniquity of the license system and the right and duty of prohibitionists. It is an invaluable handbook for all friends of prohibition........................... .50

Worse than Wasted. By Wm. Hargreaves, M.D. 12mo, 98 pp. Giving valuable and startling figures from census and other official reports, showing the relation of intoxicating drinks to labor, trade, and the general prosperity of the country.. .30

Alcohol and the State. A discussion of the problem of law as applied to the liquor-traffic. By Robert C. Pitman, LL.D., Associate Judge of Superior Court of Massachusetts. 12mo, 411 pp... .50

Talmage on Rum. By T. De Witt Talmage, D.D. 12mo, 114 pp. Consisting of Eight Sermons by this eminent pulpit orator on the twin evils of rum and tobacco... .25

Prohibition Does Prohibit; or, Prohibition Not a Failure. By J. N. Stearns. 12mo, 120 pp... .10

Prohibition, Constitutional and Statutory. By John B. Finch. 12mo, 12 pp.. .05

Constitutional Amendment on the Manufacture and Sale of Intoxicating Liquors. By Hon. H. W. Blair. 12mo, 48 pp., with covers, 10 cents; $7.00 per hundred; thin paper, 6 cents; per hundred........ 4.00

The Great Drink-Waste Diagram. 22 x 28 inches. Paper, 10 cents; cloth... .25

Prohibition. By Petroleum V. Nasby (D. R. Locke). 12mo, 24 pp. This is putting in pamphlet form the masterly article of Mr. Locke's (P. V. Nasby), which appeared in the October Number of the *North American Review* on Prohibition.. .10

High License Weighed in the Balances and—. By Herrick Johnson, D.D. 12mo, 12 pp. Cheap edition, $2.50 per hundred; with cover, per copy... .05

The Prohibition Songster. Compiled by J. N. Stearns. This is a new collection of words and music for Temperance Gatherings, with some of the most soul-stirring songs ever published. Music by some of the best composers, and words by our best poets. 12mo, 64 pp. $1.50 per dozen; $12.00 per hundred; single copies.. .15

Four-page 12mo Tracts, $3.00 per Thousand; Postage 45 cents per 1,000 additional.

No. 220. The Responsibility of Citizens for the Results of the Rum Traffic.
" 227. An Argument for Constitutional Prohibition.
No. 257. Temperance and Over-Production.
" 258. Is it Constitutional?
" 259. Christendom and the Liquor Crime.
" 260. The Saloon in Politics.

One-page Handbills, $1.00 per Thousand; Postage 30 cents per 1,000 additional.

No. 20. The Pistol and the Bottle.
" 22. Close the Bars.
" 29. Thirty Reasons for the Prohibition of the Liquor Traffic.
" 31. Constitutional Amendment.
" 42. Constitutional Prohibition.
" 90. The Great Drink Waste.
" 99. Prohibition and Business Prosperity.
No. 102. Riding Down-Hill on a Jug.
" 103. Licensed Saloons.
" 104. Is it Right?
" 105. The Mother of Crimes.
" 106. Governors of States on Prohibition.
" 107. Appeal to the Colored Race.
" 109. Senator John H. Reagan on Prohibition.

Sent by mail on receipt of price.

Address, **J. N. STEARNS, Publishing Agent,**
58 Reade Street, New York.

www.ingramcontent.com/pod-product-compliance
Lightning Source LLC
Chambersburg PA
CBHW032001230426
43672CB00010B/2235